THE HUNGARIAN TEXANS

THE
HUNGARIAN
TEXANS

James Patrick McGuire

The University of Texas
Institute of Texan Cultures at San Antonio
1993

THE TEXIANS AND THE TEXANS

A series dealing with the many peoples who have contributed to the history and heritage of Texas. Now in print:

Pamphlets — *The Afro-American Texans, The Anglo-American Texans, The Belgian Texans, The Chinese Texans, The Czech Texans, The French Texans, The German Texans, The Greek Texans, The Indian Texans, The Italian Texans, The Jewish Texans, The Lebanese Texans and the Syrian Texans, The Mexican Texans, Los Tejanos Mexicanos* (in Spanish), *The Norwegian Texans, The Spanish Texans,* and *The Swiss Texans.*

Books — *The Danish Texans, The English Texans, The German Texans, The Hungarian Texans, The Irish Texans, The Japanese Texans, The Polish Texans, The Swedish Texans,* and *The Wendish Texans.*

To the Exiles

Library of Congress Cataloging-in-Publication Data
McGuire, James Patrick.
    The Hungarian Texans / James Patrick McGuire. — 1st ed.
      p. cm. — (Texians and the Texans)
    Includes bibliographical references and index.
    ISBN 0-86701-041-X. — ISBN 0-86701-048-7 (softbound)
    1. Hungarian Americans — Texas.   I. Title. II. Series.
F395.H95M37   1991
976.4'00494511 — dc20   91-43628
                                              CIP

The Hungarian Texans
by James Patrick McGuire

Copyright ©1993
The University of Texas Institute of Texan Cultures at San Antonio
P.O. Box 1226, San Antonio, Texas 78294

Rex Ball, Executive Director
David P. Haynes, Director of Production

Production Staff: Sandra Hodsdon Carr, Jim Cosgrove,
Lynn Weiss; Alice Sackett, indexer

Library of Congress Catalog Card Number 91-43628

International Standard Book Numbers
  Hardbound 0-86701-041-X
  Softbound 0-86701-048-7

First Edition

This project was made possible in part by grants from the
San Antonio Hungarian Association, Michael Balint, the
Minnie Stevens Piper Foundation, the Franz Liszt Foundation
of Texas, the Hungarian Foundation of Texas, the Texas
Committee on the Humanities, Houghton Mifflin, and
the Houston Endowment, Inc.

Printed in the United States of America

CONTENTS

FOREWORD

This study of the history of Hungarians in Texas was begun during the summer of 1985 at the Institute of Texan Cultures. No previous attempt had been made to write a history of the Hungarians in Texas prior to that date. Identifying individual Hungarian pioneers involved combing through community, church, county, city, and Texas histories as well as the existing body of Hungarian Americana in both English and Hungarian. Further, word-of-mouth identification of previously unknown individuals in our history proved helpful. All areas of the state of Texas were searched for the Hungarians.

Problems encountered in Hungarian source materials were solved with the assistance of Hungarian readers knowledgeable in both languages. Names, often distorted by census takers, presented special problems. In cases where descendants assisted us, we accepted the current, if anglicized, spelling of family names and, often, the nonuse of diacritics. Spelling variants which appeared in the data are given, as well as nicknames and anglicized given names. The overall result may appear uneven, since we also attempted to use proper Hungarian given and surname spellings and diacritics as accurately as possible.

Places in the old Kingdom of Hungary were given their actual Hungarian names rather than the Slovak, Czech, Ukrainian, Polish, Serbian, Croatian, Rumanian, or German versions of their names. Many of Texas' Hungarians were born and lived in areas which are today part of Hungary's neighboring states.

The Hungarian research files at the Institute of Texan Cultures are available to scholars and the public. We hope that additional information will be added in the future as more data becomes available or is discovered in dusty attics and archives. Photograph negatives of historical Hungarian pioneers and their Texas descendants are also maintained for future use.

CHAPTER ONE

Hungary and Texas

Bon voyage, you horsemen!
Bon voyage, you hero!
You noble lady! In the New World
Be granted to you, you mourners and maiden,
Freedom, home, happiness, and peace.

With this poem Hermann Seele, a German immigrant, commemorated the arrival of László Újházi, the most noteworthy exile of the Hungarian Revolution of 1848-1849, and his sons and daughter as they passed through New Braunfels on their way to a new home near San Antonio in September 1853. As Hungary's first political refugees reached Texas, Seele saluted them as the heroes of a valiant nation, defeated in their quest for freedom and forced to seek haven on America's Texas frontier. Although preceded by a few Hungarian adventurers, travelers, and settlers, the arrival during the 1850's of a score or more of political émigrés fleeing the failed revolution marked the real beginning of Hungarian immigration to Texas.[1]

Hungary is a small Central European country of almost 36,000 square miles and a population of about 11 million. By contrast, Texas covers a land mass of 266,807 square miles and has more than 17 million citizens. Few Texans know that the Treaty of Trianon, which ended World War I for Hungary in 1920, awarded more than two-thirds of the ancient kingdom, or 89,700 square miles, to her neighboring states: Austria, Czechoslovakia, Rumania, and Yugoslavia. Sixty-four percent of her population, including more than 3.5 million Magyars and most of her national minorities of Slovaks, Serbs, Germans, Ruthenians,

1

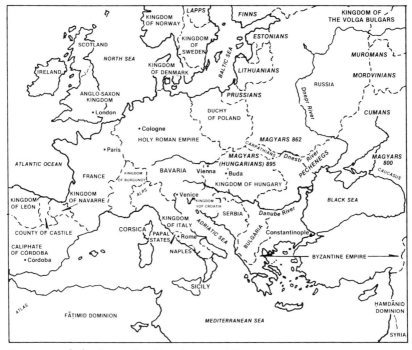

Europe and the Byzantine Empire, c. 1000

Croats, Slovenians, Rumanians, and others, were also lost. What remained was a nearly homogenous core of Magyars in what was called Inner Hungary in historic times.[2]

Hungary lies in the Carpathian Basin, surrounded on the west, north, and east by a wall of mountains of the same name. Bisected from north to south by the mighty middle Danube River, eastern and southern Hungary is largely a stepped plain. Mountainous Transylvania (Erdély in Hungarian), now part of Rumania, lies still farther eastward in the Carpathian Mountains. West of the Danube, hilly country reaches toward the Alps. This Trans-Danubian district contains the country's largest lake, Balaton. Into this mountain-protected basin marched the Magyar tribes, ancestors of the Hungarian nation, in A.D. 896.

Who are the Magyars, and where did they come from? Little is known of their origin. They speak a Finno-Ugric language, part of the larger Ural-Altaic family of languages. Only Finnish, Estonian, and a few minor languages are related to Hungarian. Coming originally from the region of the middle Ural Mountains, the ancient tribes mi-

2

grated westward from their forested homeland onto the steppes of what is now southern Russia, where they came into contact with Turkish peoples. Leading the lives of nomadic herdsmen, the Magyar tribes were gradually forced westward by fiercer neighbors in the fifth century. By the early ninth century seven hordes, or tribes, lived along the right bank of the lower Don River. There they were joined by three hordes of Turkish Khazars, the Kabars.[3]

Under pressure from superior forces from Central Asia, these nomadic tribes moved westward in 889 under the leadership of Árpád, a Magyar chieftain. They crossed the passes of the Carpathians in 895-896 and took possession of the Carpathian Basin from the weaker Slavs and Avars. The Székelys, another tribe already present, submitted and were assigned to guard the Carpathian passes in what became known as Transylvania. By 907 the conquest was complete, each tribe was allotted its own area of the conquered territory, and the house of Árpád ruled Hungary for the next four centuries.[4]

Christianity arrived from the west. Géza, the great-grandson of Árpád, received Christian baptism from Byzantine priests from Constantinople, and his son, Stephen, the "best-loved, most famous, and perhaps the most important figure" in Hungary's history, opted for Roman Catholicism and became Hungary's first Christian king. He converted his people, built churches, and laid the foundation for a feudal state. Stephen was canonized in 1087.[5]

In 1222 the Golden Bull, Hungary's Magna Carta, chartered national liberties and established Hungarian constitutionalism. But disaster struck the kingdom in 1241 when the Mongols (Tartars) under Batu Khan swept through the Carpathian passes and ravaged the land and its population for a year. With the death of the last Árpád king in 1301, the throne passed to foreign monarchs, who ruled until Austria's Habsburg dynasty came to power in the 16th century.[6]

Hungary faced a second, more lasting disaster brought on by the decline of royal power. An unsuccessful peasant revolt in 1514 paved the way for serfdom. As a result, Hungary was severely weakened when faced with aggression from the Ottoman Turks from the Balkans. In 1526 the Hungarian national army was defeated at the battle of Mohács and the king killed. For the next century and a half, the Ottomans ruled southern and central Hungary, while Austria dominated the northern and western fringes of the country. In the east Transylvania became an autonomous state subject to the Turks.[7]

Liberated from the Turks in 1699, reunited Hungary was ruled by Austria's Habsburgs until 1918. Although monarchs periodically sought to impose centralized rule over their polyglot empire, Hungary's nobility preserved ancient constitutional traditions and rights which each king swore to uphold at his coronation in Hungary. Austria was forced to compromise with those rights throughout much of its rule, and it was from the ranks of the nobility that Hungarian nationalist leaders emerged early in the 19th century to lead a linguistic, cultural, and national revival.[8]

With the meeting of the 1825 Hungarian Diet, the economically and socially underdeveloped country experienced "a powerful modernizing movement" similar to that which began earlier in Western Europe. Aimed at removing the ancient privileges of the nobility, improving life for the peasants, and gaining national freedom, this revival became known as Hungary's Age of Reform, 1825-1848. It culminated in the Revolution of 1848-1849 against Habsburg autocracy. Although some wished to retain traditional ties to the Crown, many of the lesser nobility, led by Lajos (Louis) Kossuth, demanded liberal social and economic reforms and favored radical changes in the political link to the Habsburg king which would lead to national independence.[9]

Kossuth, a young lawyer, became leader of the opposition in the Hungarian Diet in 1847. He called for a genuine, responsible national Hungarian government; an enlarged franchise on the local and national scene to include non-nobles; taxation of nobles as well as commoners; abolition of the remnants of feudal dues and serfdom (without compensation to the landlords); the equality of everyone under the law and of all recognized religions; freedom of the press and of assembly; and union with Transylvania. However, no concessions were offered by this Magyar national movement to the kingdom's minorities, especially the Croats and the Serbs. In spite of stiff minority resistance, Magyar was made the official language of public life and education.[10]

Hungary's inability to solve its minority problems, combined with goals for modernizing the nation, brought on armed conflict. The Revolution of 1848, which began in France, spread to Austria. Austrian Chancellor Metternich was deposed in Vienna, and crowned heads elsewhere fruitlessly sought to turn back the clock. In Hungary the Diet pressed its demands on the king, who appointed a government and a provisional prime minister in March 1848. The king also accepted the reform package, which became known as the April Laws. Thus

Hungary became a constitutional monarchy under its Habsburg king, and Kossuth joined the new government as minister of finance.

Events moved rapidly during the spring of 1848. Croatia, backed by Austria, rebelled against Hungary, which in turn set up its own national army (Honvéd, or National Guard). When Croatia invaded Hungary in September 1848 and mediation failed, martial law was declared by the king, and the Hungarian ministry resigned. Kossuth then became head of the Hungarian committee of public safety for national defense. In December the new Austrian ruler, Franz Joseph, embarked upon a vigorous program of uniting all lands and peoples of the empire into one great centralized state, but the Hungarians declared that policy illegal and resisted.

The war of independence lasted until August 1849. Hungary's new armies were initially successful in the north and in Transylvania, but Austrian and Croatian forces captured Buda in January 1849. The Hungarian government fled east to Debrecen, where on April 14 the Diet declared the throne vacant and Hungary an independent country with Kossuth as governor. Czarist Russia then came to the aid of Austria. Hungarian forces were driven into the southeastern part of the country and overwhelmed at Temesvár on August 8, 1849. Kossuth and his followers fled into exile. On August 13 Hungary surrendered at Világos—the struggle for national independence was over.

Many who had participated in the revolution chose exile in Europe and America. Others were not as lucky. Hundreds were executed, including the prerevolution prime minister, 13 generals (at Arad), and many other military and political figures. Austria abrogated all of Hungary's national institutions, set up a provisional administration which separated Transylvania and Croatia-Slavonia, and divided Hungary into five administrative districts. A non-Hungarian bureaucracy and police force were created, minorities and their languages were declared equal, and German became the language of administration. Taxes were raised. But the repressive and centralist policies united the Hungarian nation in passive resistance. Although many of these policies were modified during the 1850's, a solution was not reached until the Austro-Hungarian Compromise of 1867.[11]

Hungary's great statesman Ferenc Deák and Austrian Emperor Franz Joseph reached an agreement whereby Hungary regained her constitutional integrity under Austro-Hungary, the new dual monarchy. Franz Joseph was crowned King of Hungary with the Hungarian regalia

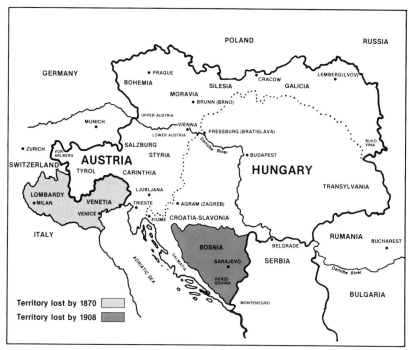

Austro-Hungarian Empire, 1914

in Buda, and a new Hungarian government controlled everything except foreign, fiscal, and military affairs, which were shared with Austria in the new system. Transylvania was reunited with Hungary and a Croatian settlement reached. In the new Hungarian constitutional monarchy, "a great economic and cultural development started," leading to a half century of "peace, progress, and prosperity." [12]

Hungary celebrated its millennium in 1896 with great fanfare. In the capital, Budapest (Buda, Pest, and Óbuda had amalgamated in 1873), the Parliament building and the Royal Palace faced each other across the Danube. Transportation, capital, industry, and modern agriculture saw vast improvement during the last decades of the century. But a rapid population increase (19,250,000 in 1900) coupled with uneven social and economic conditions among the people contributed to large-scale emigration to America by the lower classes, who sought economic opportunity unavailable within the country. Industrial workers, small farmers, craftsmen and businessmen, and others joined this migration to the United States and to Texas. [13]

The outbreak of war in 1914 brought an end to emigration from Hungary. With the defeat of Germany and Austro-Hungary in 1918, Hungary faced an uncertain future. The Treaty of Trianon dealt a serious and traumatic blow, removing two-thirds of Hungary's territory and more than half its population. Following a brief period of Bolshevik revolution and counterrevolution, an independent Hungary emerged as a constitutional monarchy governed by a regent in conjunction with Parliament. War reparations and the Great Depression of the 1930's further impoverished the truncated nation. As a result, Hungary was drawn into World War II on the side of the Axis, hoping thereby to regain lost territories from her neighbors.

The defeat of the Axis powers in 1945 doomed Hungary to military occupation by the Soviet Union. New immigrants — refugees and exiles, who were called Displaced Persons — arrived in the United States and Texas during the late 1940's and early 1950's, infusing their numbers into this country's century-old Hungarian community. Some

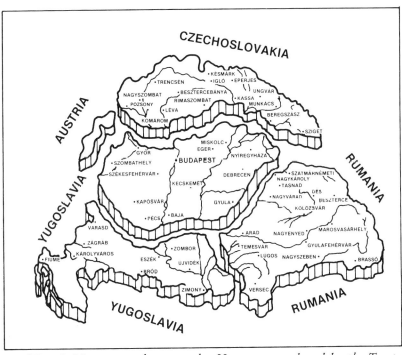

Historic Hungary and present-day Hungary as reduced by the Treaty of Trianon, 1920

of Hungary's brightest and most talented people began new lives in Texas' universities, laboratories, and industries. Still other political émigrés arrived in the months following the uprising of 1956 in Hungary. Thus, in the period bounded by the Revolution of 1848-1849 and the uprising against Russian occupation in 1956, scores and then thousands of political exiles found homes in Texas. Their numbers were strengthened greatly by many others who left Hungary in search of a better life. During that century the Hungarians joined emigrants from many nations in populating Texas, a state rapidly emerging into the modern age.

Texas welcomed the immigrants. The geographic area that had become Texas first emerged from prehistory as a remote border province of New Spain (1519-1821) and, later, of the Republic of Mexico (1821-1836). As Hungary began her Age of Reform in the 1820's, the first significant numbers of immigrants entered Texas from the United States to claim bountiful, fertile, cheap land for the cultivation of cotton. Stephen F. Austin and others promoted colonization under liberal Mexican laws which welcomed the newcomers. Europeans—individuals or families—joined the Anglo-Americans who came after 1821, and a few German and French colonies were successfully founded during the 1840's and 1850's.

By the mid-1830's political events within Mexico—principally a power struggle between those who favored centralized versus federated government—led to the Texas Revolution of 1836 wherein the victorious Texans gained sovereignty. The Republic of Texas (1836-1845) also welcomed newcomers to civilize its vast territory, much of which remained beyond the western frontier for another four decades.

Annexed in 1845 as the 28th state, Texas' story became part of the history of the United States. As the frontier slowly receded, emigrants from many other states and from Europe continued to settle in the Lone Star State. Its agricultural base was supplemented by the growth of the cattle kingdom within its western boundaries. By 1890 the frontier closed, and railroads reached across the land. Still an agricultural producer by the turn of the century, Texas faced a period of rapid industrial development with the discovery of oil at Spindletop in 1901, followed by two world wars. Fed by seemingly limitless natural resources in the state coupled with the labor of its increasing population, Texas welcomed immigrants, who became part of the ethnic mosaic of its people.

Hungary, 1993

Until the advent of the great economic migration in the 1880's, the story of Texas' Hungarian pioneers can be told in terms of individuals. Then, with the pre-World War I arrival of hundreds seeking prosperity, and later, with a second and larger wave of political refugees after World War II, Texas' Hungarian minority rapidly expanded. The history of Hungarians in Texas then broadened to include settlement patterns and the role of non-Magyar minority peoples from the ancient Hungarian kingdom who joined the migration. Hungarian community efforts became viable only after 1945 in larger cities where, for the first time, sufficient numbers permitted the formation of heritage preservation associations. Only then did the Hungarians become a visible minority within the state's population.

The stories which follow are representative of the collective experiences of all immigrants who bravely faced the future in the American Southwest. Their participation in economic, social, and political life reflected that of all who helped civilize Texas' vast land in less than two centuries. When Hungary celebrated its millennium in 1896, Texas

9

was still a young, sparsely populated state. Its potential for opportunity and advancement was shared by Hungary's political exiles and other immigrants who joined in their quest for freedom and economic security. Hermann Seele's wish for "freedom, home, happiness, and peace" in 1853 expressed Texas' promise for these people.

CHAPTER TWO

"To the Other Side of the World"

Early Hungarians in Texas

K lára Újházy Kellerschön, probably the first Hungarian woman in Texas, wrote in her diary on October 8, 1860, that her father, László Újházi, "constantly has an urge to go, either to the prairie or to the other side of the world." She saw in her father the wanderlust of many Europeans of her time, including Hungarians, who wished to explore new vistas. Although it was generally considered that Hungarians did not have any significant part in the geographical discoveries and explorations of the 15th to the 19th centuries, the first Hungarian in America may have been a man called Tyrker (Turk), who accompanied Eric the Red about A.D. 1000. He was followed by a Stephen Parmenius of Buda, who visited Newfoundland in 1583.[1]

During the next two centuries a few Hungarian missionaries worked in the English and Spanish colonies in North America, and others published their travel experiences on this continent. A few Hungarians fought for American freedom in the Revolution, including Colonel Michael Kováts and Major John Ladislaus Pollereczky. Later, information on post-Revolutionary America and its liberal, democratic political institutions reached and influenced Hungarians through translated histories and travelogues during the 1830's and 1840's, coinciding with Hungary's own Age of Reform. Scientific and cultural exchanges were also initiated at this time between the two countries. But, as far

11

George Fisher

as is known, none of these early adventurers, travelers, missionaries, and soldiers reached Texas.[2]

George Fisher was Texas' first Hungarian adventurer. When he died in San Francisco in 1873 at the age of 78, he had experienced a life filled with high adventure and accomplishment. A citizen of four countries (Hungary, the United States, Mexico, and Texas) and the husband of an equal number of wives, he had participated in important political events that led to Texas' rebellion against Mexico and the establishment of the new Republic of Texas.

Fisher's early life was obscure. He was said to have been born of Slovene (or Serbian) parents named Ribar (some sources say the family name was Sagíc) in Székesfehérvár, Hungary, on April 30, 1795. Following the early death of his father, Fisher was placed under the care of Archbishop Stephen Stratimirovich of the Orthodox Church and was sent to the College of Carlowitz to train as a priest. Fisher had other things in mind, however. He ran away from the college in 1813 to join Serbian forces under Kara George ("Black George") Petrovich to fight the Turks at Belgrade.[3]

With the defeat of the Serbian forces, Fisher joined Austria's Slavonian Legion to fight the French in Italy. After Napoleon's fall at Waterloo in 1815, Fisher found himself unemployed. Traveling from Turkey to Holland, the 20-year-old then took passage to America as a redemptioner (in order to pay his fare) and jumped ship at the mouth of the Delaware River to gain his freedom. For the next couple of years, he wandered through America, settling at Port Gibson, Mississippi, by 1817.

There he opened a tavern and a tailoring shop and applied for American citizenship in 1818. In the same year he married Elizabeth Davis and became a Free and Accepted Mason of the York Rite. Fisher assumed his first civic responsibility in 1819, as assistant commissioner of a board set up in his county to pay pensions to the veterans of the American Revolution. With a growing family, he moved in 1821 to Twin Halls, the Mississippi plantation of his wife on the Big Black River. There he became a cotton planter and in 1822 a citizen of the United States. In 1825 he went to Mexico to assist in establishing a York Rite Masonic Lodge. While there, Fisher took out Mexican naturalization papers in 1829. Ever alert to new adventures and opportunities, he embarked upon another career, which was to directly affect Texas, then part of Mexico.[4]

In Mexico Fisher applied for an empresario contract to settle 500 families in Texas within the old Haden Edwards Grant and was appointed collector of customs at Galveston in 1829. Although he did not receive official credentials, he was recognized as the administrator of the port but was suspended by order of General Manuel de Mier y Terán the next year. Fisher then became secretary of the local government (*ayuntamiento*) at San Felipe, Stephen F. Austin's colonial center in Texas, but he was again fired, this time because of suspicion that he was spying for the Mexican authorities. In 1831 General Mier y Terán appointed Fisher as Mexican customs collector at Anahuac on Galveston Bay.[5]

Unfortunately Fisher angered the Anglo-American colonists in Texas. He arbitrarily ordered that all ships leaving the little port of Brazoria, 70 miles from Anahuac, as well as other coastal points, clear their papers at Anahuac. Thus a long trip over primitive roads and bridgeless rivers was required of ship captains by the customs official, who failed to explain that his was a temporary order pending the arrival of a deputy collector for the Brazos River port. Already angered by other incidents, such as the collection of the Mexican tariff and the arrest of several popular figures, including William Barrett Travis on charges of sedition, the colonists resisted. Some ship captains ran their vessels by the Mexican fort on the Brazos, neglecting or refusing to travel to Anahuac for clearance. In one encounter a Mexican soldier was wounded. Fisher was forced to seek safety in Matamoros as the result of these disturbances at Anahuac and because of threats from the colonists.[6]

Never at a loss for a new venture, Fisher then turned to journalism, becoming the publisher of the *Mercurio del Puerto de Matamoros* in 1832. There he remained for the next three years, using his knowledge of Spanish, one of 16 modern languages (in addition to Latin and Greek) which he reportedly knew. Three years later he was dismissed for his liberal editorial policy and expelled from Mexico.[7]

Arriving in New Orleans in October 1835, Fisher immediately joined with Mexican opposition leader José Antonio Mexía in a movement to raise men and supplies to oppose the centralist dictatorship of Mexican President General Antonio López de Santa Anna. Fisher acted as the commissary general and secretary for the planned attack on Tampico, Mexico, which ended in failure because of a premature uprising of the local garrison and the arrival of enemy troops at that port city. Mexía, leading the attack, was defeated and fled to Texas. Although the invasion of Mexico by Santa Anna's political enemies failed, Fisher had established himself among the liberal opposition to the dictator's centralist rule in Mexico and ultimately on the side of the Texan colonists in the approaching revolution.[8]

After the battle of San Jacinto, April 21, 1836, Fisher appeared once again in Texas. He first visited the Texas prisoner-of-war camp on Galveston Island as an "observer" and then settled in Houston, where he became a commission merchant. There he served as a justice of the peace in 1839, was admitted to the bar, served on the Houston city council, and became president of the German Union in 1840. The next year he visited the Mexican state of Yucatán, then in rebellion against the central government, as a secret agent. The Texas government had leased its small navy to aid Yucatán, and a state of war still existed between Texas and Mexico.[9]

Fisher witnessed the annexation of Texas to the United States in 1845. When the Texas constitutional convention met in Austin that year, he served as translator and interpreter for Bexar County's Spanish-speaking delegation headed by José Antonio Navarro. Fisher also translated the new state constitution and the Ordinance of Annexation into Spanish. The next year he resigned his position as Houston's city recorder and accepted the position of Spanish translator and keeper of the Spanish records in the State's General Land Office, which he held until 1848.[10]

Fisher departed Texas in 1850 to establish York Rite Masonic lodges in Panama and then followed the rush to California's goldfields. There he remained for the rest of his life. Although he presented his library, papers, and correspondence to the State of Texas in 1856, his future arena of adventure and opportunity was San Francisco, where he practiced law until his death on June 11, 1873. He also served as the secretary for the California Land Commission from 1852 to 1856 and became the Greek consul in San Francisco in 1870.[11]

The arrival of the next Hungarian in Texas, Count Zondogi, was announced in Houston's leading newspaper, the *Telegraph and Texas Register*, on April 9, 1845. The paper wrote that George Wilkens Kendall, of "Santa Fe memory" and publisher of the New Orleans *Picayune*, and his party of hunters had arrived and were on their way to "the Commanche [*sic*] country to have another tumble among the buffaloes." The party included an English pleasure traveler, the son of a wealthy New York merchant, an old resident of Texas, a Mr.

"Life on the Prairie: the Buffalo Hunt," by Arthur F. Tait

Catlett, and the Hungarian Count Zondogi. On April 16 the Houston editor warned that this party intended "making a regular onslaught upon the shaggy tenants of the prairie" after visiting San Antonio to examine "the curiosities in that neighborhood." [12] The true identity of the Hungarian hunter, Count Zondogi, may never be known. Was he a genuine nobleman? Was Zondogi his real name? The only factual thing known about him is that he came to Texas during the spring of 1845, took part in a buffalo hunt on the San Gabriel River in Central Texas, and then left. [13]

Personal glimpses of this traveler come only from Kendall's commentary to the Houston newspaper and his own paper in New Orleans. The count's encounter with Texas conditions, especially the roads, was anything but pleasant. Kendall reported on April 26 that the trip from Houston to Washington-on-the-Brazos was a matter of "swimming, topdigging, and floundering . . . two days of the time completely weather and water bound." He went on to report that with horses the party could get along well enough, "but the Count's lameness, although he is now nearly over it, induced us to purchase a wagon at Houston, and it is not altogether so simple a matter to swim a vehicle of that particular description, neither is it so easy to draw it through the deep, heavy, black mud of the prairies." [14]

In all probability, Kendall's big-game hunt was a smoke screen for his real purpose in visiting Texas at that time. The New Orleans publicist, who "considered himself a sort of guardian of Texas" and who made the *Picayune* a reliable source of information on the neighboring frontier republic, was anxious to obtain firsthand information on Texas' plans for annexation to the United States. Hurrying as he did with the hunting party from the Texas coast to the Texan seat of government at Washington-on-the-Brazos, Kendall was determined to work for annexation and to thwart British and French diplomatic machinations to the contrary. The Hungarian count was merely an eye-witness to these momentous intrigues. [15]

Events moved rapidly during that year. On February 28, 1845, the United States Congress had offered statehood to Texas by a joint resolution by both houses. President Anson Jones of Texas then called his Congress to meet on June 16, and a convention to consider the American offer met on July 4, 1845. Both Texas houses voted for annexation, and on December 29, 1845, Texas became the 28th state in the United States. [16]

What interested Kendall were the diplomatic moves of Great Britain to prevent annexation. In an effort to block America's westward expansion toward the Pacific as well as to benefit from Texas' trade, especially in cotton and other raw materials, British foreign policy sought to gain Mexico's recognition of Texan independence, provided that the latter did not join the United States. When Britain's chargé in Texas, Captain Charles Elliot, left Galveston ostensibly bound for Charleston, South Carolina, but secretly slipped into Mexico to obtain that country's agreement to extend recognition to the Republic of Texas, Kendall's reports of his movements were published in the *Picayune* in late May 1845. From New Orleans this news reached American papers in the East. Kendall got his story and kept the reading public current on Elliot's secret negotiations with Mexico. In the end, the British effort failed.[17]

Having accomplished his goal, Kendall and his party completed their buffalo hunt and returned to Houston in late May. Unusually large herds had been found near the San Gabriel River, where Count Zondogi and his companions killed about 50 animals. The Houston newspaper revealed that "their excursion to the frontier was exceedingly agreeable, and they have returned delighted with their sport." Had the hunting party gone a little farther north, to the vicinity of the Little River, their experience may have been less agreeable because the Comanches were there, encamped near Torrey's Trading Post about eight miles below present Waco.[18]

Nothing else is known of Count Zondogi in Texas' history. One of the first Hungarians to visit, he had witnessed an important and dramatic episode of international intrigue and momentous political decision relating to the growth of the American republic. He may also have been the first Hungarian big-game hunter to visit the buffalo range in North America.

Anton Lochmar appears to have been the first Hungarian immigrant to settle permanently in Texas. Lochmar arrived as a member of John Charles Beales's projected Rio Grande Colony of 800 families who were to be recruited in New York in 1833 to settle between the Rio Grande and the Nueces River. The first group, 59 men, women, and children, arrived at Texas' Copano Bay in 1833 and traveled by oxcart to the colony site on Las Moras Creek, a tributary of the Rio Grande. There the multinational colony, including Americans, Britons, Germans, and Mexicans, built their brush hut or *jacal* (pole) homes, cleared the mesquite, prickly pear, and chaparral, dug irrigation canals, and planted their fields. A gristmill and a church were also constructed. To this beginning, Beales brought a second group of colonists, including Lochmar, from New York.[19]

However, Lochmar remained in the Rio Grande Colony, or Dolores, as it was called, for only a short time. Drought and marauding Indians in South Texas doomed the colony, and people soon began to leave for Mexico or elsewhere. One account reported that Lochmar was captured by the Indians but escaped to Dolores. Within a few years the Texas Revolution broke out, and the remaining Dolores colonists fled before the advancing Mexican army in the spring of 1836.[20]

Lochmar joined the Texas army, but too late to take part in any military engagement. Later "Antonio Lockman" and "Antonio Lockner" received two bounty land grants from the Republic of Texas government for service rendered from May to October and from November 1836 to November 1837. After his brief army career 24-year-old Lochmar moved to San Antonio. There he served as a city alderman, 1841-1842, and with two partners, Peter Fohr and George M. Dolson, opened a "house of entertainment" (a saloon and gambling hall) called the Bowie Tavern on Commerce Street.[21]

Who was this pioneer? Anton Lochmar was born in 1812 in Zengg, a seaport on the Dalmatian coast of Croatia, then part of the Kingdom of Hungary. Little is known of his family other than that a brother lived in Zagreb (Agram), Croatia, and a nephew was later a professor at the local university. How Lochmar came to the United States is not known. But, once in his new home in San Antonio, he made a brief and spectacular climb to the top. On November 30, 1839, he married Maria Apolinaria Treviño (1819-1885), granddaughter of Canary Islanders who had come to San Antonio in 1731. The Lochmars' children included a son, George W., who never married, and four daughters, Ysabel, Catarina Augusta, Adelina, and Pauline.[22]

Anton and Apolinaria, the last residents of San Antonio's famous Spanish Colonial Veramendi Palace, opened the Lochmar Hotel in 1840. It was located on Soledad Street and was described as the "best house in the city." Surrounded by a wall, the Lochmar Hotel was said to have been small. Its main entrance was through double doors wide enough for a team and wagon to enter. The dining room and sitting rooms flanked the entrance, which opened into a flowery patio with a well in its center. Around the patio were guest rooms shaded by porches. All windows facing the street were barred for protection. A back patio was used by servants for cooking and raising chickens. A rear entrance was used for carriages, horses, and cattle, and a vegetable garden and orchard were surrounded by a high wall. The Lochmar Hotel catered to many more lunch and dinner guests than overnighters. As he prospered Anton Lochmar also acquired 1,476 acres of land on Leon Creek. But his career was brief. He died suddenly on October 9, 1848, at the age of 36.[23]

As with Lochmar, Texas' next known Hungarian immigrants also arrived as part of colonizing efforts which sought to take advantage of liberal grants of public land, at first from the Mexican government and later from the Republic of Texas. Both governments sought to populate the vast and empty territory which had only about 36,000 citizens in 1836. In addition to Mexican and American empresarios (entrepreneurs and colonizers), Europeans were also attracted to the land grants in the newly independent frontier republic during the early 1840's. Germans came with the Adelsverein (Society of Nobles, also known as the Society for the Protection of German Immigrants to Texas), and Frenchmen (mainly Alsatians, with Rhineland Germans and families from the Low Countries) settled in Henri Castro's colony on vacant land west of the frontier. A single Hungarian immigrant appeared in each of these, the most successful of the European emigration efforts to Texas. The story of how each of these men found his way to Texas as a colonist reveals an interesting part of the development of the Republic of Texas. In the case of the Adelsverein, a Hungarian nobleman gave unheeded advice concerning the capitalization and planning for the proposed colony in Texas.

What is known of Baron Paul von Szirmay and his relationship to Texas comes from the records of the Adelsverein, the most successful German colonization effort in Texas. Szirmay was the only Hungarian nobleman of the 50 titled shareholders, who were mostly German nobles, reigning princes, and royalty. It was organized at Biebrich on the Rhine in 1042 to buy land in the Republic of Texas. In 1844, as a stock company, the society modified its purpose to include sponsoring German immigrants to Texas. After a series of negotiations it received rights to settle immigrants on the 3,878,000-acre Fisher-Miller Grant north of the Llano River in Indian country. New Braunfels, the first town of the colony, was founded in 1845, and Fredericksburg, the second settlement, was founded the next year. Prince Carl of Solms-Braunfels, the first commissioner general in Texas, was soon replaced by Baron Otfried Hans von Meusebach, who made a successful peace treaty in 1847 with the southern Comanches, thus opening the grant to German settlers. However, the society's efforts in Texas led to bankruptcy by the summer of 1847, and it was reorganized as the Texas Verein, still devoted to sending emigrants from Germany.[24]

How Baron Paul von Szirmay knew of the Adelsverein is not known, but in October 1845 he wrote from Hungary that he considered himself a member, being the owner of one share of its stock (valued at 5,000 forints, or $2,000 in 1845, which he purchased on credit). He wrote, "I wish to share joy and sadness with the Verein, and it is my intention to visit Texas, if possible next year. . . ." From his estate at Okruchla near Eperjes in Upper Hungary, Szirmay continued a steady stream of letters to the society's officers in Mainz for the next two years, mostly concerning his plans to visit Texas and his desire to become the second commissioner general stationed there. By May 1846 he was prepared to travel by way of Bremen in August or September on a Verein ship (he preferred a steamer). However, he was unable to attend the General Assembly of the society in Mainz, because of a six-day delay in Vienna while he waited for a travel permit. Yet, he wrote, he felt that the "personal presence of a member of the Verein can only aid the total well-being of the people." He also stated that he intended to stay in Texas for at least one year, but a society official reported from New Orleans in October 1846 that, "We have not heard from von Szirmay. However, we found out that the *Neptune* was diverted from Galveston to here, and has just arrived." Szirmay was not aboard.[25]

Szirmay wrote in November 1846 that an inheritance matter had prevented his leaving for Texas, but that he hoped to take ship in December from Bremen or Antwerp. Then, in December, he received notice that the society's October General Assembly had appointed Meusebach as the second commissioner general in Texas. Szirmay swallowed his disappointment and continued his dreams about emigrating to Texas with his wife and sons. He delayed his departure again, this time until March, asking the society for a free ship cabin, free room and food in Texas, and "some land in either New Braunfels, Fredericksburg, or in the town yet to be built on the Llano River."[26]

Baron von Szirmay must have spent considerable time thinking of the affairs of the Adelsverein during the winter of 1846-1847 at his estate in Upper Hungary. Although the society was in deep financial trouble, he urged the General Assembly to expand its horizons, increase the value and number of its shares, recruit new emigrants, and set its goals at owning several million acres within five to ten years, which would increase in value "one hundred to one thousand times." Ascribing the society's troubles to "miscalculations" and to the war between Mexico and the United States, he urged that Meusebach found a new town within the Fisher-Miller Grant (which he named Union Town and, later, Concordia). Szirmay, saying "I don't believe myself to live in Utopia," suggested that a "prime colony in the wilderness" be divided into as many parts as shareholders, who would each send one carefully selected family and build a school and church. All of "their" families would travel together from Bremen or Antwerp, and "all other expenses would be borne together. Within no time at all, the Verein would reap fabulous results from this undertaking." Szirmay ended his letter, "It is possible that I am a dreamer . . . however, I can hardly believe this, and the answer that I am a self-serving person, whose aristocratic tendencies give him such ideas, is one I cannot accept." [27]

Because of the distance from his estate in Hungary, Baron von Szirmay never attended General Assembly meetings in Mainz. Nor did he ever pay for his share, which was bought on credit. By July 1849 the Verein contemplated legal action as well as diplomatic or administrative efforts with the Austrian government to collect this debt of 5,000 forints plus interest. Finally a letter from Baroness Elotita von Szirmay was read at the General Assembly meeting on May 30, 1853, in which she said, "Since my husband left his homeland in 1849, and all of his possessions were confiscated by the [Austrian] government after he was sentenced, I am asking you to refrain from sending letters and notices to him at this address." Apparently Szirmay was exiled after the Revolution of 1848-1849. [28]

· ———————— ·

Concordia, Szirmay's Dream Town in Texas

Baron Paul von Szirmay's plan for an ideal community on Adelsverein land in Texas in 1847 was outlined in a long letter to the "Titled Members of the Society for the Protection of German Immigrants to Texas." There immigrants would find a "fruitful fatherland in Texas," sponsored by the nobles of the society, "since it is moved by ideologies only noble people have." Concordia, the name selected by Szirmay, was to center around 100 acres in which each of the 50 shareholders was to have a two-acre plot. An additional surrounding 500 acres would be distributed in ten-acre lots. Then a member of the Verein was to arrive with nine immigrants (three carpenters, three farmers, one smith, one bricklayer, and one saddler) to prepare for the following 40 families by plowing fields and building houses, a grain silo, and a sawmill. For each family, a house was to be provided as well as 20 acres of farmland, free passage to Texas, and farming tools. Food would be provided for a year by the Verein. Each family would buy its own cattle and seed, live there for five years, and provide labor for the Verein. A deposit of 1,000 forints would be paid by immigrants to the society in Germany, and half would form a credit fund for items not provided by the Verein in Texas. The other half, 500 forints, would go to the Verein for travel money, 20-acre plots, a house, and food for one year. Szirmay also outlined the types of occupations needed in "Concordia": ten farmers, eight carpenters, six bricklayers, three smiths, two tailors, two shoemakers, two cabinetmakers, two tilemakers, two beer brewers, and one each locksmith, butcher, tanner, binder, potter, hatter, harness maker, saddler, wheelwright, turner, dyer, soapmaker, baker, and stonemason. Further, "Concordia" would also need a doctor, a pastor, and a schoolteacher as well as a schoolhouse, a church, an inn, and a community house. The town was to be governed within a year by a mayor, two counselors, a secretary, and three councilmen. All but the mayor were to be elected, with each family having two voices. Szirmay figured that building this community in Texas would cost the Verein 85,000 forints. Its costs would be recovered from revenue on livestock, tools and instruments, and labor, and by building ten houses on each shareholder's two-acre plot in the town, which would be sold for profit, as could be their ten acres outside the town. The town would attract new immigrants within a few years, and land values would increase, permitting the stockholders to realize handsome gains on their investment. Szirmay offered to "oversee the entire matter in America" if his travel costs were provided. He proposed to take the first ten immigrants himself, including two or three Hungarian families at his personal expense. Concluding, he wrote, "I have given this new town the name of 'Concordia'." [29]

Information from another source suggests that Paul Szirmay later reached America with other Hungarian political exiles. The Hungarian-American historian Géza Kende wrote in 1927 that Paul Szirmay accompanied exiled poet Frigyes Kerényi to New Buda, Iowa. On May 22, 1851, Klára Újházy, then a resident of that village, wrote:

> Two weeks ago our old, very good friends, Pali Szirmay and Frigyes Kerényi arrived. My father [László Újházi] went on horseback to meet them. He met Pali Szirmay, also on horseback, who was humming "The Parisienne." Szirmay was scouting the road to New Buda because the stream was overflowing. Kerényi was waiting in the nearby village with their cart.

Géza Kende also described Szirmay as "always happy, always playing." Szirmay built a cabin at New Buda near a stream during the summer of 1851, but apparently did not stay long and may have moved to California, where he was ambiguously identified as "an ambassador." All of his Utopian plans for a German colony in Texas had come to naught.[30]

Only one Hungarian has been identified among the thousands of Adelsverein colonists who arrived during the mid-1840's. When Gottfried Joseph Petmecky emigrated to Texas in 1845 from Schönau, Nassau, Germany, he could not have foreseen events which would make him the father of two branches of a well-known Texas family. Of Hungarian ancestry, he was the son of Jakob and Anna Brünkmann Petmecky and was born in Hradisch, Bohemia, on August 1, 1809. A teacher by profession, he married Anna Hübinger (Huebner) in the Holler Catholic Church in Limburg on the Lahn on April 4, 1834. Five children, Franz, Maria, Theresa, Joseph, and Lisette, accompanied their parents to Texas through Antwerp, Belgium, on the *Strabo*.[31]

Traveling by way of Indianola, the Texas port of the Adelsverein, the Petmecky family settled in the German colony of New Braunfels. There they received a town lot and a ten-acre farming plot nearby until their headright of 320 acres could be surveyed in the Fisher-Miller Grant north of the Llano River. The society's colonial grant was located far into the interior and was controlled by hostile Comanche Indians. Therefore, the colonists stayed at New Braunfels and planted their first crop of corn. Gottfried was also employed by the immigration company as a teacher. He later became city secretary for the newly organized town of New Braunfels. In 1850 he founded and directed the first German singing society in Texas, the Germania Gesängverein.[32]

Conditions in Texas were anything but those idealized by Baron von Szirmay. Tragedy struck the Petmeckys soon after their arrival. During a terrible but unidentified epidemic that swept through the German colonies in 1846-1847, Anna died on March 19, 1847, at the age of 35. Thereafter, with five small children to support, Gottfried farmed at New Braunfels until his marriage to Johanna Kuhfuss, née Richter, on August 8, 1853. She, too, had lost her spouse during the epidemic. The Petmeckys then moved to San Antonio, where Gottfried became a music teacher. Two children, A.W. and Lena, were born to his second marriage, thus establishing the second branch of his family in Texas. Gottfried Petmecky died in San Antonio in May 1871.[33]

Following the second marriage of their father, Joseph Carl and his brother, Franz (Frank), left home. Born on August 12, 1842, Joseph Petmecky apprenticed to a gunsmith, first in San Antonio and then in Austin to a man named Owens who had a shop on Congress Avenue. Owens had observed Joseph's interest in the craft and gave him a test — to file a rough piece of iron into a square. Although the task was impossible, Joseph demonstrated his persistence and was accepted by Owens. When the gunsmith died in the mid-1850's, the 15-year-old Joseph carried on the business in his own name. A skillful and inventive man, Joseph Petmecky thus established a retail sporting goods business, Austin's oldest, which lasted for three generations—123 years.[34]

Gunsmithing was an essential trade during pioneer days in Texas. Settlers, rangers, and cowboys needed pistols and rifles for survival, and Petmecky was well known throughout the state. His most successful and memorable invention was the spring-shank steel spur, known as "the Petmecker spur." Because the spring on the spur would open and keep the spur from injuring the rider's leg if he fell from his horse during a cattle drive, Petmecky's invention became a sign of the well-dressed cowboy. His other inventions and improvements on guns included making parts for the Colt revolver as well as bullet molds and ammunition to fit every size of gun. Texas Rangers and Indian fighters came to Petmecky for their weapons, including Captain Sul Ross, who asked him to make a rifle with bullets which would penetrate the antique Spanish chain mail of the great Comanche chief Peta Nacona. It was said that Petmecky rebored the mold for a heavier bullet and charge of powder. Ross supposedly used this gun during the Rangers' attack on the Comanches at the Pease River in 1860, when Cynthia Ann Parker was recaptured and Peta Nacona was killed.[35]

Joe Petmecky and family, Austin, c. 1890 — standing, from left,
Jake, Walter, Fred, Anna, and Charlie; seated, *Adolphina,
Joseph Carl, Joe Jr., and Howell in front*

At the start of the Civil War, Petmecky closed his prosperous
shop and volunteered for the duration of the struggle for Confederate
independence. He took part in the New Mexico campaign of Sibley's
Brigade in 1862. Marching by way of El Paso, Petmecky was with the
Texan troops at the victory at Valverde on February 21, 1862, and the
subsequent advance to Albuquerque. There he was assigned to make
molds and bullets for a variety of weapons used by the Southerners.
Following the decisive defeat of the Confederate force at the battle
at Glorieta Pass, New Mexico, Petmecky joined the retreat, reaching
San Antonio in July 1862. As a private in Company C, 33rd Texas
Cavalry (Duff's Partisan Rangers, 14th Battalion Cavalry), he was detailed to work in the Ordnance Department at Fort Brown in April
1863. Captured by Union forces in November 1863, Petmecky was
listed as a prisoner of war. After the Confederates recaptured the fort
in July 1864, he was listed "absent sick at Dallas" throughout the rest
of the summer. During the remainder of the war, he continued to
make molds and bullets and repair and make guns for the Ordnance
Department. He was paroled at Austin in July 1865.[36]

Joe Petmecky at his gunsmith bench, Austin, 1925, with son Howell (left) and Robert Felis

Joseph Petmecky's brother, Frank, a blacksmith on Waller Creek near Austin, also participated in the New Mexico campaign in 1862. He enlisted in San Antonio as a private in Captain Charles L. Pyron's Company B, 2nd Regiment Texas Mounted Riflemen, on May 23, 1861, and by November he had been assigned as a blacksmith to the Quartermaster Department. Following the disastrous New Mexico campaign, Frank reenlisted in San Antonio for the remainder of the war and served in Louisiana until the fall of 1863. Thereafter, because of a fractured leg, he was assigned to detached service at the Arsenal in San Antonio, where he made percussion caps for the Ordnance Department.[37]

After the war ended Joe Petmecky reopened his store in Austin and continued to make and sell guns and ammunition for a variety of firearms. On March 11, 1867, he married Adolphina Sterzing, who bore him a daughter and six sons. He expanded his business, which became known as J.C. Petmecky Sporting Goods Store, selling bicycles, RCA Victor phonographs, and other goods. At the turn of the century, he retired to his farm near Menard. The family business was operated by his son Fred Frank until 1933 and then by another son, Jake, and a grandson, Jakie, the last of the family to own the store in Austin. Joseph Petmecky died August 16, 1929, in Austin.[38]

Family stories reported that Joe was an expert marksman and hunter. He taught his sons his skills and the proper care of weapons. At age 16 his son Fred became a world rifle champion, and his son Jake founded Austin's first skeet range. Another episode in Joe's life concerned his role in a vigilante group active in Austin during the latter years of the Civil War and Reconstruction. With the collapse of the Confederate and Texan governments during the spring of 1865, bandits attempted to rob the State Treasury. Petmecky and the Austin vigilantes stopped them from getting away with all the money during a shoot-out at the capitol.

A.W. Petmecky, Joseph's half-brother and the son of Gottfried Petmecky's second marriage, founded a notable family in Fredericksburg, which contributed much to the community. Born in San Antonio on April 1, 1859, A.W. apprenticed himself to a storekeeper in Boerne at an early age. There he also learned the skills of a stonemason, a profession which he would practice throughout his life. He moved to Fredericksburg as a young man and assisted in building many homes and businesses, including the famous White Elephant Saloon in 1880. With a mason named Thompson, A.W. supposedly borrowed a wooden elephant from a merry-go-round and made a mold in soft sand. The white elephant continues to intrigue visitors to Fredericksburg more than a century later.[39]

A.W. Petmecky established a goal of public service for his sons. He served as Justice of the Peace, Precinct 1, Gillespie County, for 42 years, from 1890 until 1932. Recognized as a compromiser and peacemaker by his fellow townsmen, he was followed in service to his community by his sons, Alfred J., who was sheriff for four years and district clerk for twelve years, and William M., who was Gillespie County assessor and collector of taxes for 20 years. Petmecky and his two sons served their community for a total of 78 years.[40]

Rudolph Schorobiny (Charobiny) was the only Hungarian identified in Henri Castro's colony, which was established in 1842 under the Republic of Texas. French by birth and Jewish by heritage, Castro received two grant contracts to settle 600 families, mainly from the French province of Alsace (but including Germans from the Rhineland and Belgians and Dutch from the Low Countries). In 1844 he established Castroville, his first colony town, on the Medina River west of

San Antonio. Within a year Castro settled more than 2,100 people, and headright grants were made in his colony to 485 families and 457 single men, including Schorobiny. During the first few years Castro's colonists suffered hunger, drought, disease, and Indian depredations on the western frontier. The experiences of Schorobiny exemplify those of the pioneers who persisted, braving great danger and hardship.[41]

Rudolph Schorobiny was born January 25, 1817, in the village of Rutzdorf, Szepes (Zips) County, Upper Hungary (now Slovakia), the son of Ferdinand Anton and Anna Magista Schorobiny. Nothing further is known of Rudolph's early life until he joined Henri Castro's colony and sailed from Le Havre, France, on the American vessel *Deaucalion* for Texas. After an eight-week Atlantic crossing, Schorobiny first landed at New Orleans and then took passage on the steamer *Galveston* for the port of Galveston, which he reached December 15, 1845. From there he joined other immigrants going to Houston by way of Buffalo Bayou on a smaller steamer. While on board, so the story goes, Schorobiny met General Sam Houston, who was taking "some fine horses . . . up the country." Noticing the shivering young men near the steamer's boiler, the Texas hero said, "Come, I will warm you up," and bought each a whiskey in the boat's saloon.[42]

After a month's stay in Houston, Schorobiny set out for San Antonio to join Castro's colony and go into farming. Traveling by ox-drawn wagon, he was hampered by rain and flooded creeks, and the small party accompanying him was alert for Indians, for they had heard of a colonist being killed between Port Lavaca and San Antonio. After a tedious trek Schorobiny arrived in San Antonio in April 1846 and then went on to Castroville, the seat of Henri Castro's colony in Medina County. Schorobiny was given a town lot and 20 acres of farmland at the satellite colony of Quihi, ten miles west of Castroville. In addition, he was entitled to a headright of 320 acres as a single man in the colony, and he received farm implements and corn and bacon until he could harvest his first crop.[43]

Schorobiny's first experience with farming on the Texas frontier ended in failure, however. In company with his traveling companions from Houston, Louis Korn and his brother and a Dr. Acke, Schorobiny said, "We for a short time tried farming, but none of us possessing either sufficient experience or means, this agricultural society in consequence of trials, disappointments, and sickness, quickly dissolved, and we parted."[44]

Rudolph Schorobiny

In August 1846 he joined the Texas Ranger company of Captain John Connor to patrol the western frontier against Indian depredations. After two months' scouting Connor's company enlisted in Peter Hansborough Bell's regiment of mounted riflemen, which mustered into the U.S. Army at the outbreak of the war with Mexico. Schorobiny served for one year in northern Mexico and South Texas as part of Bell's Regiment. He was discharged at San Antonio at the end of his enlistment in 1847 and returned to Quihi.[45]

The young Hungarian immigrant once again settled on his Castro colony headright at Quihi, which was described as having "a lovely landscape, encircled with mountain ridges, of highly fertile soil, with good water, and an abundance of building and fence material." There Schorobiny turned once again to farming and stock raising. "Grass and water were plentiful, with no brush then, but open and lovely valleys. Game and wild honey were in abundance, and living cheap. The seasons were good and splendid crops made, and the hardy pioneers began to enjoy the fruits of their labor and sacrifices," according to one writer. On a ridge above Quihi Creek which offered a commanding view of the valley, Schorobiny built his house of red sandstone.

On November 25, 1847, he married Francisca Meyer, a 16-year-old immigrant from Alsace, at Castroville in a ceremony performed by Bishop Claude-Marie Dubuis, the second Bishop of Galveston. Then, in February 1848, Schorobiny returned home from a search for his wandering cattle and made a grim discovery. Francisca was missing, and his farmhouse had been ransacked. During his absence a band of Lipan and Kickapoo Indians had made a raid. They had slain Blas Meyer, Francisca's brother, and attempted to carry her away into captivity. Choosing to escape or die trying, she jumped from the horse about a half mile from her home and raced for a thicket of oaks. The Indians fired two arrows into the fleeing woman, wounding her in the back. Fearing pursuit by the colonists, however, they fled without scalping their victim. Francisca crawled to the village of Quihi, where she was nursed back to health by the colonists. Upon her recovery, she and Rudolph were presented with a large town lot in Quihi, where they lived for six years before returning to their home two miles from the settlement. They remained there for the rest of their lives. Of six children born to them, only two, Rafael and Michael, reached maturity. They also adopted a daughter, Ottilie.[46]

The farming and ranching community of Quihi slowly prospered as the immigrant farmers from Alsace and Germany acquired farm animals and tools. The military road from San Antonio to the

Rudolph Schorobiny's house in Quihi, c. 1930

Rio Grande passed Quihi, then the last settlement on the road to the west, and the farmers also prospered by selling produce to travelers on their way to the California goldfields after 1849. A church and a school were built as the community grew in the years before the Civil War. Corn, wheat, oats, cereals, and vegetables were planted by the farmers. Schorobiny was the first to successfully plant onions.[47]

• ─────────── •

"The Wilderness Blooming with Civilization"— *A Pioneer Settler's Account*

On September 1, 1879, a third of a century afterwards, Rudolph Schorobiny wrote a glowing recollection of the founding of old Quihi settlement to Lorenzo Castro, the colonizer's son. This was published in the San Antonio *Texas Sun* in March 1880:

"In the commencement of March 1846, the first settlers, numbering about twenty-five families, started for the new colony of Quihi, on the Quihi creek, ten miles west from Castroville; it was a lovely landscape, encircled with mountain ridges, of highly fertile soil, with good water, and an abundance of building and fence material. To every family a city lot of twenty acres was gratuitously given by the founder, Mr. H[enri] Castro, apart from the head right of 320 or 160 acres. Mr. Castro appointed two men, James Brown and David Burnham, to provide the colonists with game, which abounded in the neighborhood, and as they were experienced and practical men, to advise and superintend the colonists. A Mexican by the name of Aug[ustine?] Treviño proved himself very useful as teamster and instructor in cattle raising. The agriculturists were furnished with corn meal and bacon, together with some implements. Everything was progressing finely, and everybody was busy to build houses and plant corn when a dreadful blow was dealt to our Colony. The family of Brinkhoff, consisting of five persons located in the so called lower village, were murdered by Commanche [*sic*] Indians; which sad event caused a portion of the colonists to leave the place, and to move to San Antonio or other regions. . . . At first our colony made but little headway in agriculture, as the settlers lacked suitable draught animals and necessary implements[.] [M]oreover the continual danger or fear and prevailing insecurity of life and property caused by Indian raids caused our settlers to be despondent and apathetic, yet perseverance, as it will everywhere, carried us through our troubles. The military road built from San Antonio to the Rio Grande, via Quihi, soon led to a marked improvement

31

of our condition; our productions found a good and ready market at the forts which the U.S. Government erected along the Mexican boundary. Our Quihi became a gathering place for the farmers of the neighborhood, and easily and quickly acquired a stately church building, as well as a spacious school. The settlement gradually began to expand; hundreds of acres were put under fence and plow; cattle raising was a paying business, as the military posts required a large amount of beef every year. Altogether, the period immediately preceding the rebellion was one of the highest prosperity for our village and colony. . . . Then came the civil war, and with it a period of Progression, as fields and habitations became desolated and fell a prey to temporary decay. Since then, however, our colony has quickly recovered from its deplorable effects, and has entered on a new era, of which we hope it will endure for many, many years to come. Our village population is increasing steadily; our mode of agriculture is being improved by the appliance of time-saving machines; cattle raising alone suffers somewhat from losses through thieves and raiders. Everybody is busy now—even those who were lazy before, now vigorously take a part in the general activity of our settlement. Thus, we look forward to a happy future with hopefulness and cheerful hearts."

Schorobiny then summarized the 1879 condition of Quihi, reporting that cultivated land lay three to four miles on each side of the village. Of these 3,000 acres, two-thirds were planted in corn and the rest in other grains and vegetables. Annual yields from the fertile soils averaged 25 to 40 bushels of corn, 10 to 20 bushels of wheat, and 50 to 75 bushels of oats per acre. By that year the settlers had acquired machinery and draft animals, enjoyed good health "as the climate is so very salubrious and mild," and lived in the well-built houses of the earliest settlers. Schorobiny concluded: "Still, there are some yet living, who after hard struggles and severe trials, are now enjoying the fruits of their labors in peace and contentment." [48]

• ——————— •

Schorobiny served as Justice of the Peace for Precinct 2 of Medina County, beginning in 1851. He was later followed in this office by his son Rafael (c. 1855-1894) in 1885, and then by his other son, Judge Michael Schorobiny (1858-1939), who held the office for more than 43 years. "It is possible the position has been in the Schorobiny family since its creation." Rudolph Schorobiny also was a founding member

Judge Michael Schorobiny

of the Quihi Schützenverein (target-shooting club) in 1890. In 1894 he applied for a pension as a veteran of the Mexican War. It was said that he had lived under five flags (Hungary, Mexico, Texas, the United States, and the Confederacy). Schorobiny died at his home on April 24, 1908, at the age of 91 and was buried in the private family cemetery on his ranch.[49]

Judge Michael Schorobiny carried on his father's public service as justice of the peace until his death in 1939. He also was a founder of the Quihi Schützenverein and served as chairman of the Medina County Republican Executive Committee. In 1937 he served as Medina County chairman of the United States Constitution Sesquicentennial Celebration committee. It was said that he was "the last of the direct descendants of the original Castro colonists to spend his entire life on his father's headright." Michael Schorobiny never married, and so, with him, the family ended.[50]

The experiences of Rudolph Schorobiny were as typical of the Texas frontier as those of his fellow Texans, most of whom were farmers and ranchers. All faced common dangers. As the lone farmer among the Hungarians who came to Texas prior to the Revolution of 1848-1849 and the only Hungarian-Texan Mexican War veteran, he became a respected community leader in a county heavily populated by Germans and Alsatians.

Economic possibilities as well as the spirit of wanderlust brought the earliest Hungarians to Texas. Seeking a better livelihood where land was plentiful and cheap and opportunity boundless appealed to Lochmar, Petmecky, and Schorobiny. On the other hand, Fisher and Count Zondogi sought adventure or seized opportunities where they existed in the fast-changing political arena of Texas during the 1830's and 1840's. Perhaps seeking the "other side of the world," these men witnessed dramatic changes which led to Texas' future as part of the United States and then departed, while the others stayed and became part of the state's history. Interestingly, none of them started a chain of immigration of friends and relatives who might have followed them to America and to Texas. Other pioneer Hungarians may also have found their way to Texas, but their stories are not known.

A new kind of Hungarian immigrant began to appear in Texas in the early 1850's. Thousands of political refugees from the Hungarian Revolution of 1848-1849 chose exile in America, and a score or more found Texas an inviting new homeland. Led by a former Hungarian government official, László Újházi, some began appearing in the San Antonio area, and others scattered to towns around the state. Called the 48ers, they formed the first significant Hungarian presence in Texas. Újházi's story is known in greater detail than that of others, and it marks the beginning of this new immigration.

CHAPTER THREE

"If one has to be in America, one is better off in Texas."
László Újházi, the Great Exile

The first significant wave of Hungarian emigrants, albeit few in number, began to arrive in the state during the 1850's. "If one has to be in America . . . one is better off in Texas," was László Újházi's observation to Louis Kossuth in 1852. Újházi, who had been to Texas for the first time that year, liked the mild climate and recommended the state as a favorable destination for the exiles and refugees of Hungary's failed struggle for freedom from Austria in 1848-1849.

László Újházi was the leader of the Hungarian exiles who fled to America. He identified Texas as a prime site for emigration and moved there, abandoning his attempt to form a Hungarian colony on the Iowa prairies. The details of Újházi's American and Texas career are better known than in the case of many other Hungarian 48ers. His letters, with those of his family, friends, and political associates of the revolution, have been preserved in Hungarian archives, and his role and significance as a participant in the revolution and as the leader of the émigrés in America has been analyzed and widely published in Hungarian literature.

Described as a man of strong but inflexible character, Újházi was reputedly one of the most radical among Hungarian liberal politicians during the revolution, supporting Hungary's independence and stubbornly maintaining with great integrity his resolution never to

László Újházi

recognize a Habsburg as the Hungarian monarch. He unfailingly upheld these principles until his death, refusing to accept amnesty and return to his homeland. As a result of his staunch republicanism and admiration for democracy, he became an American citizen and a farmer and rancher on Texas' frontier near San Antonio.[1]

László Újházi was born January 20, 1795, on his family's estate of Budamér between Kassa and Eperjes in Sáros County, Upper Hungary (now Czechoslovakia). Part of the large and powerful Protestant lesser nobility, the Újházy family of Budamér (and Bogdány, Böki, Kőszeg, Lemes, Terebő, and Vargony) traced its line from 1669, when its patent of nobility was granted by King Leopold I, a Habsburg. (The "y" ending of the family name indicated its nobility, and László used that spelling until his exile. At that time he symbolically adopted the democratic "i", which he retained until his death. His children, however, did not use the "i" even in the United States.) The son of Sámuel Újházy (1764-1816) and Polixina Radvánszky, László attended the lower schools in Eperjes and Debrecen and received his degree in law at Sárospatak.[2]

As a member of Hungary's lesser, untitled nobility, Újházi's status in Hungarian society was assured from birth. Powerful in the politics of their local counties, the lesser nobles jealously protected their

36

Louis Kossuth in 1848

ancient rights of freedom from taxation, the right of habeas corpus, free ownership of land, and the right to bear arms when the country was invaded. Their elected representatives sat in the Lower House of the Hungarian Diet. It was said that these "so-called *bene possessionati* landowners with a few thousand acres of land . . . usually wielded great influence in politics, national as well as local."[3]

Újházi married Teréz Várady Szakmáry, the daughter of Róza Benyovszky and Donát Várady Szakmáry, about 1818. Her grandfather, Count Móric Benyovszky, was a world traveler who had been killed in Madagascar in 1786. To László and Teréz were born four sons and four daughters. Of their close knit family, five children later accompanied their parents to the United States in 1849: Klára (Mrs. Joseph Kellerschön, 1821-189?), Farkas (1827-1898), Tivadar (1832-1870), Ilona (Helen Mrs. Vilmos Madarász, 1838-1899), and László Jr. (1841-1906). Two daughters, Pauline (Mrs. Károly Nagy, 1819-1872) and Klementine (Mrs. Gusztáv Fáy, 1822-1888), and a son, Sándor (1824-1864), remained in Hungary.[4]

An early convert to the Hungarian Reform Movement of the 1820's and 1830's, Újházi came into contact with Louis Kossuth (1802-1894) as early as 1831. He remained a staunch and loyal follower of

Buda and Pest in 1848

Kossuth, the Hungarian Reform Movement's most radical leader, all of his life. Újházi's role in county and national politics began early. He was a member of the liberal opposition, both in the Sáros County Assembly and in the National Diet. He distributed Kossuth's hand-written parliamentary reports in Sáros County and was recognized as an opposition leader in support of reforms; as such he came under police surveillance.[5]

Early in 1837 Újházi was accused of treason by the conservative forces in the County Assembly, but no legal proceedings were brought, and he and others of the "Parliamentary youth" were given amnesty in 1840. Újházi advocated republican governmental ideals and the abolition of ancient feudal practices and serfdom, making him an enemy of his own noble class in the County Assembly. In April 1848 he was appointed lord-lieutenant (one source called him the county judge) of Sáros County by the newly created Hungarian government. Although local reactionaries in the Sáros Assembly tried to depose and arrest him, Újházi was vindicated by a government commissioner and continued to carry out the reforms of the April Laws. In July he became a member of the Upper House of the Hungarian Parliament in Pest.[6]

With the outbreak of hostilities and the invasion of Hungary by a Croatian army, followed by that of the Austrians in the fall of 1848, Újházi ordered the formation of three regiments in Sáros County to defend the homeland. One, called the Újházi Hunters, fought in northern Hungary with General Arthur Görgey during the winter of 1848-1849. Újházi was then sent as government commissioner to Pozsony (another source reported that he went to Sopron) late in September to recruit troops and supply the new national army (called the Honvéd Army, or "defender of the fatherland"). Supposedly a fusilier corps was named for him. On October 20 he and his 16-year-old son, Tivadar, fought at the Battle of Schwechat, a suburb of Vienna, and his older son, Farkas, was wounded while fighting under General Mór Perczel. When the Austrian forces captured Buda in December, Újházi and his family fled eastward to Debrecen with Kossuth and the Hungarian government and Parliament.[7]

In the nationalist Hungarian Parliament at Debrecen, Újházi was president of the Democratic Republican Club and the Radical Party. A red feather worn in the hatband, symbolic of republicanism, distinguished the members of this group. Újházi was among the first to support Kossuth in the deposition of the Habsburg dynasty and the call for establishment of a Hungarian republic in April 1849. The next month the government sent him as civilian commissioner to the gigantic and virtually impregnable fortress of Komárom on the Danube. His mission was to ensure the loyalty of its defenders, recruit new soldiers, and obtain supplies. With Újházi went his wife, daughters Klára and Helen, and sons Tivadar, Farkas, and young László Jr. In Komárom Újházi had one vote on the military council. His powers were coequal

A sally of Huszárs from the fortress of Komárom,
February 24, 1849

with the military commander, General György Klapka. Even after the surrender of the last Hungarian field army at Világos in August 1849, Komárom held out for two months before negotiating a surrender with amnesty on October 3. Újházi did not sign the capitulation.[8]

The amnesty provided that all officers could either return home or leave the country with a passport. The Austrians had previously marked Újházi for execution, and to prevent this General Klapka commissioned him a major. Újházi chose exile. On October 11, 1849, he was given a passport, without privilege of return to Hungary, to emigrate to the United States. Following the surrender, Újházi and others formed an American emigration society, which gathered in Hamburg by the end of October for the Atlantic voyage. Újházi, his family, and others sailed on the *Hermann* for New York, arriving in America, "the freest country" of their time, on December 16, 1849. Thus, in his midfifties, Újházi's permanent—and, later, self-imposed—exile began.[9]

The Hungarian Revolution aroused great sympathy in the United States. Even in the remote community of New Braunfels, Texas citizens were eager for news, asking the postmaster to "read something to us. No news from Hungary?" When Újházi and his first group of refugees reached America, they were welcomed as heroes.[10]

While waiting in Hamburg during the fall of 1849, Újházi had been anxious for the future of the émigrés. He made a short trip to England, where he asked the American minister to petition President Zachary Taylor to grant asylum to the exiles. This the president did, "offering them the benefits and protection of a free country." The exiles' arrival in New York was greeted by overwhelming enthusiasm. Astor House, and, later, Hungarian House, had been rented for them by a committee of welcome. The city and state of New York gave receptions, and Újházi, his family, and a delegation were invited to visit Washington, D.C. On the way Újházi spoke to a gathering in Philadelphia's Independence Square in German, his "universal" language. The Hungarians were treated to serenades and torchlight processions. In the national capital Újházi and his delegation were received by the president and invited to dine at the White House.[11]

At Újházi's request, Senators Lewis Cass and William H. Seward submitted a bill in Congress to provide the refugees with free land "in recognition of their great services for human freedom," but the bill failed. The Hungarians then returned to New York, where Újházi and his two older sons, Tivadar and Farkas, made their declarations of intent to become citizens of the United States on December 31, 1849, just two weeks after their arrival. As American public enthusiasm for the exiles began to wane, Újházi and other exiles sought to raise funds and achieve their political goals, but dissension soon arose among them, and Újházi left in April 1850 to start a Hungarian colony in the American West.[12]

Újházi set two goals during his first months in the United States. The first was to work for Louis Kossuth's liberation from internment in Turkey, and the second was to establish a Hungarian agricultural colony which would serve to keep the exiles together until the revolution could be renewed to gain Hungarian independence. Újházi wanted to establish a community in which "political life should be patterned after the American model, while social and domestic life should preserve the features of life in Hungary." On March 27, 1850, while still in New York, he was named by Kossuth as his envoy plenipotentiary and representative to America. Although Újházi never attempted to present his credentials as the representative of a now-defunct government to the American secretary of state, he pursued his goals, the first succeeding and the latter failing, for his first two years in America.[13]

Újházi, his family, and a few other émigrés traveled westward by canal boat, lake steamer, railroad, and stagecoach through the Great Lakes to Chicago and St. Louis. He established his proposed Hungarian colony on vacant government land on the prairies of Decatur County, Iowa, in the late summer of 1850 and named it New Buda. Újházi described the location of New Buda, in southern Iowa on the Thompson River, to a friend: the soil was fertile, the woods were untouched, and the view was beautiful. He went on to say that "We found suitable rolling hills to plant grapes; our next aim is to plant them as soon as possible." Újházi preempted twelve sections of land (640 acres to a section) and began to build his log "castle." Other Hungarians settled nearby. Thereafter, when not laboring to build, fence, and cultivate the land, and care for his newly acquired livestock, Újházi took care of his large correspondence. This included communication with Kossuth, official papers, arrangements for more Hungarians to come to America, publications, and translations of Kossuth's speeches to be presented to Congress.[14]

Újházi was appointed postmaster for New Buda (with an annual salary of $200) in 1850 and entertained visiting exiles, many of whom stayed but a short time before moving on. The scattered farm community never exceeded 75 inhabitants and later became a ghost town. It was said that the Hungarians' "agricultural methods greatly amused their frontier neighbors." In New Buda Újházi and his family attempted to maintain their accustomed aristocratic way of life while performing manual labor as a frontier farm family.[15]

Winter had arrived by the time the Újházis' house was completed. They invited their American and Hungarian neighbors to a dedication and celebration which lasted for three days. A document signed by the family and their friends was sealed in a bottle and buried under the cornerstone to mark the foundation of New Buda. During the cold blasts of winter, the family gathered in the house, while Újházi smoked his pipe and engaged in long conversations with fellow exiles on plans for the future. He was described as a "quiet, nonostentatious man, whose main goal was to achieve personal integrity for himself and his companions by means of self-sufficient hard labor on free soil" in the western wilderness. In his communications to friends in Europe, Újházi pointed out that "We enjoy liberty already, and the land which is nourishing us will be loved by all of us; it will be our future country. We will love it, but we will not forget our mother country either."[16]

During his time in New Buda, Újházi corresponded with President Millard Fillmore, the secretary of state, and other high officials. His letters concerned Kossuth's release from internment in Turkey and possible arrival in the United States. Obtaining free government land for the exiles and the settlement of New Buda also occupied his attention. Then, on October 6, 1851, tragedy struck the struggling family. Újházi's wife died. Already in ill health before leaving Hungary, Teréz Újházi died as a result of the stress of exile as well as the hard physical labor which she was forced to perform for the first time in her life. She was buried on the family farm without religious services, since her husband disliked priests.[17]

In his depression over his beloved wife's death, Újházi wrote to his father-in-law on October 25, 1851, pouring out his grief and loneliness in a foreign land. His mourning was deep for the mother of his children, who had followed him into exile. He wrote that "I would rather have given up my own happiness and offer my freedom to my enemies to take my life in order to lengthen the life of the best mother in her old country." As a result of her death, Újházi became restless and began to think of moving to the milder climate of Arkansas or Texas, where he could cultivate vineyards.[18]

Louis Kossuth landing in America

His mood brightened considerably with the arrival of Louis Kossuth in America December 5, 1851. The Hungarian leader-in-exile arrived on the American war vessel *Mississippi*, which had been sent to bring him from Turkey. He was hailed as the "Hungarian George Washington" and was greeted with banquets, parades, and speeches. From New York Kossuth went to Washington, where he met the president and members of Congress but failed to gain support for the resumption of the Hungarian Revolution. Thereafter he began a national tour which lasted for six months. Traveling westward to the Mississippi Valley, he reached St. Louis on March 9, 1852.[19]

Unable to afford a longer trip, Újházi and a fellow exile from New Buda, György Pomutz, went to meet Kossuth in St. Louis. There Újházi and Kossuth had an hour-long private visit. Újházi hoped that Kossuth would become the leader of the exiles in New Buda and was also prepared to follow him elsewhere. But Kossuth rejected the idea, choosing to return to Europe to continue his struggle for Hungarian independence. He had been offered land in several states, including 1,000 acres in Texas, and he asked Újházi to take possession of it for him. Thus Újházi, although disappointed that Kossuth would not settle in a Hungarian colony in America, had an opportunity to seek land for himself in Texas. He considered himself still in Kossuth's service and retained the hope that Kossuth would support a Hungarian colony in the United States at some future time.[20]

$5 Kossuth Bond, to be paid on demand "one year after the establishment in fact of the Independent Hungarian Government"

Újházi made his first trip to Texas during the spring of 1852 shortly after leaving Kossuth. He traveled first by riverboat and then overland in March and April by way of Little Rock, Arkansas. He rode the first 650 miles on horseback and then walked for the last 200 miles when his horse became lame. Újházi wrote to Kossuth on April 22, 1852, that he stayed in Austin one night to see the governor and inquire about land at the General Land Office. He found the citizens of Austin recovering from the big April 21 celebration of San Jacinto Day, and Governor Peter Hansborough Bell had been too exhausted to receive him. He wrote that "After many hardships we arrived in Austin, the capital of this state, but what kind of a capital? . . . It looks as filthy as a Turkish town. . . . To call such as this a 'city' is decidedly an exaggeration. Even the smaller settlements in Texas were much nicer than this Capital. We walk around in a disgusting accumulation of trash." A local German told Újházi that Austin "had no importance, the population no money and no excellence in high moral standing." Újházi then traveled to Corpus Christi to inspect the land given to Kossuth by land promoter Henry L. Kinney. [21]

In informing Kossuth of conditions in Texas, where the federal government owned no public lands, Újházi wrote:

> If one has to be in America (may the good Lord protect you from this), one is better off in Texas, which gives you certain advantages . . . for instance, the climate. . . . The only possible

way to live here without backbreaking labor is the growing of cattle, which occupation gives you plenty of opportunity to live without worry and pain. In this case one could have a spiritual life, and one could concentrate himself in cultural pursuits. Everyone who has seen the surroundings of the Nueces [River] is very enthusiastic about it. . . . There is no great difference between Arkansas and Texas; the soil improved slowly after we entered Texas. The trouble was that the more fertile grew the plains, the more miserable were the forests.

We found many blessed plains which looked very similar to those in Hungary, undulating in the breezes, and on those places we shed many tears over the velvety grass. We had to think how happy we could have been if tyranny had not expelled us from the land of our forefathers. And I had to think how unhappy I am, a wanderer without a country, who never can find the least surrogate for a fatherland. I, who would never be happy even in Eldorado, since I have lost part of my life — my wife.[22]

Újházi met Kinney in Corpus Christi, inspected the 1,000 acres which were bordered by the Nueces River on the Barranco Blanco (now the Calallen area), and accepted the deed for Kossuth. Kossuth never made use of the gift, and in all probability Kinney's ownership and sale of the land was fraudulent. In telling Kossuth about Corpus Christi, which was located where the Nueces River flowed into the Gulf of Mexico, Újházi wrote:

. . . there is no woodland, only prairie; most of the forest is on the shore of the river, and its extension is not wider than a hundred feet on both sides of the river, and the wood is crippled and crooked. On the prairie there are some stunted trees and bushes, so that the fences are made out of shrubs. Moreover, there is a great lack of drinking water.

Nothing more is known of Újházi's meeting with Kinney.[23]

In recording his observations in Corpus Christi, Újházi stated that the "endless prairie" between the Nueces and the Rio Grande in South Texas were grazed by thousands upon thousands of wild mustangs. These horses were rounded up by people from Mexico, who tamed some and sold them in Corpus Christi for $6 to $10 a head.[24]

Even before leaving for St. Louis to meet Kossuth, Újházi had urged a London banker to forward money which was being sent to him by his sister and his children in Hungary as soon as possible, for "without the money, we are not able to pay for our ranch in Texas." Whether he received this money before leaving Iowa is not known.

During the trip Újházi and his companion, Pomutz, camped out at night, often near a farmhouse where they could obtain milk to drink. After visiting Corpus Christi he reported to Kossuth that he and Pomutz had only $100 left and that they would have to work their way back to St. Louis and Iowa. How the 57-year-old man earned money during the return to New Buda is unknown. He arrived at the end of August 1852, having been away from home for six months. [25] In her diary on September 14, 1852, Klára Újházy quoted her father's reaction to his Texas journey:

> I almost gave up on finding a place which I liked, when finally, in the State of Texas 130 miles from the city of Corpus Christi, traveling northwest, I arrived on the beautiful banks of the Guadalupe River. I found there, all in all, the best land, excellent water, and pleasant climate. The fields are green even during the winter. One does not need any stable or fodder, so keeping cattle is easy and profitable. Nature alone makes one the owner of great herds of horses and cattle.
>
> However, they don't give Paradise away free. There are no free lands in Texas. We can't go there with our hands empty as we came to Iowa. We must buy the land there for good money. [26]

During the harvest season and winter of 1852-1853, Újházi made preparations to sell his preemption rights and most of his livestock on his Iowa farm. He had probably visited San Antonio, a frontier town of 16,000, in 1852. There he explored the surrounding farmland and employed local attorney C.N. Riotte to begin purchases for him on Olmos Creek above the headwaters of the San Antonio River, four miles north of the city. In November 1852 Riotte bought 139 acres in two parcels of land for $530 from the City of San Antonio, of which only 20 percent was paid down. [27]

In March 1853 Újházi wrote to a friend in London that all future correspondence was to be addressed to him in care of C.N. Riotte in San Antonio (by way of New Orleans). However, it was June before Újházi and his daughter Klára and sons Tivadar, Farkas, and László Jr. left for Texas. To his great disappointment and disapproval, his youngest daughter, 15-year-old Helen (Ilona, Ilka), married Vilmos Madarász, the teenaged son of László Madarász, who had been Kossuth's police commissioner during the revolution and was now an exile in New Buda. The young couple were married on June 4, 1853, in Gentry County, Missouri, by a justice of the peace. Újházi opposed the marriage and was estranged from his daughter for the next five years. [28]

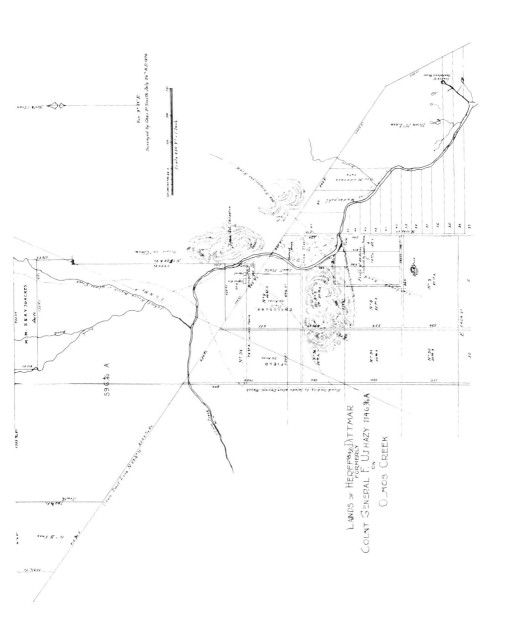

Survey map of the Újházi property, bought by Dr. Ferdinand Herff and Judge Albert Dittmar

47

One of Újházi's last acts in New Buda was to exhume his wife's coffin and load it on one of the ox wagons for the long overland journey to San Antonio. In a March 4, 1853, letter to his daughter Pauline Nagy in Hungary, Újházi wrote:

> My friend Riotte, whom I commissioned in Texas, bought a small but very handsome land, only 196 *hold* [one *hold* equals 1.42 acres], for us for $1620.00. I have to pay only one fifth of the price now, the rest over fifty years with eight percent interest. It is not exactly cheap, but it is near the city of San Antonio along the banks of the river of the same name, and that increases its value. We plan to leave on the first of May when the roads are safe, [going] partly by river, partly by horse and by wagon. According to our travel experience, we should arrive in our destination by the end of August. With the others, a longer but not noticeable crate is prepared in which we will take the body of your mother of blessed memory because it would not be permissible that her remains should be left here, her grave sunk into forgetfulness with strange and indifferent feet trampling over it. We rather will take her casket with us and will put her to eternal rest on our new and final farm. For this reason, I [will] call that manor Sírmező [Hungarian for "field of sighing," or "cemetery"].

How many other exiles accompanied the Újházis to Texas is not known, although one source reported that a Lajos Farkas from Zemplen County, Hungary, made the journey of over a thousand miles.[29]

On April 29, 1853, Klára Újházy recorded in her diary that the wagons had been packed in preparation for the "journey through unknown lands on a longer and more endless road to find a new country." Although engaged to Joseph Kellerschön, son of a local German immigrant farmer, 32-year-old Klára, who the family thought would never marry, dutifully accompanied her father and three brothers, who would need her to run their new household.[30]

Traveling first by riverboat and then overland through Missouri, Arkansas, and the Indian Territory, the slow-moving wagon train approached Texas during the late summer of 1853. The German newspaper, *San Antonio Zeitung*, noted on July 30, 1853, that "the old Hungarian hero and patriot may now shortly be expected in our midst. On July 2 he left Missouri . . . to move to the Texas border through the steppes. He carries with him the remains of his wife . . . as a dear relic." As they passed through New Braunfels on the final leg of their journey, the local newspaper noted their arrival on September 1, and the next day a San Antonio paper reported that "General Újházi, the former Governor of Komárom," had arrived there.[31]

Újházi's record of his move to Texas included interesting comments on the land and people of the West. In choosing the shortest road to San Antonio, he traveled through Arkansas and entered the Indian Territory before reaching the Red River and Texas. Although he wanted to see the Indians, he was afraid that his 15 horses would be stolen. But, he wrote:

> We started toward Indian land. After ten days of horseback riding, without any problem, we crossed two nations, the Choctaw and the Chickasaw. This road was even better . . . because many of the Indians knew English. Our horses found rich pastures, and we found enough food.

Újházi saw in the Indian Territory "one of the most beautiful lands I have seen so far in America," bought peaches from a half-blooded Indian, and commented on the fate of America's Indians, who had "lost the strength of their ancestors" and adopted the "sins of the white world." [32]

• —————————— •

New Braunfels teacher, lawyer, and civic leader Hermann Seele wrote on September 7, 1853, that "When Újházi, after he had camped at the foot of the mountain [at New Braunfels] during the night, rode on with his horses in the morning, his daughter wept and followed alone after the wagons. Újházi moved on with his people towards San Antonio." Seele's poem commemorated the event.

> In the east the sun dawns red,
> Encased in a thick blanket of fog.
> The mist rises and falls on the reddish light
> And flees to the west as balls of cloud.
>
> What means the ringing of bells there
> And the trampling of horses along the road?
> So early that timidly the cows stand
> At the corral and turn toward the sounds.
>
> Now there arises a mighty cloud of dust,
> A troupe of horses approaches at high speed,
> And riders come flying.

They fly like a storm over the waves of the sea,
Then, in a flash, they again turn back
To him, who with an old man's solemn glance
At a slow, deliberate pace
Rides after the troupe.

The beard flows white around his face,
Ill, tanned in the sun's rays,
And over the brow, filled with sublime thought,
Is seen on the hat the [red] feather waving.
Straight ahead the staunch hero looks
To the west, where over heaven's vault
The sun will in a wide arc
Have advanced by evening to its rest.

He well thinks that, like it, he
Will find there in the west the place
Where the star of freedom will shine
And, after the battle, beckon to rest.
The bold column has rushed past;
There follows, as migratory birds in flight
Are often followed by a straggler, tall in the saddle,
A noble woman, a woman that weeps!

From her eyes fall tears
Down upon the horse's mane.
Oh tears, fall like flowing iron
Into that bloodhound's tiger heart
    [the Austrian emperor]
Searing it, that from your wounds
It may never more recover,
Into the heart of him who banished them
From their dear fatherland,
That they know to be enslaved by him!

Bon voyage, you horsemen!
Bon voyage, you hero!
You noble lady! In the New World
Be granted to you, you mourners and maiden,
Freedom, home, happiness, and peace.[33]

• ——————————— •

The arrival of Újházi and his family in Texas marked the beginning of a recognizable Hungarian presence in the state. Throughout his remaining years there, Újházi and his family attempted to adapt to the land. He also participated in local politics, maintained correspondence with other exiles and his relatives in Europe as well as with U.S. government officials, and sought to surround himself with a small Hungarian émigré community. A staunch democrat and citizen, he sided with the anti-slavery faction in San Antonio, thus placing himself in opposition to prevailing social and political sentiments in Texas. He also attempted to preserve something of his former aristocratic lifestyle in Hungary, planting a vineyard of cuttings from his ancestral estate and treating his friends to hunts with his imported dogs. At first the family stayed in a hotel in San Antonio and, on September 11, were serenaded by a local German singing society.

Two years later, on July 16, 1855, Újházi wrote to his daughter Pauline, who lived on her estate of Hazsina in Hungary, that the family had stayed in "strange quarters" in San Antonio for more than a year while their two-room frame house was being renovated on his land on Olmos Creek near the crossing of the Old Nacogdoches Road. He wrote, "Until that time, living in a tent, we took turns with the boys to protect the cattle. . . . Our small land lies near San Antonio. The location was worth the higher price because of its closeness to the city." The Újházi farm included three 50-acre fields. They and an adjacent pecan grove were enclosed with fences. Across the creek to the east rose a stony ridge called the "Loma del Chilpetine" (now part of the city of Alamo Heights).[34]

During that first autumn in San Antonio, Újházi's horse herd was stolen. After chasing the horse thieves for two weeks into the Hill Country north and west of San Antonio, Farkas, assisted by a Mexican herdsman and Újházi riding in a wagon, found the horses, which had been sold singly or in pairs to local farmers. The recovery of the horses cost Újházi $200 for rent on the wagon and horses and the fee for the people who had bought his horses from the "Mexican thieves." He observed further that "riff-raff" lived in the neighborhood of San Antonio and that he would have preferred living 15 to 20 miles away "where there is more rest and quietness."[35]

In November 1853 Újházi began purchasing additional land next to his property, which eventually totaled 550 acres along Olmos Creek, surrounded by rocky hills and rolling prairies. He named his estate Sírmező and planned to rebury his wife's coffin on a hillside facing east toward his homeland. On the same hillside he planted a half-acre vineyard enclosed by a rock fence.[36]

Újházi anxiously anticipated the arrival of supplies shipped by his children in Hungary. The crates were filled with engineering tools, Hungarian books to educate his youngest son, László Jr., bottled wine, two small glass boxes of soil from Budamér, and other such items. In return, the Texas family sent exotic souvenirs to their relatives in Hungary, including a coconut, sweet potatoes, nuts, flower seeds, coconut spoons, an American washboard, two Indian tobacco pouches, a "tiger" skin hunting bag, two Indian whips, and an Indian needle and thread holder, all packed in moss.[37]

During his first years in Texas, Újházi registered his cattle brand, UL (for Újházi László, the traditional Hungarian form for names) at the Bexar County Courthouse. In this way he sought to protect his cattle, which grazed freely along Olmos Creek in the vicinity of the headwaters of the San Antonio River.[38]

The family moved into their house at Sírmező on March 1, 1854. An older frame house had been refurbished with much expense and labor, with the addition of two stone chimneys, floors, windows, and doors. The rooms, including the kitchen, were paneled, and the yard was fenced in and covered with gravel. Near the house was a well house, servants' house, chicken house, and corral. During the following year they fenced their fields, digging 1,200 postholes and nailing 36,000 board feet of lumber (with 600 pounds of nails). Because he did not own the 20 acres on which the house stood, it took Újházi more than three years to acquire title to this part of Sírmező. In addition, he continued buying land, especially that already encircled by Sírmező, paying $1,500 for the final 57 acres, which lay on a shady hill facing eastward "toward our unhappy fatherland." There, in the autumn of 1856, he buried the remains of his wife under a large and spreading live oak tree.[39]

On his journey through Texas in the mid-1850's, Frederick Law Olmsted visited Újházi at this farm and recorded:

> About four miles from San Antonio we passed the stock farm of Mr. Újházy [*sic*], late governor of Comorn [Komárom]. We stopped a few moments to pay our respects and were very cordially received. He had but recently entered his new log-house and was hardly yet established. . . . He had moved by the long

52

inland route to Texas, driving his herd of valuable mares through the friendly Indian country and camping nightly with all his family while on the journey. He had spent some time in looking over the State and finally purchased a large tract of land here, on which he was now making a new home. His wife having died during his residence in Iowa, he lives secluded with his faithful daughter [Klára], the very picture of a staunch, hale old gentleman, who supports with quiet dignity what fortunes the gods have decreed. He finds the climate here not to differ greatly from that to which he was accustomed in Hungary and thinks it more salubrious than that of Iowa.[40]

During the first year at Sírmező, Újházi reported that he had ten cows, eleven calves, 20 horses and colts, and an assortment of other domestic animals, including his favorite dog, Holló (Raven), which he had brought from Hungary. In addition, he had beehives, plows, and other farm implements (brought from Iowa), and other tools for carpentry, masonry, and gardening. He learned to sow corn by hand from the American neighbors and noted: "The American farmer is an unusual creature. The day before yesterday, I plowed and sowed. Yesterday, I had to write an article for the newspaper, and tomorrow I am going to clean my boots because I am going to the city."[41]

In describing his life at Sírmező, Újházi wrote to his daughter Pauline that 14-year-old László Jr. (Laci) had been enrolled in "the school of the Jesuits," which was far superior to others in San Antonio. In fact, his son attended St. Mary's College, established by the Brothers of Mary from France in 1852. Újházi said that he had "suppressed my antagonism toward priests and monks" because the school offered English, French, German, Spanish, sciences, mathematics, physics, geography, and history. Újházi was anxious that his youngest son obtain a good education. At the same time, he also contemplated sending László Jr. to learn the saddlemaking trade from Benjamin Varga, "a Hungarian man who works here."[42]

Újházi described his daily routine in July 1855, writing that he arose at dawn and brought out the horse and wagon for his son to drive to school, where the Brothers provided a shed for the rig during the day. László Jr. milked the cows while Klára prepared breakfast. The boy then left for school at 7:00 a.m., delivering milk to a local military camp along the way. He took his noon meal at school and began his return journey of four miles at 4:30 p.m. Once at Sírmező, he milked the cows again. Újházi went on to report:

Our ranch is beautiful and fertile —I think I picked it right—
if the usual drought would not torture us during the summer.
The corn thinned out, and caterpillars got into the corn. One day
last week, while Laci was in school and Klári [Klára] in the city
to buy pots, I went to sell the hay. While Farkas read on the porch,
a few cattle, following the dried-out creek, came up to the garden
and destroyed my carefully planted, . . . registered melons. I was
very depressed because probably all the melons added together
would not have as much moisture in them as the sweat that
dripped from my forehead while cultivating them.

Újházi also described the local poisonous snakes (water mocca-
sins) in the dried-up Olmos Creek as well as the rattlesnakes, one of
which had gotten into Klára's room.

The late 1850's were drought years in Texas, and the Újházis,
whose fields had just been cultivated, suffered. Writing to his daughter
in August 1855, he thanked her for sending $2,250 from his estates
in Hungary and said, "We need the money badly because the drought
is incredible. Even the older folks don't remember such heat. I, too,
got hot from the sun while I was loading the haystack and I fainted."
His son Tivadar sold hay in San Antonio during that year. Újházi's
favorite three-year-old horse, Villám (Lightning), was stolen, but local
officials recovered it and asked Újházi for a $10 reward as a prize as
well as to cover their expenses. He went on to tell that

Along with our great deal of loss we had some profit, too.
My land tolerates the drought better than others, and the cattle
recognize that. Wherever they come from, they end up on my
land. When the owner comes, he can take them, but if nobody
looks for them, which is quite common, I will brand them during
the winter. The law permits it. In the beginning, I just looked
at these as kinds of gifts, but now I am smarter. I immediately
start using the intruders, and let my own cattle rest.

In the same letter Újházi said that the men of the family had
"successfully completed a tremendous job." They fenced Sírmező's fields;
otherwise they would have had to guard them day and night against
foraging cattle. The family then had a feast since Klára had killed a
large turkey, and Újházi obtained a couple of bottles of red French
wine in San Antonio. He said, "This is the way the Hungarian peasantry
of Texas feasted, happy that the labor of the future will not be exposed
to the destruction of the cattle." [43]

Újházi's son Tivadar tried to help the family fortunes, for he had asked for his maternal inheritance and borrowed from his family to become partners "with a yankee and open a store in the city [San Antonio]." Unfortunately, the unidentified "yankee" went to buy merchandise for the store in New Orleans and did not return, leaving Tivadar bankrupt. Újházi said, "He escaped back to here" since he did not wish to remain in the city and be hounded by his creditors. Thereafter Tivadar sold hay and produce from his own cows and chickens for cash. Although his father and brother loaned him money, Tivadar, in Újházi's words, was "completely gone." Although Újházi hoped that the local military commander could find employment for Tivadar, he wrote to his daughter in July 1855 that "things are getting very difficult, because the years go fast, and the sympathy toward the Hungarians disappeared a long time ago. This is no surprise because many behaved very badly." In the end, Tivadar was forced to auction off his wagon, horse, and the remainder of his possessions in Texas.[44]

In May 1856 Újházi wrote to his daughter Klementine (Mrs. Gusztáv Fáy, who lived at Nyustya, Gömör County, Hungary) that he had been ill for two weeks and incapable of writing but had recovered. In his letter he informed his children in Hungary that he wanted to divide his Hungarian estates, freed by an amnesty from the Austrian government in that year, among his eight children in exchange for $6,000, "for my survival in America." He planned a trip to meet them in Switzerland to complete the gift, asking that the expenses of such trip be paid equally by his children in Hungary. It was two more years, however, before he could make the journey.[45]

Meanwhile, Újházi's daughter Klára finally married Joseph Kellerschön, the son of the German farmer who had bought Újházi's preemption of his New Buda farm in 1853. Two years had passed before 30-year-old Joseph could follow her to Sírmező. They were married on August 18, 1855. Thereafter they remained at Sírmező, Klára keeping house for the men and Joseph working with Farkas and the others in farming and cattle raising. In those next few years they had two children, a daughter named Tini and a son named Gyula [Julius]. The reaction of Klára's family to her marriage was mixed. Farkas and some of the relatives in Hungary were outraged because Joseph Kellerschön was neither Hungarian nor of the nobility. In addition, he was less educated than his wife. Yet Újházi blessed the marriage, fearing that, at his death, his daughter would be unprotected in a foreign land.[46]

Not all of Újházi's attention was focused on his family and farming problems. Local and national politics interested him, and he informed his family and friends in Europe of the issues and candidates of the presidential election of 1856 in which James Buchanan defeated John C. Fremont. As the slavery controversy heated up at all political levels during the 1850's, opposing sides became even more divided and uncompromising. Interests of Northern workers conflicted with those of the slave owners of the South. As an abolitionist living in a Southern state, Újházi watched the anti-foreign Know-Nothing Party in Texas and San Antonio and reported on the burning of abolitionist Adolph Douai's *San Antonio Zeitung* office by a mob in 1856. Even the mayor of the city was attacked, defended himself, and killed his opponent in a gunfight. German and French immigrants then protected the local jail in order to prevent the mayor's lynching. It was a time of "tremendous excitement in the city." [47]

At the same time, the severe seven-year drought continued to plague Central Texas, and Újházi became restless. In October 1856 he wrote Klementine that although a partial amnesty had been declared by the Austrians and many former rebels were regaining their estates, "I will never ask for any kind of clemency." In February 1857 he wrote to his family in Hungary that the drought continued with no rain for five months and that cattle from as far away as 15 miles came to Sírmező to drink. "Sooner or later, we will have to have some rain, and therefore, we are in a great hurry with the plowing. . . . We started plowing at the beginning of February, and since that time I am following the plow in a shirt and pants." [48]

The drought continued unabated in Texas during much of 1857. On August 10 Újházi wrote:

> In 20 days it will be one long year that neither rain or even dew brought a little life to suffering Nature. . . . On hills, in the meadows, and on the land, everything is dead, and a yellow-brown picture meets the eyes, almost blinded by the continuous clear sunshine.
> The daily, regular southeastern wind, which in previous years brought relief and cool, now became the burning hot wind of the Sahara since the soil, which is burned out like a brick, picks up the reflected heat of the sun and brings it into every nook and corner of our house through the doors and windows. We can hardly stand it in the daytime and cannot sleep during the night.

Újházi went on to say that his garden was being destroyed by starving rabbits, who chewed their way through the mosquito nets with which he covered his favorite melons. Finally he was forced to chain two of his dogs in the garden to protect the family's food supply.[49]

In February 1857 Tivadar Újházy (who, with his father and brother Farkas, had become a U.S. citizen on April 7, 1855) requested an American passport in order to return to his native land. Never successful in Texas, he departed Sírmező on March 27, accompanied by László Jr., who traveled with him for the first day and then returned home. Tivadar sailed from Galveston for Germany, where he had to wait at Hamburg for travel funds from his sister Klementine Fáy and for Austrian permission to enter Hungary. He later married, farmed at Pusztahát, and died of typhoid in 1870.[50]

László Újházi also continued his own plans during the fall of 1857 for a trip to Europe and described a proposed route to Switzerland, avoiding New York, London, and Germany. He said of those places, "I hate New York, anyway, as well as the life in London where everything is hypocritical and misleading. I never liked the life of high-society people, and now I like it even less since I became a peasant [farmer] of the desert [Texas] eight years ago." He sailed from the port of Indianola to New Orleans and then traveled by steamship to Le Havre. The journey lasted about 35 days and included calls in Cuba, Puerto Rico, the Canary Islands, and the Madeiras. He remarked that the climate of the latter islands was pleasant and the landscape beautiful, and that the wine was superb in the Canary and the Madeira islands. From Cádiz, Spain, he planned to travel by way of Le Havre to Paris and then to Geneva to meet his children.[51]

Before leaving Texas, on August 4, 1857, Újházi gave Farkas his power of attorney. More than a month later, on September 10, Újházi wrote his son-in-law, Károly Nagy, that he was ready to depart Sírmező for the journey. He said, ". . . on August 8th the fountains of heaven opened, and Nature started a new life. Man, animals, and plants got a new lease on life when they hardly had any hopes."

On December 2 he wrote his daughter Pauline Nagy from Geneva, announcing his arrival:

> I am sorry that I, who traveled thousands of miles with great trouble to get closer to you, am unable to make the final few hundreds. But, as long as our country suffers under the yoke of

the tyrant, however sweet some consider this imprisonment as tolerable, for me it is neither tolerable nor acceptable, and never will be. So I only came to the mountainous country of Switzerland, which is the closest among the free countries." [52]

Although Helen, who was afraid to confront her father, and Pauline, who was pregnant, did not accompany others of the family from Hungary to Switzerland, a reunion was held that winter. Upon her return, Klementine Fáy wrote to Pauline that the tearful reunion found Újházi "just as active and determined as he always was." His appearance had not changed, she wrote:

> . . . as if he had spent his time in Budamér with quiet farm-ing and hunting and had not broken the soil of Texas or cut forests in Iowa. Perhaps it is so because seven years ago when we separated he already had a long white beard, and with his small stature he looked like a very old person rather than only a fifty-year-old man.

In Geneva the family completed the division of Újházi's Hun-garian estates and discussed family problems, including plans to send László Jr. from Texas to Switzerland for his university education. They also decided that Helen Madarász, now living in Hungary abandoned by her husband, Vilmos, would accompany Újházi back to Texas with her sons, Ladislaus W. and Béla. In Texas Farkas would assume the duties of guardianship over her and her children. [53]

Following the family gathering in Geneva, Újházi stopped in the German states to shoot quail with a new rifle. He then waited in Hamburg from mid-March until mid-May for Helen and her sons to arrive from Hungary and for Tivadar to bring him Hungarian hunting dogs. Meanwhile, he made arrangements for Pauline Nagy to buy Helen's half of the estate at Hazsina, which they jointly shared in the division of his lands in Hungary. Pauline was to pay Helen 15,100 forints (two forints equaled one dollar in 1858) over a period of three years, so that she would have money to settle in Texas.

Újházi purchased only one ticket for Helen's passage on the steamer which left Hamburg for New York on the 1st and the 15th of each month. His son-in-law Vilmos Madarász, having squandered his inheritance, meekly came to Hamburg with Helen, but Újházi was determined that Vilmos would not accompany the family to America. In a conversation between the two men, Újházi casually proceeded to clean his new rifle, load it, and take a practice aim. How Vilmos interpreted this is not known—when Újházi lowered the weapon, the young man had disappeared and did not return. Later Újházi mused that "if by accident I had suddenly remembered that, at the last moment, he had made my unfortunate daughter pregnant again, I don't know whether I could have resisted pulling the trigger." But the old patriarch had forgiven Helen, observing that "her mind is quick and fertile; only her horizon is narrow, and [she] remains still childish."

While he waited at Hamburg Újházi received a letter from Texas in which Farkas reported that the devastating drought continued and that the "locust[s] ate everything, melon harvest, garden [and] grapes. After the drought, the locust[s]; what is bringing upon us the curses of Egypt?" When Tivadar, with the dogs (*agárs*) and money, arrived in Hamburg on June 10, Újházi wrote that he had great plans for the dogs in Texas, where he would breed them to hunt rabbits on the prairie. "The fast-running hunting dog is practically unknown" in Texas. Újházi with his daughter and her sons finally sailed on the *Borrusia* from Hamburg on June 15.

The *Borrusia* crossed the stormy Atlantic Ocean in two weeks and arrived in New York on June 30, 1858. Újházi and his family then rested at the farm of Mrs. Louise Ruttkay, Kossuth's sister, for nine days before continuing on to Texas. From New York City they sailed to Savannah, Georgia, where they boarded a train to Montgomery, Alabama. The next leg was by river steamer to New Orleans, and the last was another sea voyage to Indianola and Lavaca on the Texas coast, the nearest point to San Antonio.

On August 10 Újházi reported to Pauline from Sírmező:

> A few days ago we arrived at the permanent station of our life and our post from which I doubt I will move away in my lifetime. Our journey was difficult and unpleasant, full of misfortunes. The Atlantic Ocean in June is always cold and stormy. On the other hand, from New York, we traveled in constant stifling heat, especially from the seashore of Texas to here [Sírmező].
>
> We spent nine days in New York, which means that we also spent that much money taking care of our customs, mails, and financial affairs and looking for a ship which would bring us cheaply closer to Texas. I shipped the luggage of Ilka [Helen] and the wine on a separate sailboat, which goes much slower but carries the goods much cheaper to Lavaca, the last seaport.

Újházi went on to describe their route, saying that their money was so depleted they were forced to take "a very bad ordinary mule

59

wagon" for the final leg of the trip to Sírmező. The greatest tragedy of the journey was the death of Béla, Helen's infant son, who became ill and died in Galveston. Újházi wrote that "I could not bring my dead grandchild, the beautiful little Béla, to the land of Texas where our graves are multiplying." Although the family wanted to bring his body to Sírmező for burial next to Újházi's wife, the summer heat forced them to bury him in a small cemetery at Lavaca.

Újházi found that local conditions had changed little during his absence. Although newspaper reports had promised "shining and encouraging news . . . about the crop of Texas this year," he found that locusts had destroyed the first planting, and although his children had replanted, the crop did not live long because of the lack of rain during the summer of 1858.

The four hunting dogs given to Újházi by his children during his visit to Europe survived their trip to Texas. Called *agárs,* which some have translated as "greyhounds," in all probability the dogs were Hungarian *vizslas,* smooth-skinned, brown pointers which excelled in hunting birds and rabbits. A yellow dog, Híres (Famous), had been stolen at Lavaca during the trip, something Újházi very much regretted because so much labor and money had been spent on him. Újházi planned to breed the hunters, sell some, and amuse himself hunting in the neighborhood.[54]

In addition to occupying himself with the hunting dogs, Újházi also brought a large store of Hungarian wines from Europe to San Antonio. During the fall and winter of 1858, a local firm, Groesbeeck and Smyth, advertised a "choice lot" of Hungarian wines for sale, including such labels and types as Pesti, Nussberger, Ruszti Bor, Ruszti Bor 1822, Szekszardi, Budai, and Budai 1846 as well as Somlói, Tokay Maslas (Mazsolás), and Tokay Aszú. In addition, the liquor importers also stocked Hungarian Hock and Stein wines for local consumption. Though Újházi's name was not mentioned in the newspaper in connection with these wines, it is likely that he was responsible for their appearance on the local market, and he probably made a good profit.[55]

In October 1858 Helen wrote to Pauline that Újházi was healthy and busy looking after his newly acquired dogs, one of which had had a litter. Újházi fed the dogs himself, but "did not go duck hunting yet because of the extreme heat."[56]

Újházi's youngest son, László Jr., left Sírmező December 18, 1858, to attend school in Geneva, Switzerland, and Helen gave birth to her third son, Louis (Lajos), on January 20, 1859, at almost the same time that Klára bore her second child, Gyula. The Újházi home became even more crowded. In a letter to Pauline at the end of January 1859, Helen wrote that the first flowers had bloomed, the bees were swarming, and the oaks, green through the winter, were now shedding their leaves. Northers were followed by warm weather, and the "climate was most unusual." Her older son, Ladislaus, was learning Slavic "since he is continuously playing with the Polish children" whose father was among the tenants who worked for Farkas Újházy at Sírmező.[57]

In a letter to Pauline on February 27, 1859, Helen said:

> Father already planted the cantaloupes, and he would like to go hunting with his dogs, but he cannot because Pletyka [Gossip] had babies, and without her, the dog hunt is worthless. You know what a devotee father is to the dogs. He feeds them himself, bathes the little dogs, makes beds for them, and talks to them as we used to talk to our children. With the young ones together, we already have eleven dogs. They cause a great deal of trouble for Klári because she has to give lots of milk to them and they come to play in the kitchen.[58]

During the spring of 1859 Helen again wrote to Pauline that she continued living at Sírmező and that "here nothing indicates that it is Easter day." She reported that

> Father went for a hunt with the dogs and Farkas, yesterday, too. They found one rabbit and they caught it. Father took the three young dogs out two weeks ago, the ones he raised with such great care as very few mothers raise their children, and up to now they have caught about thirty rabbits. Father finally sold one puppy for $25. If he had raised it to maturity, he could have gotten $50. The grapes [cuttings] you sent from Hungary are doing really well in spite of the drought. . . . Twice a day we water them. He who does not irrigate cannot even have lettuce this year. The spring is long gone and now there is already summer's heat in April. If only we had some kind of water nearby in which one could cool off a little. But Father lives along the shores of a river [Olmos Creek] which also has no water in it.[59]

In writing to a relative on May 19, 1859, Újházi described his routine at Sírmező. Arising at dawn, he first fed his dogs, breakfasted, and then worked in his vineyard with his hoe. He planted flowers at his dear wife's grave in the vineyard, but regretted that the "small sea [?] rabbits and field rats" had damaged his vines. His arms had turned "as brown as an Indian's" from working in shirtsleeves. His lunch, consisting of boiled beef or soup and noodles, was prepared by Klára and served at 2:00 p.m. and was followed by rest during the hot afternoons. His bathing place was in a clear pool of water about one mile from his house. Reading his German and English newspapers also occupied his days. Work resumed on the farm in the late afternoon and was followed by supper and a night's rest. Rather than having slaves to do the labor, Újházi wrote:

> If I, a Hungarian at the age of sixty-five, without ever doing physical work [in Hungary] am able to spend six hours in one of the Southern states without damaging my health, then you [the Southern farmer] could do the same, because you are made out of the same clay; you have even the advantage of having been born in this country, while I came from the highest Hungarian [Tatra] mountains. [60]

Újházi's opinion of conditions in America and in Texas were also expressed in a letter to his sister, Valerie Szinnyei, written September 29, 1860:

> Times are gone when the trend of immigration was toward America. In the old days the needy found bread; the mercenary, a field in which to make money quickly; the unlucky or persecuted, a hiding place. But now, even the poor should not come here, because a helping hand nobody will give him. Here, a well-educated man will forever miss the culture of Europe. Here I am . . . pushed into a western state. . . . I brought my tents here from a distance of more than 1,000 miles on horseback, and now I am surrounded by strange people who do not understand the voice of my soul. [61]

The prolonged drought in Texas depressed Újházi, and he and Farkas thought of moving to Sicily. With the outbreak of war between Austria and Italy, assisted by France, in 1859, Újházi's attention returned to the cause of Hungary's freedom. Kossuth, who hoped for Austria's defeat and Hungary's liberation, organized a Hungarian Legion to fight for Italian unification, and "the exiles, even those who lived in America, were preparing to join them, too. The hope, mixed with excitement, reached Texas." Although the war was short and France was victorious at Solferino, the European balance of power was retained, and nothing was done for Hungary's liberation. In a letter to Klementine on June 8, 1859, Újházi wrote that Kossuth had counseled the Hungarians in America to stay there, for, in case of defeat, he could not pay their return fare. And Újházi lamented that no ocean cable existed to bring the news from Europe faster than the one month needed for the mail.[62]

In the same letter Újházi again gave a picture of conditions at Sírmező:

> It is the third year that our river has dried up. We were forced to dig a well in the yard of our house. Fortunately, we found good-tasting, clear water about twenty-five feet down. We put an iron pump, which is available and cheap here, into the well.
>
> In addition to the drought, a cattle disease broke out. Even the deer are dying on the prairie. If we don't get some rain within the next few days, no vegetation will remain. The vegetable garden is completely dead.
>
> Who would have expected this? When I came down the first time [from Iowa] to examine this territory, the fresh and living Nature smiled at me everywhere.

Rain did come in June 1859, but a month too late to save the Újházi garden and fields. Meanwhile, Farkas and his father collected some of their funds which had been lent out for high interest, expecting to depart for Europe and the war which might free Hungary. Instead, the family harvested the corn for fodder that year, and Helen wrote to Pauline that they kept encouraging themselves about the drought conditions because their neighbors reported that "in the past they very rarely missed a harvest."

In September 1859 Újházi wrote to Pauline condemning Napoleon III of France for failing to exploit his victory over Austria — "I always said that the tyrants only look out for their own interests and never for those of the people." He reported that the family in Texas continued their "accustomed position," although they would never be able to become completely adjusted to it. He also wrote that he had helped Helen buy a farm on Cibolo Creek in northeastern Devon County and that he had received news that a ship carrying wine and brandy from his children in Hungary had sunk, forcing him to buy "a barrel of Hungarian wine for myself from New York." His letter ended:

> In the ten years that we have been struggling in America, we have never had such a bad and unhappy life. The drought, [the like of] which has never been experienced in this area before, burned everything standing; neither in the field nor in the garden did we have any harvest worth the black [soil] under our fingernails. Now, finally, the rain has arrived, but only when we were through with everything."

In the fall of 1859 Újházi had a serious accident while rabbit hunting. His horse stepped in a hole, throwing him over its head and rolling over on him. Újházi was unconscious, his "eyes were bulging," and there was a egg-sized swelling on his bloody forehead. Helen and Farkas rushed to his aid, and, fortunately, he recovered after a week. Thereafter he promised his children that he would not hunt with his dogs in the "pitted prairie, . . . although he is going all over the place with his dogs."

Klára Kellerschön wrote in her diary on October 8, 1860, that rains had returned after everything had burned up. Újházi, still thinking of his plans of the previous year to move to Sicily, had almost reached a decision. "The dry and hot years will turn Texas into a desert of Africa," and in Italy he and Farkas would be nearer the revolutionary movements led by Garibaldi. Of her father, she said:

> He is a marvelous man that he cannot rest. Others who have reached his age are broken or mellowed old people, who are sitting on the bench and smoking a pipe. He constantly has an urge to go, either to the prairie or to the other side of the world. Farkas would follow him to the ends of the earth. It is true that for him it is easier because he lives mostly from cattle and not from farming, and there is little profit in that. In the city [San Antonio], where there is always less money, the demand for rapid expansion enables one to invest his profit very well and turn it over.

Újházi, a firm opponent of slavery, wrote in a long letter to Klementine on January 6, 1861, about the American political situation. He saw that the Union was breaking up as the South looked to its own interests alone. The free states, which he described as superior in population, intellect, industry, and commerce, would not tolerate the policies of the Southern "aristocratic minority" and would elect a new president, Abraham Lincoln, who would take office in March. He continued:

> The Southerners look upon the Northern president with such disfavor that they would rather break away from the Union than tolerate him. South Carolina has already declared the rift, on December 21st, and very likely the others will follow her, too. They are planning to establish a new Southern Confederation. Very likely our Texas will also join them, although here there are fewer slaves, and there are many European immigrants. The only reason for the separation is to uphold slavery. Therefore, one can assume that they are going to pass some tyrannical laws; they will sacrifice personal freedom as well as freedom of speech and the

press. . . . Obviously one can uphold a tyrannical institution only through tyrannical laws.

If that happens, we will not be able to stay here any longer, and we will have to pick up the wanderer's staff once more. We have to look out for our own skin because who could predict the severity of a Civil War in advance.

With the outbreak of the American Civil War, Újházi, his staunch antislavery view well known in the local community, would not stay in Texas. On April 6, 1861, he wrote to Secretary of State William H. Seward, outlining his situation as an abolitionist in the South. Because of conditions, he could not sell his land and move to a free state. He thought of joining Garibaldi, but that door too was closed to him because of the peace policy which then prevailed in Italy. Therefore, Újházi, capitalizing on his prestige in America's Hungarian community, asked to be named American consul to Hungary (since the United States imported Hungarian wines), where he could spend his last days among his fellow Hungarians without molestation by the Austrian government. He closed his letter with a postscript, saying: "Being said, communications directed to persons of consideration in the North, are opened by our Southern postoffices—this letter is forwarded to New York by a merchant's firm. Already all our New York newspapers are confiscated by the postmasters." [63]

Since the United States had no consulate in Buda-Pest, President Abraham Lincoln appointed Újházi as American consul at Ancona, Italy, on the Adriatic Sea. This post commanded an annual salary of $1,500 plus travel expenses. Újházi preferred to be located in Italy since he expected it to place him relatively close to his old homeland. There he believed that he might continue to serve the cause of Hungarian freedom and have close contact with other exiles, including Kossuth, who lived in Turin. [64]

Before leaving Texas Újházi advertised in a local newspaper during the spring of 1861 that he was selling half-breed saddle horses at his ranch. He also gift-deeded Sírmező to Farkas Újházy and Klára Kellerschön, on September 14, 1861. The gift included 550 acres, all claims, mortgages and securities, household and kitchen furniture, tools, 75 horses with two stallions, and 125 cattle including several yoke of working oxen. In this way, if he did not return, he would not have to be concerned with a will or legal details of his American estate while in Europe. [65]

THE PRESIDENT OF THE UNITED STATES OF AMERICA,

TO ALL WHO SHALL SEE THESE PRESENTS, GREETING:

Know ye, That, reposing special trust and confidence in the abilities and integrity of *Ladislaus Ujhazi, of Texas,* I have nominated, and by and with the advice and consent of the Senate, do appoint him CONSUL _____ of the United States of America, for the *at Ancona;* _____ and such other parts as shall be nearer thereto than to the residence of any other CONSUL or VICE CONSUL of the United States within the same allegiance, and do authorize and empower him to *HAVE AND TO HOLD* the said office, and to exercise and enjoy all the rights, pre-eminences, privileges, and authorities to the same of right appertaining, during the pleasure of the President of the United States, for the time being: He demanding and receiving no fees or perquisites of office whatever, which shall not be expressly established by some law of the said United States. And I do hereby enjoin all Captains, Masters, and Commanders of ships and other vessels, armed or unarmed, sailing under the flag of the said States, as well as all other of their citizens, to acknowledge and consider him, the said *Ladislaus Ujhazi,* _____ accordingly.

AND I DO HEREBY PRAY AND REQUEST *His Majesty, The King of Italy,* _____ *His* Governors and Officers to permit the said *Ladislaus Ujhazi,* _____ fully and peaceably to enjoy and exercise the said office, without giving or suffering to be given unto him any molestation or trouble; but, on the contrary, to afford him all proper countenance and assistance; I offering to do the same for all those who shall, in like manner, be recommended to me by *His said Majesty.* _____

In testimony whereof, *I have caused these Letters to be made Patent, and the Seal of the United States to be hereunto affixed.* GIVEN under my hand at the City of Washington, the *Twelfth* — day of *July,* — in the year of our Lord one thousand eight hundred and *forty-two,* and of the Independence of the United States of America the *Eighty-seventh. Abraham Lincoln*

BY THE PRESIDENT:

William H. Seward, SECRETARY OF STATE.

László Újházi's certificate of appointment as U.S. consul to Ancona, Italy, July 12, 1862

President Abraham Lincoln's appointment of Újházi as U.S. Consul at Ancona was signed on November 27, 1861, and he received his consular passport the next month. King Victor Emmanuel II of Italy issued the exquatur for Újházi's appointment on January 5, 1862. Accompanied by Farkas on the journey to Italy, Újházi sailed from New York in January 1862 and reached Ancona by way of Liverpool, Paris, and Turin. He assumed his post on January 18, 1862, and Farkas returned to Texas.

Újházi found Ancona an expensive backwater port where few American vessels called. In March 1862 László Jr., who had been at school in Geneva and with relatives in Hungary, joined him and became his secretary at the consulate. There they lived for the next two years in a rented villa three miles from the town. Újházi cultivated his favorite melons, as he had in Texas. He continued his correspondence with Hungarian exiles in Italy and took keen interest in the Italian unification movement and its possible effect in helping to free Hungary. But Újházi carefully committed no act contrary to his diplomatic status as an

American consul. Apparently he traveled through the Neapolitan Provinces in 1862 and observed the Italian people and economy.[66]

In November 1863 Újházi was visited in Italy by members of his family from Hungary, including his daughters Pauline Nagy and Klementine Fáy with Klementine's husband. His sons Sándor and Tivadar came also, as did old friends Joseph Hámos and Ferenc Erdélyi. While there the family and friends had a group photograph made to commemorate the visit. All the while, the Austrian secret police watched Újházi and his family, both in Italy and in Hungary, for revolutionary agitation and activities on behalf of Hungarian independence.

Újházi's age and health, as well as his concern for the safety of his children in Texas during the Civil War, led him to resign his post on December 11, 1863. His resignation was accepted by the secretary of state on February 6, 1864. One of the reasons he gave for his resignation was his wish to return to "share the fate of our Union on our own soil." Also, László Jr. wanted to enlist in the Union army.[67]

The Újházi family and friends, Turin, Italy, 1863—standing, from left, *Joseph Hámos, László Jr., Sándor, Tivadar, Ferenc Erdélyi;* seated, *Pauline Nagy, László Sr., Klementine Fáy, Rosa Fáy, and Gusztáv Fáy*

67

Leaving Italy, Újházi and László Jr. traveled by way of London and reached New York in April 1864. Going on to Washington to conclude his business with the government, Újházi wrote to Klementine on the 10th of that month that he had inquired about Farkas and his daughters in Texas and had sent a message under a government flag of truce. In New York he learned that the Union troops no longer controlled all the Texas coastal ports and that the occupation of the interior and of San Antonio had been delayed. He also sought to obtain an officer's commission for László Jr. while in New York.[68]

On April 22, 1864, Újházi wrote an informative letter to Tivadar, saying that he had heard from the family at Sírmező—they were all right, and Farkas and Joseph Kellerschön had not been drafted into the Confederate army. Although Újházi anticipated being at Sírmező within a month, his travel plans required him to skirt the blockade and go to Matamoros, Mexico. From there he and László would have to cross the Rio Grande and then proceed to San Antonio. Újházi also had learned that Sírmező was in "acceptable condition." He informed Tivadar that he wanted to enroll László Jr. as a lieutenant in a cavalry unit under the Hungarian émigré General Julius Stahel, who was stationed in Virginia, and wrote that "if he finds a proper place for me, I will move my tent over to the vicinity of the camp."

From New York Újházi wrote on July 1 to Pauline concerning financial matters relating to Helen and the money exchange rate between gold and paper dollars. He also said that László Jr. was "an assistant quartermaster in the camp with $80 a month salary, plus food and horse." He ended his letter with "I can write nothing about the people in Texas."

At Sírmező Klára Kellerschön recorded in her diary on September 5, 1864, that she was worried her father would not be safe from marauders who roamed around San Antonio during the last year of the war. As for Helen, she was seemingly not afraid to continue living alone on the Cibolo, even though "the war is getting closer and the Confederacy is about to lose. The deserters, the vagrants, beggars, and thieves multiplied." Helen spent much time at Sírmező, but returned to watch over her crops and cattle at her own farm, where "the crop will burn out anyway and the cattle exist without any guardians."

Conditions were dangerous for Újházi's family at Sírmező as well. On October 14 Klára wrote in her diary that Farkas and Kellerschön were almost conscripted into the army. The enrolling patrol in

San Antonio stopped every man under 50 and searched for others who were in hiding in the forests and hills. At one point Farkas had been stopped in the city, but because he knew one of the recruiting officers, he was released and "ran home during the night." On October 11 the family members at Sírmező were awakened during the night by their Mexican horseboy, who warned them that the soldiers were nearby. Gunshots were heard in the distance as Farkas and Kellerschön dressed, climbed out the window, and fled into the darkness. They hid out in the bush for two days before coming home. Klára worried that László Jr. would be drafted but knew that her father's age exempted him from service. She concluded, "Who would have thought when we came to Texas what we would be mixed up in? There isn't the smallest mouse hole in this world where one could hide from fate."

Újházi, accompanied by László Jr., who resigned his commission in order to accompany his father home on the long, dangerous journey, arrived at Sírmező late in November 1864. There he found the family healthy. The farm was a bit run-down, partly because of his absence and partly because of the ravages of war. Implements were missing, and the drought continued. He observed to Klementine November 29 that, "Last year it [the drought] was worse than we've seen since we came to Texas. Yet, in 1862, the fields brought beautiful crops, to everybody's surprise." The family there had not profited, however, because of military confiscations of foodstuffs for a nearby camp.

Újházi's journey from Matamoros, Mexico, was trying. At a crossing point at Rio Grande City, he hired some mule wagons. The trip to San Antonio took seven days; part of one was spent in repairing a broken wheel. He and his son drank water found in holes, cooked and baked for themselves, and were entertained by the Black coachman, who accompanied himself on a guitar. Újházi hoped that László Jr.'s European passport would protect him from the recruiting officers.

> As far as I am concerned, the people here [San Antonio] already know that I arrived, but there is no news that they want to bother me. I went to the city, met several leading people, and they did not grind their teeth against me. They took my return as natural. Of course, none of them know where and for what I was away. . . . I believe, therefore, that . . . they will let me be in peace.

While on his way to Texas, Újházi had been robbed at his New Orleans hotel of his watch, ring, seal, and paper money, among other things. He lamented, "My poor good old watch, faithful companion of fifty years, which showed my life in happy and unhappy minutes. He deserted me also, and I do not know if I will have another which will slow my last minutes." A more serious misfortune also occurred immediately following Újházi's return to Texas. At the Mexican border a merchant entrusted $1,500 in gold to Újházi to deliver in San Antonio. But, when Farkas took the money into the city, he lost the saddlebag, and the money was not recovered. Újházi gave one third of his insurance premium as security and entrusted a panel of three judges to decide whether he was at fault for the money's loss.[69]

Újházi had only been back at Sírmező a few months before a more immediate danger threatened his family. One night in February 1865 three strangers, possibly deserters from the Confederate army, came to Sírmező. Farkas was shot in the thigh and László Jr. in the groin when they answered a knock on the door. Without light or the help of a doctor, Újházi managed to staunch the heavy arterial bleeding of László Jr.'s wound. This "horrifying and terrifying night" was described as a "fight between life and death" for Újházi's sons. Although Farkas quickly recovered, László Jr. required a longer convalescence.[70]

During the spring of 1865 another serious incident occurred. Sírmező was flooded one night by a storm which struck the headwaters of the Olmos Basin. Újházi wrote:

> An unheard-of downpour occurred in our part, and the river [Olmos Creek] which was about two hundred steps from the house rose so rapidly that every five minutes the water level rose one foot. When it began to seep into the house, we left everything behind, picked up only our documents, and started toward the hill, carrying our grandchildren on our backs. . . . It was only by the light of the lightning . . . [and] at first light that we saw that our house was still there. When we returned, we saw the tremendous destruction. The fences of our farm were taken away and the plants washed out. Our damage is greater than what we poor folks can take.[71]

But the family survived their misfortunes. On July 27, 1866, Klára Kellerschön and Farkas Újházy gave László Jr. a one-third share in Sírmező (for which he paid one dollar) with its improvements and livestock. At the same time, Klára deeded her two brothers her share in the farm, known locally as the Újházi Place, with the exception of ten cows, in return for $5,000 in silver. Thereafter Sírmező was owned by the brothers, each with an undivided half interest.[72]

With the Civil War at an end, Újházi and his family settled into their routine on the Olmos, and he drove his four matched white mules when visiting the city. With the restoration of peace and arrival of the U.S. Army during the summer of 1865, Újházi joined with pre-war Unionists, Germans, and other European immigrants and freedmen in forming the Bexar County Union Association, the predecessor of the local Republican Party. Its committee of arrangement and invitations asked him to a public meeting of voters (those who could qualify as non-Confederate participants and officeholders) to discuss candidates for the nominating convention, which was scheduled to be held on December 27, 1865.

As a dignified and respected elder statesman who had held a consular post under Abraham Lincoln, Újházi was closely associated with those of his political leanings in local affairs. On July 4, 1867, he gave a speech at the Independence Day Celebration, drawing parallels between that event and the Compromise of 1867 and the coronation of Franz Joseph as King of Hungary. Újházi attended party meetings and conventions throughout the late 1860's and, in January 1868, served as presiding officer of the Republican (Union) Nominating Convention in San Antonio. He was chosen because he "held himself aloof from all political affairs," probably meaning that he did not side with either the radical or the moderate factions of the Republican Party at the convention.[73]

In addition to his interest in local politics, Újházi maintained his great interest in Hungarian affairs. The important Compromise of 1867 had been negotiated by politician-statesman Ferenc Deák, and Hungary regained her constitution, Transylvania was reunited with the kingdom, and the Austro-Hungarian Empire came into being. Emperor Franz Joseph of Austria was crowned King of Hungary on June 8, 1867, in Buda-Pest. Although a majority of Hungarians welcomed the Compromise, Újházi, from his now self-imposed exile in Texas, remained adamant. He submitted an article, written from Sírmező on March 15 to the New York *Tribune* (published August 20, 1867) in which he repudiated the Compromise and publicly announced his continued refusal, on principle, to accept the amnesty which had been granted to the émigrés. In reaching his final decision Újházi resolved never to return. He wrote, "Deák's cursed document probably will last longer than my unhappy life." In a San Antonio newspaper he challenged the Compromise:

71

Go forward, Hungarians, with courage, with your strong arm erase the cowardly year of 1867 from your national calendar. Do not let this year be one of your independence's gravestone. A brother sends his worried, desperate words from the land of liberty and fraternity.[74]

One of his paternal concerns was the future of László Jr., who had returned to Texas with him in 1864. In April 1867 Újházi, again counting on his prestige, wrote to Secretary of State William H. Seward asking that the United States establish a consulate in Buda-Pest and that László Jr. be appointed to the post. (The separate communities of Óbuda, Buda, and Pest amalgamated in 1873 and henceforth were know as one city, Budapest.) Újházi reported that his son spoke French, Italian, German, English, and Hungarian, and had experience as his secretary at the consulate in Ancona, Italy. His letter was seconded by Congressman Edward Degener of San Antonio, who wrote that the "political creed of young Újházi is the same [Republican] as of his father," and that "Father Újházi himself is at this place the most respected supporter of the Union, . . . the most consistent Republican." Degener and Újházi also wrote to Senator Charles Sumner, chairman of the Committee on Foreign Affairs, and Texas Governor Elisha M. Pease asking for their support. However, the government did not act, although Újházi again wrote to Secretary Seward in December.[75]

Not all of Újházi's attention was devoted to politics, his children's futures, and Sírmező—he seemed to find time for relaxation with his favorite sport. During the fall of 1866 he invited his Hungarian neighbors, Gabriel Katona and Francis Böröndi, two colonels, a major, several captains and lieutenants of the U.S. Army, and members of his family, including Helen, Farkas, and László Jr., to a rabbit hunt on the prairie about six miles north of Sírmező. Also included were the local chief justice, a bank director, and an attorney. In describing this hunt to the editor of a Buda-Pest newspaper, *Vasárnapi Újság* (*Sunday News*), which published it on February 27, 1867, Újházi refrained from political topics concerning Hungary and reported:

I usually keep six greyhounds and we took all of them to the hunting ground. My dogs are of pure Hungarian origin. The two male *törzskutya* [registered pedigreed dogs] were given by my old friends in Hungary. I brought them . . . from Geneva in 1858 through Hamburg to Texas with many difficulties and infinite care. They were new and excited much admiration here in Texas among the populace. The rabbits in Texas are smaller than those in Hungary; on the other hand, they have much longer ears. This is the reason they are called jackrabbits by the natives. This particular species thrives in Texas and neighboring Mexico.[76]

The hunting party of 16 left Sírmező, accompanied by carts for those who did not ride and the luncheon supplies. The hunt, complete with hunting horn, began with the riders assembled in right and left wings, with Újházi and László Jr. in the center. The dogs flushed the first rabbit, which dodged into a thicket but was pursued and killed within 15 minutes. Thereafter the hunters, spread out for two miles, continued the hunt. At lunchtime the ladies, including Helen and the judge's wife, served excellent food (roast turkey, suckling pig, head cheese, and pastries) on a white tablecloth by a small lake. The repast was accompanied by Hungarian wines, the red Egri Bikavér (Bull's Blood), Tokay, and brandy (acquired from his Hungarian relatives who owned vineyards). After a rest the dogs were again released, and the hunt continued, with a few minor accidents, possibly caused by the Americans' unfamiliarity with strong Hungarian wines.[77]

At the meal Újházi had toasted the U.S. Army for saving the republic and liberating the South from the "tyranny of the slave-owning aristocracy." He also expressed his pity for President Andrew Johnson, whom he wished to see impeached by Congress. On the way home from the hunt Újházi and his party were refreshed with champagne by the colonels. Újházi complimented himself at the end of the hunt, saying that he, a 72-year-old man, had ridden as well as the younger men from seven in the morning until five in the evening. Thus he continued his old Hungarian custom of hunting with his dogs.[78]

Very little else of the family during the late 1860's is known. In September 1867 Újházi and Farkas offered to rent a 50-acre fenced field "in a high state of cultivation," thus continuing a practice established prior to the war that of leasing land on shares of the crops. Their ad in the local paper ran until the first week of October.[79]

László Újházi's symbolic value in the Hungarian political arena had not ended in 1869, although he knew nothing of it at the time. In the elections for Parliament in Hungary that year, he was nominated by the left-wing opposition (the political following of Kossuth) for a seat from the Inner City of Pest to stand against the leading Hungarian statesman of the time, Ferenc Deák. Újházi was considered an honorable but safe candidate to oppose Deák, although he was now a U.S. citizen living in Texas. Deák won the election by a large majority. In Hungary

Újházi's children were outraged that his name had been used without his permission. When Újházi found out about his nomination, he took it as a grave insult to his intelligence. He thought that his supporters in Hungary did not credit him with a realistic view of the political situation in his former homeland. Further, Újházi had always rejected Austrian amnesty and would not return to his native land.[80]

In 1869 Klára and Joseph Kellerschön left Sírmező to take up residence at Schönbornslust, Germany. In her diary, on February 2, 1870, written in Hungary while visiting her relatives, Klára recalled the move. With the remainder of her share of Sírmező and land in Iowa which her husband had inherited from his father, as well as his earnings at Sírmező, she mused that she owned more than all her siblings, both in Texas and in Hungary. Her husband, for whom she felt respect and honor for his "diligence, his straightforwardness and . . . quietness," had determined to invest their money in his homeland and raise his children as Germans in Germany. Before leaving Texas Kellerschön gave László Jr. his power of attorney to transact business for him. Thereafter Klára remained in Germany, with periodic visits to her relatives in Hungary, until her death, the date of which is not known. Her years of hard physical toil — cooking, washing, housekeeping, child-rearing, and farming — in Iowa and Texas had ended.[81]

László Újházi's life was also near its end. He died at Sírmező on March 7, 1870. The 75-year-old exile had been in declining health, and "his mind was occupied exclusively with death. He did not read newspapers — he hardly ever stepped out of his room," wrote Farkas to his relatives on March 10. The day of Újházi's death, Helen, who was again living at Sírmező, accompanied her son Ladislaus to school in the city. Only Farkas and his young nephew Louis were at home with Újházi. There, wrote Farkas, the family's patriarch died sitting before the fire in his armchair during the middle of the afternoon. No mention was made in the sad letter of suicide. Farkas expressed the wishes of his father and of the family to transport the remains of his parents from Sírmező to the ancient family crypt beneath the little Lutheran church at Budamér. Farkas concluded, "We buried his holy remains [at Sírmező] yesterday. . . . We embalmed him so that we can bring the blessed ashes of both [parents] home so that all of their children could make a pilgrimage to their grave."[82]

A San Antonio newspaper, which gave the cause of his death as suicide, reported:

Yesterday we chronicled the death of our honored and venerable citizen, Governor Ladislaus Újházi.

Truly a great and good man has fallen. His name is enrolled among the patriots and reformers of the world.

The love of liberty was a passion for him. Although born to fortune and privilege, he espoused the cause of freedom in Hungary against the despotism of Austria, and gave the best energies of his life to its support.

He was the intimate friend and compatriot of Kossuth, Klapka, and the other leaders of the Hungarian revolution.

The great hope of Gov. Újházi's life was to see his native land freed from Austrian tyranny. But his sympathies were by no means confined to his own oppressed country. He was the friend of freedom throughout the earth. At the close of the Hungarian revolution Gov.Újházi fled to the United States. For a time he lived in Iowa. He then moved to Texas, and settled near San Antonio in 1853 and here he resided until his death. He was universally respected and beloved by the whole community.

The local paper's report of his death was repeated in East Coast and Hungarian newspapers, which called him the "Cato of the 19th Century." A San Antonio German newspaper, *Freie Presse für Texas*, commented that Újházi "always stood on the side of the radical freedom party. He was a man of extreme strength of character and with a force of conviction, a republican of the purest intentions. During the slavery rebellion he stood with all his heart on the side of the Union." [83]

The *Magyar Újság* (*Hungarian News*) in Pest paid Újházi a final tribute when it published a letter, written in March 1870, from a Hungarian 48er in New York City:

The liberal American Hungarians were shaken by sad news today. Of those few who since 1849 are still struggling here and work for the better life of the Republic and for their country [Hungary], a cruel fate took away another star—a star, the memory of whom will continue to live. . . . He was born in a free country—he should die in a free country. Peace upon his ashes. [84]

In a diary entry made in Hungary on May 3, 1870, Klára remembered her father: "Oh, father. Every word of his was bitter, yet he lived happily. Otherwise, he barely could have tolerated what he had to go through. It was assigned to him." On June 17 Farkas wrote to Pauline that his "one holy, sacred duty toward our two parents" dictated that he return their remains to Budamér, but it was nine years before this was accomplished and László and Teréz Újházi were finally laid to rest among their ancestors in 1879. [85]

Local gossip about Újházi's life at Sírmező was wildly embellished, especially with the passing of time. According to the story told in the Ferdinand Herff family, Újházi, described as a flamboyant nobleman, had lived in a luxurious style at his showplace home, which was filled with rare art objects. Large profits from his Hungarian lands enabled him, a "lover of art and lavish living," to lead a profligate existence. His "famous salon" was frequented by prominent San Antonians and visiting dignitaries, including military elite, ministers, consuls, and foreign plenipotentiaries during the Civil War.

A visit to Sírmező was a memorable event since his "banquets were epicurean, his wine cellar matchless, and the entertainment superb." Újházi was even remembered by his San Antonio associates as importing "professional vocalists, instrumentalists, and stage notables." Finally, when his Hungarian incomes decreased, Újházi was cast into poverty. After borrowing from Dr. Herff to pay off his servants, the old Hungarian committed suicide. The Herff tale also reported that shortly after his death, the house at Sírmező burned, and "Every trace of the splendor, and the ruin, of Count Újházi's career disappeared into ashes." [86] (The various titles, e.g., Governor, Count, General, by which Újházi was addressed, were strictly honorary, bestowed on him by those who vastly respected him and perhaps made assumptions from stories of his past exploits. He had no legitimate title or military rank.)

If the western frontier of Texas at mid-19th century was peopled by a variety of characters and personalities, László Újházi certainly found a suitable place to settle. There the idiosyncratic Hungarian nobleman-turned-democrat became an American citizen and participated avidly in his adopted country's political processes. At the same time, he remained faithful to the ideals of Louis Kossuth, which called for the true independence of Hungary and the modernization of its antiquated social, economic, and legal institutions. As the result of Újházi's participation in Hungary's Age of Reform and its subsequent Revolution of 1848-1849, he became a victim, choosing to spend the remainder of his life in exile, always faithful to his republican principles and his aversion to continued Austrian Habsburg rule in Hungary. In the end, he died in a land which he never completely called home.

Újházi was a victim of his birth, generation, and education. In spite of his resolve to be a democratic member of American society, he never completely shed the attitude of a nobleman. Even on the edge of the western frontier in Texas, he sought to duplicate his earlier life as a Hungarian country squire. As a result, he was an anomaly among his Texas neighbors. Keeping pedigreed Hungarian hunting dogs, importing Hungarian wines, and driving four matched white mules when he visited San Antonio, his lifestyle and that of his family elicited local gossip and legends of his supposed wealth. Had he established a large Hungarian colony in Iowa or San Antonio, Újházi might have derived some satisfaction by keeping the refugees together in order to resume Hungary's quest for freedom. Reality held otherwise, and he spent his last years in the small circle of his family and a few other 48ers who adapted to Texas conditions, including the epic drought of the 1850's and the Civil War, as best they could.

CHAPTER FOUR

"Once I am settled, I will not move."

Újházi's Family in Texas after 1870

A nd what was the fate of László Újházi's children after his death in 1870? (Of eight children, five came to America—Klára, Tivadar, Farkas, László Jr., and Helen. All shared his exile in Iowa and at Sírmező in Texas.) Tivadar and Klára had returned to Europe before 1870. After Újházi's death László Jr. and Farkas, disheartened by their years of struggling to succeed in farming and stock raising, had no compelling reason to remain and also returned to Hungary. Only his youngest daughter, Helen Madarász, who came to Texas to live with her family in 1858, chose to remain, endeavoring to support herself and raise and educate her children.

Much of what is known of Helen's life comes from a handful of unique and highly personal letters written from Iowa and Texas to her relatives in Hungary. Her father's letters and Klára's correspondence and diary likewise give insight into Helen's character. Born about 1838, Helen was still a child with her family inside Komárom when Hungary's last fortress surrendered to the Austrians in the fall of 1849. She accompanied the family to Hamburg and then to New York, where her father and the other Hungarian refugees were heartily welcomed by the American people. Klára described their arrival and first view of the city in her diary. The wharves were lined with warehouses and hundreds of ships' masts and smokestacks. A Hungarian welcoming committee

Helen Újházy Madarász

met the new arrivals, and its leader, Colonel John Prágay, proclaimed, "God brought you here to the free American soil." Installed at Astor House, the Újházis were repeatedly called to the windows by an enthusiastic crowd, and the menfolk participated in a parade composed of Hungarian, Scottish, Irish, and other national guard cavalry units in uniform. It must have all been very exciting for young Helen.

Described in Klára's diary as "still a child" who was always enthusiastic to travel but who understood only Hungarian, Helen, with other members of the family, accompanied her father to Philadelphia briefly, then returned to New York while he went to Washington to meet the American president and members of Congress. Even after the family's decision to move to Iowa during the summer of 1850 was made, Helen was not expected to assume much responsibility in the pioneering family, although her sister wrote that she would mature and blossom in a year. For the first time, the Újházi ladies would have no servants.[1]

Although Klára, 17 years Helen's senior, judged that her sister got "terribly bored" doing meticulous work such as needlepoint, Helen proved valuable during the family's overland trek to their new home on the Thompson River. She was an excellent horsewoman, and, riding sidesaddle, she was responsible for herding the family's newly purchased livestock. At times Mrs. Újházi and Klára had to alight from the wagons to help Helen round up the sheep, but Klára admitted that her sister was doing well in the heavy work. "She handles the horse well and tolerates the heat, and even her patience does not diminish."

Helen's first letter to her beloved sister Pauline Nagy was written on August 20, 1850, as she witnessed her family's efforts to build a house and fence the fields on the Iowa prairie. She wrote, "I became a guardian of a goose; could you ever imagine that? I really don't care because I don't have to do anything, just walk the land, although, in this high grass, the animals disappear. I can call them to no avail. I could daydream at will if I would only know what about."

Helen was excited over the new farm, yet bored. She felt that "life is not too terribly happy" with the adults working and no playmates available. Then, almost boastfully, she told her sister that she was no longer a little girl. As she grew taller she felt that she was maturing into womanhood and that hers was no longer the mind of a child. In describing the available men at New Buda, Helen said that the neighbors who came to raise the house were all Americans of Irish peasant stock and were rough, drank, and laughed loudly. The adolescent Helen vowed to marry none of those and, in a dramatic, childish way, declared she would stay an old maid or else run away.

Helen called her sister Pauline, 19 years her senior, her "little mother." In a letter written in February of 1851, Helen said that she was healthy despite the harsh winter and was making an overcoat from stag hide, which she had obtained from visiting Indians for eight scarves bought in Hamburg. In describing the Indians Helen wrote that they

> . . . came from the other side of the Thompson [River], where they live and hunt. Gentle and peaceful people are they. They just kill all of the animals because they live from that which they are able to hunt. The farmers say that sooner or later we have to get rid of them because no wild animals will remain for the farmers to shoot when they hunt. Dad said that the end will be that the Indians won't want to go away and both the Reds and the Whites will suffer if a war breaks out. But it is also true that as long as there are Indians somewhere, the farmers have no rest. On the other hand, as soon as the farmers settle someplace, the Indians have no rest.[2]

The entire Újházi family attended a country dance at an Irish neighbor's house to celebrate the harvest of 1851. A rapidly maturing Helen was allowed to go with her first date, Vilmos Madarász, teen-aged son of László Madarász, a Hungarian exile who lived 14 miles from New Buda. The ladies rode to the dance in a wagon, sitting on chairs so that their wide crinoline skirts, brought from Hungary, would have space. Music for the dance was provided by an "orchestra" of two Blacks "who, like our gypsies at home, play from memory without scores." Klára recorded that the single "American national dance, which was only twelve notes" was easy to remember and that "the dance itself is very similar to the *csárdás* [a folk dance] of the peasants of Somogy [County, Hungary]. The couples are all jumping up and down in one spot, and they are stamping their feet." Helen and Vilmos were also "jumping up and down," reported Klára. The following morning the ladies slept in the wagon on their way home.

Helen's mother died shortly thereafter, on October 5, 1851, and was buried on the farm at New Buda. Klára assumed heavy house-hold duties in caring for the men. She wrote to a sister in Hungary:

> Ilka [Helen] is still a child, although the siblings don't con-sider her as such. They are misled by the sudden development of the body. . . . I, however, know our little sister better than the boys, and I know that in the suddenly blossomed body a still-childish temperament lives. She knows nothing about the world and doesn't understand anything of it, which would be all right if she could grow up at home in the manor of Budamér, like any other girl of the Hungarian gentry, within the protecting, defend-ing circle of her family. But being transplanted into a strange land, and even in that strange land in its wilderness, where, instead of the entertainment and studies befitting a noble girl, she is forced to take on hard manual work and trials and tribulations, and, in addition, without a mother—what will become of her, only the good heaven knows.

Without her mother's supervision, Helen rapidly developed into a rebellious teenager. Her father's attention was distracted by both his mourning and his heavy work schedule. Although she helped her sister, she lived "as she wants to and loafs around as a foal escaped from the corral." She disappeared for "half a day from the house and comes home only for supper." A teenage romance soon formed between Helen and Vilmos Madarász. He began filling her head with dreams of mar-riage and their returning together to Hungary, where she would live like a lady with servants. In writing to Pauline in January 1852, Helen revealed her secret plans to marry Vilmos:

> My face is red . . . caused by too much and inevitable outdoor activities. But here one cannot carry a parasol. . . . Vili [Vilmos] says I shouldn't despair because I will become a white-faced lady. . . . We, in spite of how fate undermined our life, are still Hungarians and a gentleman's family.

Her determination to marry strengthened while her father was absent in Texas during the spring and summer of 1852. Klára wrote that her sister's "rebellious temperament is taking over, and she is living a completely vagabond life." Upon his return to New Buda, Újházi learned of his 15-year-old daughter's decision to marry young Madarász. Although she fearlessly made her wishes known to him, Újházi opposed it, judging Vilmos to be "immature in age [and] also mentally and in character." Yet he reluctantly gave his blessing after the young couple did marry on June 4, 1853. Helen was estranged from her father but fortunately not from her siblings in Texas and Hungary.

Helen and Vilmos lived with his father, László Madarász, near New Buda for two years, during which time a son, Ladislaus W., was born to them. Helen's adolescent desire to become a fine lady with servants was partially fulfilled. The Madarász family kept a German girl to wash, cook, sew, milk, and do other light housekeeping for her. In writing to Pauline, Helen revealed that she could speak and understand English now, but that she did not know her own age. She requested that her sister obtain this information from a Book of Registry so that she could "know how old I was when I got married." [3]

In December of 1855 Helen wrote to Pauline that she and Vilmos had returned to Europe. He had had to obtain a passport to enter Hungary from the Austrian government. Vilmos's maternal grandmother, a wealthy noblewoman, had promised to finance their journey, so the young family had set out. They had planned to meet the elderly lady in Belgium and live there until a passport could be obtained. Unfortunately, the grandmother had died before she could journey to Belgium, but, in any case, Vilmos had succeeded in obtaining permission to enter his homeland.

When she wrote this letter Helen, now expecting a second child, was living at her sister Klementine Fáy's estate at Nyustya, Hungary. She had been left there by Vilmos, who was elsewhere settling matters concerning his inheritance from his grandmother. From Nyustya she wrote to Pauline that she was "finally a lady" — she had her own maid! But she felt that she and her son had been abandoned by her husband, who was wasting his inheritance in rich living and flirting with women in another part of Hungary. This situation created a scandal in both their families. Described as uncontrollable as well as childish, lonely, and weak, Madarász let it be known that he considered his American civil marriage invalid in Hungary. He also accused Helen of infidelity in London during a visit on the way to Hungary.[4]

By April 1856 the young couple had reached an impasse. Helen wrote to Vilmos that in his continued absence, she considered herself "the master of my own person." Although the families of both expected a divorce, Helen and Vilmos were reconciled briefly in the late summer of 1857 through the efforts of relatives and friends. A second son, Béla, had been born during their separation. During this period of reconciliation Vilmos wished to legitimize his two children, and Helen agreed to a Catholic marriage ceremony. But, by the end of August, they again separated because of Vilmos's continued uncontrolled behavior. Thereafter Helen lived with one of her sisters, Pauline or Klementine, and awaited the arrival of her father for a reunion in Switzerland in the winter of 1858.[5]

In Geneva the family decided to send Helen and her two sons to Texas with their father when he returned in mid-1858. Helen, with her sons and Vilmos, who tagged along, arrived in Hamburg by way of Vienna on May 23 to join her father. Although she had to rely on her father's generosity for her travel funds, Helen's real concern was that she would have no money upon which to live in Texas. And she was expecting a third child. Újházi had planned to sail on the first of June for New York but was delayed because he had to wait for Tivadar to arrive with four hunting dogs. Meanwhile, he was determined that Vilmos would not accompany them to America and so frightened him off.

Having become accustomed once again to servants during her three years in Hungary, Helen brought with her a maid, Julia, to help and to care for the children during the voyage and in Texas. Julia had been an outdoor maid at Klementine's estate at Nyustya and was described as a "handsome, quick young lady," who packed for the journey on short notice. Helen observed, "What a good thing she will be for me in America. At least I will have somebody to look after me if something happens to me." As the family prepared to board the *Borrusia* for the June 15 sailing, Helen lamented to Pauline that if the ship sank during the voyage, "then think sometimes, my dears, about your unfortunate relative to whom God did only good that He saved her with one single blow from further bitterness and disappointments."

The transatlantic voyage lasted two weeks. Upon arriving in New York, Újházi and his party rested for some days before leaving for Texas. On July 12, 1858, Helen wrote to Pauline about the terrible heat they encountered in New York and throughout their journey. Helen informed her sister from Savannah, Georgia, that

> My body and soul are bored with the journey. It is terrible how much I suffer because of the heat. I didn't write you from New York because my hand stuck to the paper from the heat. We really didn't live, only suffered. [Even] If Texas will be the same, I do not wish to leave. . . . Only God knows how much I suffer, even now as I am writing. The ship is rolling, shaking; sweat is pouring from me. . . . Yesterday I was forced to interrupt this gorgeous scritch-scratch because I got sick.

But, except for the heat, Helen traveled in comfort. She reported that she was "the queen" of the voyage since the only other lady passenger did not show herself. Food was plentiful and good, and the beds had linens, "which is rare in America." However, Julia became seasick for the first time during the last segment of the trip, and Helen complained that "just when I need it most, I don't have any help."

The young woman's description of her journey to Texas continued to chronicle her complaints. During the train ride from Savannah to Montgomery, Alabama, Helen's small sons "were eaten up by the mosquitos," and once there, she reported that an "omnibus ran over the foot of my little dog." But she was relieved to be able to "wash leisurely and dress myself."

A great personal tragedy marked Helen Madarász's introduction to Texas. On August 8 she wrote from Sírmező:

> I cannot say that we were lucky with our trip because I was hit with the greatest misfortune so far. I had two sons, and all my happiness and joy was in them. But Fate thought that was too much for me and took it away from me. Oh, my God, how did I sin against You that You are still not satisfied with my misfortune?

Béla, her younger son, became ill during the trip from New Orleans. Although Újházi wrapped him in cold, wet sheets and the ship put into Galveston for a doctor, the little boy died July 20. The family quickly made a small casket and in their sorrow tried to bring the body to Sírmező for burial. But, after a day's sail to Lavaca, they were forced to bury him immediately. Helen vowed to retrieve Béla for reburial the next winter next to his grandmother at Sírmező. She wrote to her sister, "Oh, it was even more painful for my soul that I had to leave him there in the desolate prairie. My poor little one, we scratched him into the dirt as an abandoned orphan. . . ." [6]

Following a six-day wagon trip inland to San Antonio, Helen and her surviving son, Ladislaus, settled with her family at Sírmező. Fresh from the comforts of her relatives' estates in Hungary, she found conditions at Sírmező primitive by comparison. Her greatest shock, however, came when she first saw Klára, who was now married and had a child:

> "When I saw Klári, I could only cry. . . . If I had met her in a strange place, it is possible that I wouldn't even recognize her. For one, she has aged a great deal, and the misery clearly shows on her. She has let herself go in her clothing, so she really looks miserable. . . . I cannot but marvel how she could take all the misery that has befallen her."

Obviously, the difference in their situations during the five-year separation was to blame. Klára had remained with her father in Iowa, made the long overland trip to Texas, and done all of the kitchen and household work at Sírmező, while her younger sister enjoyed the comfortable life of a lady in Hungary.

For the next year Helen remained at Sírmező. Her immediate goal was to purchase a farm and become independent. Friction soon developed between the sisters, who shared the two-room home. Klára, with her husband, Joseph Kellerschön, and daughter, Tini, occupied one room, and Helen and her son shared the other with her father and brothers. In good weather the men slept outside on the porches. Having lent out her capital of $1,000 at 12 percent, Helen had already spent her first year's $120 interest for the Atlantic crossing and was forced to borrow or accept charity from her family. She told Pauline in a letter dated August 9, 1858:

> I don't like Texas at all. The land is miserable; nothing grows on it. . . . Here one can almost never count on a good harvest. If the drought does not kill the crop, then the locusts come and eat everything. . . . Even if I am not satisfied, I am forced to settle here, and once I am settled, I will not leave.

To support her son and herself, Helen immediately went into San Antonio to obtain sewing customers. By early October she reported to Pauline:

> Presently I am stitching some shirts for a Yankee lady and she will not really offer much pay. You . . . would have smiled when I was sewing a dress for a Black lady and we went to the store to buy the lining. They looked at me in the store as if I had lost my senses. As I came out of the store, I couldn't keep from laughing. You see, my sweet Poli, that is why America is good. A person is never afraid or ashamed to do something here.

But Helen said that the meager few dollars which she earned were soon spent. She asked her sister to send "two little buckets of dried plums," which her brother Farkas could sell for a great profit in the city. And she promised Pauline half of the profits if "you can send me a few barrels [of plums]." Unfortunately, no plums arrived at Sírmező, and Helen continued to live on her family's charity.

Her daily routine included helping Klára at Sírmező. In late August she reported to Pauline that she was busy making jams and that "the peaches were rather cheap in the city and we bought some for preserves." In a postscript to her letter, she added, "If you wish, you could send some plum brandy to try out. I believe that the profit would be great on that, too." Even though she did not feel homesick for Hungary, the tedium of hard work and the friction with Klára soon became evident. Helen's son and Klára's "spoiled little girl" fought when they played together, and Ladislaus often received a scolding from the Kellerschöns. Helen began to write that she wanted to be free as quickly as possible. She said, "You can't even imagine how bitter my lot is here. There is an ice wall between Klári and myself which, I believe, will never melt."

Helen complained to Pauline that Klára was miserly, begrudging even a small piece of bread for her little black dog. In addition, Klára let her appearance go and dressed in a shirt and apron or a little vest and never wore stockings, which "rot in the cupboard. She puts on an even fancier outfit when she milks the cow." For her part, Klára poured out her disapproval of her youngest sister in her diary. Among things which irritated her about Helen was that she was "endlessly nosy," wore a corset so "that her thin waist should not become disfigured" during pregnancy, was accustomed to "live by the hands of maids," and had made a "stupid marriage." But, perhaps most of all, Klára resented Helen's attempt to remain a gentlewoman at Sírmező, and wrote, "Now she is doing some sewing, but I will see how she will go out to hoe in a silk skirt and milk the cow in patent leather shoes once she is on her own."

Perhaps their irritability with one another resulted from the fact that they were both pregnant and expected the births of their babies that winter. Helen was forced to cast aside her fashionable girdle and appear in San Antonio wearing a sleeping jacket. Although she wanted a girl this time, both she and Klára bore sons a month apart. Klára named hers Gyula, and Helen chose Louis (Lajos). In a letter to Klementine, Újházi expressed his fervent wish, "May love reign between them in the future." But peace between the sisters did not return immediately. Helen continued to criticize Klára for spoiling her daughter and for her constantly crying newborn son. Klára returned the criticism, recording in her diary that Helen, in spite of a narrow pelvis, had had an easy delivery, while her own had been difficult, but she did admit that her sister had a difficult time when Béla died. However, she could not understand Helen's using a little whip to discipline Ladislaus. She wrote, "When was she whipped?"

Their disagreements continued, each complaining to their father. By February 1859 Helen suggested to Újházi that he send a tenant away and rent some land and a house to her, even though she would have to borrow the money from him. She wished to buy cows, a horse, and other small farm animals in order to set up housekeeping on her own. Almost at the same time, she encountered a problem with her Hungarian maid, Julia. An unnamed suitor asked permission to court the domestic, but Helen sent Gabriel Katona, a Hungarian exile who periodically worked at Sírmező, to intervene: "Tell him that he shouldn't even try; Julcsa [Julia] is not for sale and won't be." Although the suitor continued for a time, Helen prevailed and wrote that "If I would only be in my own house, I would really show the door to such kinds of people. I can imagine that they are drooling after such an attractive Hungarian girl. I don't know what I would do if Julcsa would leave me. Then my life as a farmer would come to an end."[7]

During her first year in Texas, Helen continually asked Pauline to send her the latest fashion magazines from Hungary. However, in spite of her desire to live as a gentlewoman, Helen experienced the drudgery of a farmer. At the end of February she wrote to Pauline that she was working every day in the fields. Újházi's farm tenant had moved away, and she was helping to kill weeds and grass in preparation for sowing corn. Although she hired Katona to plow, she and Julia cultivated a small garden, where they planted "the most necessary things." She added, "I have never started working as seriously as now. . . . If the weather permits, I will take my little boy with me [to the fields] to work with such a good spirit as the girls [in Hungary] go to dances." She continued:

> The house is still in the greatest disarray, but I will put it in order after I finish the field and when I have some money. I can hardly wait for the hour when I can move in. I am often angry that I cannot change myself into a man for a few hours. Then I would have to rely even less on others. As long as I am young, I can take it. I will work like an ox so that I can live a quieter life when I am older. . . . One cannot hope for a better place to make money than this; not as much from the field, but rather from the cattle which can live on the grazing land. That is, if we have rain.

At Eastertime Helen wrote to Pauline that she was forced from lack of money to delay moving Béla's remains to Sírmező and would wait until the next winter. She also began pleading with her sister to send payments and interest on her share of the estate at Haszina. Although she tried unsuccessfully to borrow the rent on a field from her father, Helen was broke and failed to harvest a "single ounce of crop" because of the drought. As a result, she was forced to continue living with the family, but wrote, "It will be an unforgettable day for me when I will eat from my own [labors] the first time. The bread of pity, even if it is prepared well, tastes the worst."

At the end of June Helen again wrote to Pauline about conditions in Texas. Her children were growing rapidly, and she continued to work in the fields. The crops failed again in 1859, and she lamented.

> I harvested my corn weeks ago for fodder. Much of it was already dry by that time. I can see that one can be satisfied here if he gains the planted seed back. Then one doesn't have to buy the seeds with money for sowing next year. Oh, how good it would have been to have had a little harvest. I would have had something to give to my hen and to my little horse. Father gave me a horse as a gift, a horse I like very much. They raised him and broke him to the saddle only now. I will have to ride every day so that he should not become wild again. Even so, when I mounted him the other day, he threw me off immediately. My dress was finished. This was my most favorite (silk) dress; I bought it in Pest.

In the same letter Helen again expressed her heartfelt desire to leave Sírmező and Klára's watching eyes, saying, "There is hardly a day that I don't ask God to liberate me from here." Having received the $1,000 in capital which had been loaned out the previous year, she repaid her debts to her father and hoped to have enough left to equip a new home and farm of her own. Again she asked Pauline to send payments and interest on her share of Haszina; she had received nothing since arriving in Texas. She also missed the chance to buy a nearby farm because of her poverty.[8]

In September 1859 Helen finally realized her dream. László Újházi wrote to Pauline that Farkas, as trustee for Helen's sons, bought a 221-acre farm of flat, fertile land on the stage route on Cibolo Creek halfway between San Antonio and Seguin. Forty acres were already fenced for a field, and the remainder was used for grazing cattle. A five-room brick house, a separate brick kitchen, a corn crib, and a stone-lined well made up the improvements on the property. Helen paid $2,700 for the property ($1,000 of her capital plus $1,700 borrowed from her father at 12 percent interest). There, separated by 18 miles of dusty roads from Sírmező, Helen and her small family attempted to survive by farming and stock raising, with only the help of hired hands and two rented oxen.[9]

By mid-October 21-year-old Helen had moved to the Cibolo farm, much to the relief of Klára, who still considered her a "light-headed girl." Rain had briefly returned to Texas: streams were flowing, and wells had water in the San Antonio region. Helen reported that "all of nature sprang to life. The trees are blooming again, occasionally even with flowers on them." Helen wrote to Pauline that "I am completely alone with two children." In December, however, she reported that she had fired her maid, Julia, who "wanted to become the lady of the house." Thereafter slaves were hired from neighbors, or free laborers cultivated her land and watched her cattle.

• ——————— •

An Indian Scare on the Cibolo

Helen Madarász and her two sons had barely settled themselves on the Cibolo Creek farm in the fall of 1859, when the neighborhood experienced an Indian scare. In her letter to Pauline on November 20, she said:

. . . the other day the Yankees really frightened me. I went to the second neighbor to rent a Black girl to be with the children, but I did not find anyone at home except an old, sick Black man. He said, crying and screaming, "My, oh my, my lady! There is nobody here anymore. Don't go any farther. The Indians are coming and will kill everybody and steal everything. Escape, my lady, and quickly!"

That's all I needed. Even so, I went to the next neighbor just down the river [creek] from me, and in the third neighbor's I found the women. They were as white as the wall and immediately asked me, "Didn't you hear anything about the Indians? They're saying that they are on our necks, and you're just walking up and down on the prairies. You could really have problems." "I didn't hear anything about any Indians," I answered, but they didn't believe me. "They're only about six miles from here," the women screamed. "They've killed innumerable people."

I was a bit afraid, but I still didn't believe them. It was impossible that I, living farther on up [the creek] than they, did not hear anything at all about the Red ones. As soon as I got home, I sent one of the masons over to the upriver neighbor, to the Englishman, to find out what was going on. They hadn't heard about them [the Indians] in this area, said the message of my neighbor. They say that not six, but sixty miles from here, they [the Indians] really were going around and killing and robbing. But, if we go there, it probably would turn out that even there, they were just talking about them sixty miles farther away. So are we with the Indians. And, that is the way I live by myself on the prairie.

• ———————————— •

Helen put her new home on the Cibolo in order and looked about for someone to help with the housekeeping and in the fields. "A very good Englishman," her neighbor, rented her a slave, although she maintained that "I would not keep a slave for any money, but I am forced to take one for wages. I like it even better than if I had gotten a useless White one. If you treat a Black well, there is more honesty in her than in a White." Helen also observed, "I imagined the solitude much more terrifying than it really proved to be. In the evenings before I slumber off, I ask God that He should not abandon me and that He should keep me from illness and misfortune." She also said that she had "such a beautiful house, that even in Hungary, it would not be looked down upon among the gentry houses." Thus she remained true to her self-image as a Hungarian noblewoman, although she worked with her own hands.

Helen continued to plead for her share of Haszina, writing in November 1859 that she needed something to "keep my miserable life going. If my pantry empties, I have nothing anymore to fill it with." She owed interest and principal on her notes to her father and needed to hire field hands for the spring planting. She added that working alone on her feet each day left her exhausted, so that she slept "through the long winter nights when my sewing material is accumulating." Part of her supplies of cereal, rice, peas, and dried apples had been infested with ants—the "entire area and neighborhood is an antheap." Five-year-old Ladislaus began helping by babysitting his brother, Louis, who was being weaned, so that his mother would have more time in the fields. Helen bought Ladislaus a saddle, so that he could ride as soon as she could afford to buy him a pony. And she again found, to her disgust, that her new house was infested, this time with scorpions![10]

The very real threat of hunger and other difficulties faced Helen on her farm, as it did the rest of her relatives at Sírmező, during the fall and winter of 1859-1860. In spite of her happiness at living independently, she again appealed to Pauline for money to meet her obligations and keep food in the pantry. Although rains came in the springtime, making a garden possible, Újházi wrote to Pauline that April:

> Your blood [relative], Ilka, is struggling, lonely on her isolated land. Sometimes we visit her, and then she revives a little bit. Her material existence, however, is in such a state that if she does not get a part of her portion [of the Haszina estate] very quickly, she will have to fail completely in her undertaking and will lose her daily bread.

He then added that if they did not receive more rain within a few weeks, the "already dying Nature" would not revive, and "we can say that in this strange and wide land we are living the years of the seven starving cows."

At Christmastime 1860 Helen and her children visited Sírmező, and she learned that her husband, Vilmos, had arrived in San Antonio in November in order to reconcile with her. Apparently this did not happen. At first Újházi refused to tell him where Helen lived but mellowed when his son-in-law showed him a note for a thousand pounds on the Duke of Newcastle. The older man then agreed to take Madarász to the Cibolo farm. Fortunately, however, Újházi's banker quickly determined by a telegram to the British consul in New Orleans that the note was forged and that Madarász was wanted by the British police. Vilmos escaped from San Antonio before the sheriff caught him and left Texas by way of Galveston.[11]

How long Madarász remained in San Antonio is uncertain. As early as April 1860 Újházi had heard that he was coming to Texas. In the census of that year, Madarász was listed as the 28-year-old head of a household which also included Helen and the two boys. In July Madarász's lawyer also filed a petition for habeas corpus in the 4th District Court in Bexar County against Újházi and Helen, asking only for custody of one son, Ladislaus. However, Vilmos failed to prove that Helen was an unfit mother. The petition was dismissed, and he was assigned the costs of the proceedings.[12] Thereafter Helen and her sons apparently had little communication with Vilmos.

In January 1864 she filed a petition for divorce and asked for custody of her children during the spring term of the 4th District Court, alleging that she and her children had been abandoned for more than three years by Madarász. The divorce, by default, was granted by a jury in September, and Helen obtained custody of her sons. Madarász, whose whereabouts were apparently unknown at that point, failed to appear in court, and so ended Helen's unhappy marriage.[13]

During 1860 Helen continued to plead with Pauline for her share of Haszina, for large notes were due the next March to her father. In addition, she wanted to send Ladislaus, now learning English, to school in San Antonio rather than to the local country school, which was filled with "many terrible German kids." She owed money also to several of her neighbors; to the owner of her maid ($10.00), who was willing to wait one or two months; to a day worker who sowed corn; and for two milk cows, which she bought on credit from her English neighbor. Helen wrote to her sister, "I can tell you that very few women can do what I am doing." But she could not hope to keep her creditors at bay for long, and so she asked Pauline for $1,500 and the interest for one year. To lose the Cibolo farm would have been, to Helen, "to fall from paradise into hell," for, in spite of her many problems, she was satisfied there. To give up the farm and move to San Antonio, where she would have to take in washing and sewing, would have been a terrible blow to her.

By April Helen reported to Pauline that Ladislaus had become "a real farm child," who worked in the garden and had quickly learned to speak English. There was "no wilder child" than Louis, who still could not talk. Helen was in good health except for her legs, which felt like "those of a fifty-year-old woman" from squatting and standing in the field. That spring she planted only ten acres, leaving the remainder of her farm in grass, for she had "neither the strength nor the money to cultivate the rest." Fortunately, she received a payment from Hungary and paid for her two cows and a $400 note which was past due.

Klára, who saw her sister at Sírmező during Christmas 1860 for the first time in many months, was shocked by Helen's appearance: "Such a short time, and such a tremendous change! Her face is rough and brown from the unending work in the fields. She showed [me] her legs; they are thick and the blood vessels swell bluish on them. My God, she isn't even twenty-five years of age! What will the tremendous pain and unaccustomed work make of a person?" The sisters fell into each other's arms and cried during their reunion. A reconciliation began between them as Klára realized that the "still-childish girl" had matured at last.[14]

Following Újházi's departure for his consular post in Italy in 1861, Helen and her relatives in Texas faced poverty and many dangers. Helen wrote to Pauline in 1863 asking for the remaining payment on her portion of Haszina to be made in silver dollars (worth six paper dollars each during the latter part of the war because of inflation). She described the condition of her farm on the Cibolo:

> This is the fourth year that I have tried to grow some corn. Up to now, all my labor has been for nothing. Even the little crop which I harvested during the bad years was lost because the cattle trampled it. This year the cattle ate everything while it was growing. And why? For no other reason than until now I haven't had enough money to build a good fence around the field.

She also said that the roving cattle and hogs ate the crops, which consequently had to be guarded day and night. She and a twelve-year-old Black boy had done all the cultivating that year. She continued:

> If Farkas had not helped during the winter with corn meal, and, occasionally, some money, I would not have started this. My only income was from needlepoint, and from that I could not have bought the $8.00 [seed] corn. During the whole winter, almost without exception, we lived on coffee made of barley, salted beef, and corn bread made with water. The wheat flour is $40.00 to $50.00 per one hundred pounds. The coffee costs $10.00 a pound, and everything is expensive in this proportion. During the spring, I bought thirty bushels of wheat for $4.00 per bushel.

Helen ended her letter by pleading for money, to be sent by Pauline through Újházi in Italy, for he knew a safe route by which to send it to Texas. Helen vowed that "we will leave here [the Cibolo] as soon as we can sell the land!" [15]

Upon his return to San Antonio in November 1864, Újházi wrote to Klementine about conditions on the Cibolo farm. Helen owned 50 head of cattle, but half had starved. She had a Black woman and her teenaged son to help, paying them $8.00 in gold a month. But it was only through the assistance of her relatives that she survived at all. Klára recorded in her diary on September 4, 1864, that "all the anger has dissolved in my soul against her, and she is gentler too. Where is now the young lady? She became exactly the kind of farmer I am myself. The grinder grinds without asking who was put inside." [16]

How long Helen continued living on the Cibolo during the late 1860's is unknown. In late August 1867 she sought to sell or rent the 240-acre farm. Her newspaper ad in San Antonio touted 40 acres "under perfect culture," a comfortable five-room brick house, a detached kitchen, and "continual running water." The ad ran in the paper until October 12 of that year, but it is not known whether she had already returned to Sírmező with her sons. Pauline was slow in paying her for Haszina but sent $100 early in 1867. Helen wrote that "I owe several hundred dollars to my bloods [relatives] here, and after all, they are going to get tired of listening to my empty, promising words." In July of that year she wrote that she had borrowed the school tuition for her sons, while waiting for payments from Hungary. As taught by her father, she accounted for every penny and its interest from her relatives. There is some indication that she moved into San Antonio after the Civil War, for in 1867 she reportedly bought a house for $4,000 with her two brothers, paying 12 percent interest on the lien. [17]

In 1869 Helen began transacting business in her own name for the first time. Previously this service had been performed by her brother Farkas acting as guardian of her children. On January 2 she paid $9,000 for a town lot on San Antonio's busy Commerce Street to her brother László Jr. and Alexander Varga, a fellow Hungarian, who had jointly purchased it in 1866. She then sold the western half of the lot for $3,000 in gold on September 19, 1872, taking a 12 percent lien from the purchaser. On February 17, 1870, she sold the Cibolo farm for $1,700. The next month László Újházi died, and his children were forced to decide about their futures. [18]

After the death of the old patriarch, Sírmező became even more deserted. Klára and Joseph Kellerschön had left in 1869. In midsummer of 1870 László Jr. returned to Hungary, where he became a farmer at Putnok in Gömör County. There he was married twice, first to Katinka Tornallyi (or Torpallyai) and later to Viktoria Stroda. He became the father of three children: László, Árpád, and Elektra. A grandson, also named László, was born in 1907. László Jr. died in 1906 and was buried in the family's crypt at Budamér.[19]

In his last letter from Sírmező, on June 30, 1870, László Jr. informed Pauline of his calculations on her outstanding debt to Helen, who had decided to remain in Texas. He reported that she had rented out the farm and planned to survive on her rents as well as on her share of Sírmező, "not richly, [but] quietly and sufficiently." Helen had decided to remain in Texas because her children had grown up there, knew the language and customs, and faced a bright future "if they gather sufficient knowledge." László Jr. concluded his comments by saying that she "lives exclusively for her sons, and in their interest she must stay in America."[20]

Farkas Újházy wanted to sell Sírmező immediately after his father's death and return to Hungary. His brother László wrote that Farkas had lost all desire to work at Sírmező, even though 1870 crops had been good. The load of work was too much for one man alone. Further, László wrote, "If our poor, dear, good father could have seen it [the good crops], he would have been assured that bad luck and not the unlucky selection [of the Sírmező site] was the reason for the many years of bad harvests." The Agricultural Census of that year indicated that Sírmező was one of the more prosperous farms in Bexar County. Of its land, valued at $3,000, 100 acres were improved, 400 unimproved, and 100 covered with woodlands. Farm implements and machinery were valued at $125, and $150 had been paid out in wages during the past year. Livestock included three horses, five mules, 16 milk cows, twelve oxen, and 400 wild cattle, the total valued at $9,500. In addition, there were 1,400 bushels of corn and 200 bushels of grass seed on hand. The estimated value of all farm products at Sírmező, including betterments and additions to the stock, amounted to $2,500. But, even if the farm could not be sold immediately, the brothers were determined to rent it: "once we settle everything, we are going."[21]

Helen wrote to Pauline on December 15, 1870, concerning the final payment of her share of Haszina. The twelve-year struggle to collect her half of the Hungarian estate was over, having caused a decided cooling of her feelings for her "little mother." In lamenting Klára's departure from Texas in this letter, she remarked that "Although America does not give me a Fatherland, it gives me security." Her son Ladislaus, who had attended St. Mary's College in San Antonio, was studying engineering in a Northern university. She mused that his behavior and progress satisfied her and gave her happiness.[22]

László Jr.'s final act concerning the family property at Sírmező was to give Farkas power of attorney on July 10, 1872. This was done from Putnok, and László never returned to America. Thereafter Farkas's decisions determined the fate of the family estate in which the brothers owned equal, undivided interests. Farkas did not record the power of attorney at the San Antonio courthouse until September 15, 1878.[23]

Although Farkas himself had wanted to return to Hungary in 1870, he spent another eight years in Texas. The economic depression brought on by the panic of 1873 adversely affected the profitability of the farm as he attempted to dispose of it. In 1875, for an unknown reason, he bought the Pedro Camarillo tract to the north of Sírmező, bringing the total acreage of the estate to almost 1,147 acres (although he sold 36 acres in April 1875).[24]

Farkas's activities during his last years in Texas were varied. He was appointed Bexar County commissioner in January 1870 by Brevet Major General J. J. Reynolds, commander of the Fifth Military District in Austin, but it is not known how long he served in that capacity. In December 1873 he was elected justice of the peace on the Democratic ticket and, interestingly, was named a delegate to the Bexar County Republican Nominating Convention in September 1874.[25]

Insight into his continued operation of Sírmező indicated that Farkas purchased a threshing machine during the spring of 1870 to use on his farm and to rent to neighboring landowners. Likewise, a steam-powered cotton gin was installed to serve Sírmező and nearby farms. On the night of October 13, 1875, it caught fire while he was ginning for a neighbor who wanted to exhibit his cotton at a fair in San Antonio. A lamp exploded, causing $1,000 in damage and the loss of nine bales of cotton. Fortunately, the engine survived undamaged, and Farkas determined to rebuild the gin. However, "nothing on earth will ever [again] induce [him] to do ginning at night."[26]

To meet obligations and expenses, Farkas began early in 1873 to mortgage the original 550 acres of Sírmező. He gave promissory notes and liens at 12 percent interest. Among the principal holders of his notes were Dr. Ferdinand Herff, San Antonio's pioneer physician, and Judge Albert Dittmar, a local attorney, who lent him $700 in September 1873. This lien was sold to A. Vogt, who extended an additional $300 in July 1874. Farkas continued borrowing on the farm, including $2,000 from the Hungarian Francis Böröndi in 1875. In all, mortgages on Sírmező, including the Camarillo tract, totaled over $5,700 by 1877.[27]

Farkas was unable to meet his notes and so lost the family estate. As early as November 1877, a trustee's sale handbill had been posted in San Antonio, and notice was published on December 22 in the local *Daily Express* of its forced sale. Among his chief creditors were Dr. Herff and Judge Dittmar. Others included A. Vogt, Friedrich Ackermann, Francis Böröndi, and Elmendorf & Company (from whom he had bought lumber for fencing). László Jr.'s undivided half interest was to be sold first, followed by that of Farkas. Sírmező was sold from the steps of the Bexar County Courthouse on December 22, 1877, and Herff and Dittmar became its owners.[28]

The new owners of Sírmező (thereafter known as the "Old Újházi Place") leased the fields to sharecroppers. They also used it for hunting and outings. As late as 1917 it was reportedly a wilderness covered with mesquite trees and cactus, and was then called the Herff and Dittmar pastures. In 1925 the heirs of Herff and Dittmar sold part to the City of San Antonio to use as a park and flood control basin for construction of the Olmos Flood Control Dam to protect the city. The smaller City of Olmos Park, established in 1927, was built entirely on the oldest section of Sírmező as San Antonio's urban area and population expanded. No trace of Újházi's buildings survived.[29]

Before the sale of Sírmező, on November 5, 1877, Farkas deeded all movable property and livestock to Helen Madarász. This property included Újházi's four famous white mules, a bay mare, a light buggy, the cotton gin with revolving cotton press, a mower, two combine reapers, a gang plow, a corn planter, and a cultivator. Also included were a pulverizer harrow, three harrows, eight plows, seed covers, a cabinetmaker's bench with tools, hay forks, field and grubbing hoes, sets of ambulance and light wagon harnesses, buggy harnesses, and three mule harnesses. Valued at $1,000, these goods and livestock were to be applied as partial payment of a note held by Helen.[30]

Then, during his last year in Texas, 50-year-old Farkas married Phillipina Wolf on March 10, 1877. His witnesses were his nephew

Ladislaus W. Madarász and his old Hungarian friend Joseph Varga. Where the new couple lived during those last months in San Antonio is not known—the house at Sírmező had reportedly burned after László Újházi's death. Their first child, a daughter they named Palma, was born in 1877 in San Antonio (a son, Dénes, was born in Hungary in 1882). Farkas and his family remained in San Antonio until the fall of 1878, when he exhumed the remains of his parents at Sírmező and left for Hungary (his parents were reburied in the family crypt at Budamér). Farkas Újházy died at the old family estate in Upper Hungary in 1898.[31]

Helen Madarász remained in Texas for the remainder of her life. With her sons, Ladislaus W. and Louis, she had survived the economic hardships and war conditions of the 1860's with the greatest difficulty. Putting aside her fine clothing, she did the normal hard physical work required in farming and also sewed for others. With the receipt of the final installment of $1,503 of her share of Haszina in 1870, she erased all outstanding debts to her siblings.[32]

Helen never remarried, although Klára had advised her to consider her English neighbor on the Cibolo, who had helped her. He was described as diligent and honest, and a man who could give Helen security and peace and quiet. Klára also pointed out that Helen's first marriage, "according to American customs [a civil marriage]," had ended in divorce and that the Catholic rite at Haszina in 1858 did not count in Texas. However, Helen resolutely maintained that she did not want a man in her house whose orders she must obey. Rather, she chose to devote her life to her sons.[33]

Described as a "capable businesswoman with high standing in the community," Helen supported her family primarily by real estate deals and by lending her capital at high interest rates. For example, she gave a deed of trust on a house on Commerce Street, probably that which she acquired earlier from László Jr. and Alexander Varga, for a loan of 72 Mexican gold doubloons on February 1, 1870. She repaid that debt by April 1873. In 1870 she bought 16½ acres of woodland near Sírmező for $700. She also bought a lot on the Upper Labor Ditch on 3rd Street for $800 in March 1872. Although she borrowed $1,500 on that lot, she repaid the debt by April 1873.[34]

At the time of her arrival in Texas, she had a total capital of $1,000, which she loaned at 12 percent annually, planning to live on the interest. After being vested in 1869 by the local District Court to conduct business in her own name, she continued lending money derived from her share of Haszina and from real estate sales at substantial interest rates. During 1874 and 1875 she loaned a total of $9,625 in seven transactions, taking liens on various pieces of property, including town lots and rural acreage.[35]

In the Census of 1870 Helen was listed as "keeping house" for her sons, who were then attending school. She probably moved to her house on 3rd Street between 6th and 7th Avenues as early as 1872. When the street names were changed in the early 1880's, her address became Dallas Street at the corner of Atlantic Avenue. By 1877-1878 Louis reportedly was clerking in the real estate firm of John Eckford and Company, and the next year Ladislaus was a secretary at the Occidental Land Company.[36]

Louis Madarász

Little is known of the early life of Helen's youngest son, Louis. He attended St. Mary's College, where he excelled in penmanship and

Louis Madarász demonstrating correct writing position for
The Madarasz Book *(1911)*

calligraphy. He was still listed as a student in his mother's household in the Census of 1880. Three years later he was no longer listed in the city directory. Louis Madarász moved to Rochester, New York, "leaving on the first train that went out of San Antonio," and enrolled in the Rochester Business University. There he came to be known as the "wonder boy penman." After further schooling in Brockport he worked in Rochester and elsewhere throughout New York until settling in Manchester. Thereafter, famous for his "Madarász Style" of calligraphy, which was in great demand, he lived for short times in Jersey City, New Jersey; Sterling, Illinois; and Poughkeepsie, New York, where he worked at the Eastman Business College.[37]

Then, following a tour of the Southwest and a visit to his family in Texas, Louis Madarász settled in New York City, where he briefly attempted an acting role in a Shakespearean play. He married Clara

Kalish on March 26, 1889, but they had no children. Madarász later taught calligraphy and penmanship in Iowa, Nebraska, Ohio, Nevada, and Arkansas, but always returned to New York City. In 1907 he visited his relatives in Hungary. Described as a broadminded and well-educated man who was also "peculiar in his tastes and habits, loyal to the few friends he cultivated," Louis died of pneumonia, complicated by diabetes, on December 23, 1910, in New York. Grandson of two old Hungarian revolutionary exiles, László Újházi and László Madarász, he had earned a national reputation for his skills in penmanship.[38]

Known in San Antonio as a "prominent young society man," Ladislaus W. Madarász remained with his mother and became a leading social and business figure during the 1880's and early 1890's. Most of what is known of his life comes from local newspapers, which seemed to report his every move. For example, on July 16, 1877, it was reported that he had been badly bitten by a swarm of bees while working on a hive, but that he survived! As he matured, he participated actively in a number of local groups, including the recently organized Free Literary Society, which formed in September 1877 to discuss religious, political, philosophical, and scientific topics. In November 1879 he was also listed as a member, along with the socially elite boys of the city, of the first football team organized in San Antonio.[39]

· ———————— ·

San Antonio's First Football Game, 1879

"The football game was indeed a novelty to our people [in San Antonio]. Never before had they seen anything of the kind, and it is doubtful whether there was ever such a game played in this State before. Though incurring an immense amount of work upon the contestants, the game is of all games most amusing to spectators. Few had believed that sides could be organized which would prove anything like equally matched, but no difficulty was experienced in selecting good men. . . . The contest was warm and spirited, fully fifteen hundred spectators being present. After two efforts, however, neither side being able to make the 'go,' the game was given up. The continuous applause and laughter and cheers of the lookers-on was an evidence of the general interest taken in the game."[40]

· ———————— ·

Madarász's interest in his grandfather's political party, the Republicans, was soon evident. He made the final speech at a large Republican celebration held at Krisch's Hall, sponsored by the Garfield and Arthur Club, to hail election victories in Indiana and Ohio in October 1880. He also developed an early interest in horticulture, which resulted in the establishment of Ilka Nursery (after his mother's nickname) about 1879-1880. A local paper noted on November 12, 1880:

> It has been customary to send off for plants and shrubs and the experience has been that 50 percent or more of the plants were dead by the time San Antonians received them. Mr. Madarácz [sic] has altered the situation and has built green houses and experimented with shrubs for about a year. The Madarácz Place is located opposite Maverick's Grove on the west side of the river near the rock quarries. Mr. Madarácz has also purchased an additional piece of land from Col. [George W.] Brackenridge. Mr. Madarácz has designated Friday and Saturday as open-day for all flower lovers.

The next year he was reported to have displayed leafy plants in a pyramid arrangement at the local agricultural fair.[41]

Ilka Nursery was established on three and a half acres of land between the old Spanish Upper Labor Ditch and the San Antonio River. The land was purchased by Helen Madarász from George Brackenridge for $765 in June 1883. In October she also bought a small adjoining property for $2,400 from Brackenridge, who retained the water rights of the river for his San Antonio Water Works, which supplied the city. Helen's land, formerly the site of a Civil War tannery, also adjoined the Brackenridge estate, Fernridge (also called Head of the River).[42]

Ladislaus Madarász's article, "Fruits and Flowers," was published in Stephen Gould's *Alamo City Guide* in 1882. In addition to his botanical interests, he maintained an active role in local political circles. Madarász served as a delegate to the Bexar County Republican Convention in August 1882, and the next year he announced his candidacy for alderman of the Third Ward of the city. In 1884 the always-active young man started a machine hay-bailing factory in partnership with Ferdinand Herff and was secretary of the Blaine-Logan political club.[43]

Helen Madarász built her home at Ilka Nursery about 1884-1885 and lived there for the rest of her life. Her address was "on the Rock Quarry Road near the head of the river." About the same time, her son began working as a bookkeeper at George W. Brackenridge's San

ILKA NURSERIES

W. L. MADARASZ, Proprietor.   Nurseries, Near Rock Quarries

THE FINEST ASSORTMENT OF

Green-House AND Bedding Plants

IN THE STATE.

Also Grows a limited quantity of the Best Grades of Evergreens and Ornamental and Flowering Shrubs.

Patronize Home Firms and secure Home-grown and Reliable Stock, fully acclimated, Fresh and Carefully Packed.

ROSES A SPECIALTY.

Wholesale and Retail Orders Solicited and Supplied at Short Notice.

CITY STAND AND DEPOT, 309 EAST HOUSTON STREET.

1887-1888 San Antonio City Directory ad

Antonio National Bank, leaving the operation of the nursery to his mother. In December 1885 they opened a retail outlet for the flowers and plants on San Antonio's busy, fashionable Houston Street.[44]

Ladislaus mixed in San Antonio's elite circles. Perhaps as a beneficiary of Brackenridge's patronage and generosity, he continued his civic activities during 1886, serving on the arrangements committee for the entertainment of the San Antonio convention of the Press Association of Texas in May. In July he was listed as a founder of the prestigious San Antonio Cavalry, an elaborately uniformed drill team used for parades, and served as its first president. On August 21, 1886, the local paper reported on his heroic three-mile horseback ride from the center of the city to Ilka Nursery and Fernridge during a great storm. Although his horse was blown over by the force of the wind, he was unhurt, and he found the greenhouses and his mother's home undamaged. About a third of the large river-bottom trees had been blown down or damaged, perhaps by a tornado resulting from the inland progress of a great hurricane which had struck the Texas coast.[45]

The local papers continued to chronicle his activities. In February 1887 he reportedly suffered a financial loss when a barn full of hay which he and a Mr. Herff owned in the northwestern part of town burned. The loss amounted to several thousand dollars, according to the paper. During the June term of the District Court of Bexar County, Madarász reportedly served as foreman of the jury which convicted the murderer Jim McCoy, who had killed the sheriff of La Salle County. McCoy, described as one of the most "notorious desperados" in the Southwest in a decade, had been a member of the Altita Pen Gang and was sentenced to death. He reportedly mounted the gallows calmly smoking a cigarette before his execution.[46]

During the next few years Madarász continued his active participation in political and social events. He served as county treasurer of the Republican Party for the election in the 10th Congressional District in September 1888. For recreation he accompanied Colonel Brackenridge and his party (Miss Eleanor Brackenridge, Miss Handy, Drs. Ferdinand Herff Sr. and Jr., Mr. and Mrs. Ben Stribbling, John James, and a Mrs. Bennett) on an excursion to Mexico City in March 1889. He also represented "Hungary" in the San Antonio Casino Club's Mardi Gras celebration. Furthermore, the ever-attentive local paper reported that he was building a "fine residence" at the head of the river at Ilka Nursery.[47]

Helen Madarász's social life seems to have revolved around that of her son and a small group of ladies surrounding Miss Eleanor Brackenridge, a nationally known clubwoman, philanthropist, feminist, and suffragette, and sister of the banker. Helen probably was a member of Miss Brackenridge's Mutual Admiration and Reprovement Society. Colonel Brackenridge, also Helen's close friend and a lifelong bachelor, possibly provided wise financial advice for her investments, and their names were linked in local gossip.[48]

Although her relatives in Hungary had hoped that Helen would pay them a visit as early as 1885, she and Ladislaus made the trip in 1889. They went by train to New York and sailed for Liverpool on May 14. After visiting London and Paris they went on to see the Kellerschöns at Schönbornslust near Koblenz, Germany, before visiting relatives in Pest and Egar as well as in Gömör, Sáros, Zemplen, and Bihar counties in Hungary. Among those they visited were her sister Klementine Fáy's family and László Jr., but they did not see Farkas. Helen and Ladislaus returned to Texas in September by way of New York.[49]

As a socially prominent member of San Antonio's emerging elite, Helen participated in the first Battle of Flowers Parade in 1891. The procession, organized to welcome President Benjamin Harrison to the city, comprised over 100 flower-bedecked carriages and wagons, "all gaily decorated and many containing decorations of real artistic merit." The parade was delayed for three days by rain, but, when it was finally held, Helen and Mrs. Will Herff rode in a stylish phaeton trimmed with pure white lilies and variegated grasses and honeysuckle. As two lines of carriages circled around Alamo Plaza in front of the old mission, the participants pelted others with fresh flowers.[50]

Insights into Helen Madarász's life were given in letters from Klára, living in Germany, to her relatives in Hungary during the early 1890's. On September 17, 1890, she reported that Helen had complained in a letter of the summer heat and drought which kept her busy watering her nursery beds. The following March Klára reported that Helen had built a sixth greenhouse at Ilka Nursery. And in June 1891 the report from Texas indicated that Helen had experienced a good winter business but had trouble finding competent hired hands. Klára observed that her sister should have been contented with only five greenhouses, since all that work exhausted her.[51]

During 1891 Helen wrote to Klára about her health. She complained that she was now terribly busy taking care of her six greenhouses and her flowerbeds, and her strength was diminishing. She was tired, and her business had suffered because of a mild and overly long autumn which permitted roses to bloom all over San Antonio until late November. In addition, Helen could not sell her town lot profitably, and the building of the new house which Ladislaus planned at Ilka Nursery had been postponed, although the foundation had been laid the previous summer.[52]

Helen's life began to change about this time. In 1893 she reportedly experienced "internal bitterness and external difficulties." Her son left home for the first time and moved to the Lakeside Hotel in the city, leaving the operation of the nursery to his mother and her hired help. Especially time-consuming was Helen's need to write in English, a task which she found difficult and which Ladislaus had previously performed. However, she soon learned English spelling with the aid of a dictionary during winter evenings and, with the help of a Slovak boy, Andris, whom she brought back from Hungary in 1889, continued operation of her business.[53]

The apparent cause of the rift between Helen and her son was his marriage on April 19, 1893, to Louise (Lulu) Kingsberry in El Paso. The daughter of an army captain who probably had previously served at San Antonio's Fort Sam Houston, the bride was described as having "a very beautiful and very noble face" and being "very cultured and very noble in character" by Klára in her continuing reports on the Texas family to relatives in Hungary. Although Helen was soon reconciled with her daughter-in-law, they did not immediately come to know each other well. The new couple lived at the Lakeside Hotel until their new home on Camden Street was completed. In the next two years two children, Erma A. and Jessie A., were born to them.[54]

Chicago's World's Columbian Exposition in 1893 attracted public attention, and Helen traveled to the Windy City. There she met Klára's Texas-born son, Gyula, a Berlin-educated mining engineer, who had worked in the North since 1882, as well as Louis, who spent two weeks viewing the exhibits before hurrying back to New York. Klára informed the relatives, "It made me very happy that at this meeting the two close relatives [the cousins] had a chance to get to know each other better, and it appears from Gyula's words, they really got to like each other." After Helen's return to San Antonio, Ladislaus and his new wife also visited the fair in Chicago.[55]

A year later Klára's spinster daughter, Tini, returned to the city of her birth for a visit with her aunt and cousin. She sailed for America on April 20, 1894, on the North German Lloyd liner *Sale*. On board she met a Hungarian-Jewish couple known to her family. In writing about her daughter's shipboard meeting, Klára observed that the couple knew of László Újházi, "who fought with vigor for the Emancipation of the Jews" in Hungary during the 1840's. From New York Tini Kellerschön made the four-day train ride to San Antonio, where she had a happy reunion with her relatives.[56]

But happiness quickly disappeared from Helen Madarász's life. Disaster struck the next year. On May 1, 1895, the San Antonio *Daily Express* announced "Madarász Out of Town, Thought to Be Short in His Accounts." The San Antonio National Bank, where he was a bookkeeper, planned to begin a new policy of rotating duties among its employees on a Monday. Ladislaus Madarász left San Antonio suddenly on the Sunday night train for Galveston, after informing his mother and his wife that his accounts were short by approximately $3,000. On Monday morning Helen grimly marched into the bank and told officials that her son had run away. No previous suspicion had touched his character during a successful career of more than a decade as a book-keeper in Brackenridge's bank — his reputation had been excellent.[57]

Ladislaus fled to Hungary and then to South America, where he worked for a time for a British railroad in Argentina. He died in Buenos Aires in a British hospital of kidney disease and tuberculosis on July 11, 1904. The scandal of his crime badly shook Helen and her daughter-in-law, who moved to the Ilka Nursery at the time. Louise Madarász later moved to Denver, Colorado, with her children. It is not known whether Helen attempted, or made, restitution to her old friend's bank.[58]

After her son's flight Helen withdrew from society and lived as a recluse. At that time she was characterized as an industrious woman engaged in horticulture at her valuable nursery. Her home was described in the local paper:

> Her house was located in a beautiful Eden-like grove near the head of the San Antonio River; on it and its shrubs, flowers and foliage, as well as the grounds, she expended considerable of her means, and their beauty was famous.
>
> The old Madarász home is in one of the most beautiful natural parks in Texas. It is a grove of tall, thick-boughed trees, under which rise several of the large springs that form the San Antonio River. A footway over a stile directly in front of Limburger's garden on River Avenue [Broadway] is one entrance to the place, but the main gateway is reached from the Rock Quarry Road on the west side of the river after passing the Alamo Cement Works. In the midst of this grove, with beds of former lagoons and spring feeders to the river, and the head arm of the river itself flowing close by, stood the neat little old-style cottage of Mrs. Madarász. On the large tract of land were numerous beautiful flower gardens and hothouses containing the Ilka Nursery of which Mrs. Madarász was the proprietor.[59]

The final and most shocking tragedy of the Újházi and Madarász families in Texas was Helen's brutal murder on April 30, 1899. That night she was robbed and raped, her skull bashed in, and her body burned in a fire set to hide the evidence. Her home was totally consumed. Robbery was thought to have been the motive for the crime, since she reputedly had a large sum of money in her house from the sale of flowers for the recent Battle of Flowers parade. Her funeral was held at Madison Square Presbyterian Church, and she was buried in

Madarasz Brackenridge Park Bridge at the head of the
San Antonio River

the City Cemetery (one source said the Dignowity Family Cemetery), although no tombstone was erected. Two men were apprehended in June 1899 in San Diego, Texas, and confessed to the crime.[60]

Helen Madarász's arrival in Texas at the age of 20 in 1858 had been marked by the tragedy of her son Béla's sudden death as well as by her failed marriage. Her brutal murder marked the end of the more than four decades of her struggle to survive and succeed as a single parent and businesswoman during the late Victorian Age. During those years she matured from a pretentious, immature noblewoman to a strong, yet feminine businesswoman filled with purpose and grace. By hard work and perseverance she maintained her independence following her father's death and her siblings' exodus to their homeland. Perhaps Texas' first Hungarian-born businesswoman, she survived and succeeded by her own merits.

The Madarász name was remembered for a short time after Helen's death with the naming of the Madarasz Family Park in 1901 on the site of Ilka Nursery. There families could enjoy "picnics and jollifications" and could obtain sandwiches, ice cream, cream cheese, milk, beer, soda water, and cigars. An old stone bridge, called the Madarasz Brackenridge Park Bridge, spanned the river. Otto Koehler, owner of the local Pearl Brewery, then acquired 15 acres, including

109

Postcard of Madarasz Family Park

the old Madarász property, and his widow gave the land to the City of San Antonio in 1915. Known thereafter as Koehler Park, a recreation area where malt liquors could be sold, it adjoined Brackenridge Park, donated to the city by Colonel Brackenridge in 1899, where alcoholic beverages were forbidden. No trace of Ilka Nursery remained, and the San Antonio Zoo covered part of Helen's land. It is interesting to think that parts of old Sírmező as well as of Ilka Nursery became public parks which have since been enjoyed by generations of San Antonians and their visitors.[61]

CHAPTER FIVE

"Texas is the place to go, the sooner the better."

Hungarian 48ers in Bexar County, Texas

In a burst of enthusiasm John Xantus, a former lieutenant of the Hungarian revolutionary army, expressed his impression of Texas as a place to settle during a brief visit in 1853: writing to his mother, he said that "Texas is the place to go, the sooner the better." As one of the several thousand refugees of the Hungarian Revolution who had sought haven in America, Xantus hoped for a new life and swift advancement. Most, including Xantus, had realized that the "cause of Hungary's independence could not be resurrected in the near future, and they were determined to make it in the United States." [1]

The idea of a Hungarian exile colony in America dated from the fall of 1849 when an American emigration society formed under László Újházi's leadership at the besieged fortress of Komárom. After its surrender about 50 former soldiers followed Újházi to Hamburg, and many others made the United States their destination as well. During the winter of 1849-1850 the émigrés reaching New York continued their plans for a "united agricultural colony," raised funds, and sought free land from the American government. However, factionalism soon arose among them, and Újházi was replaced as head of the Komárom American society by Major Imre Hamvasy (Emir Hamvasy). Újházi and his family and followers then departed for Iowa and established New Buda in 1850. [2]

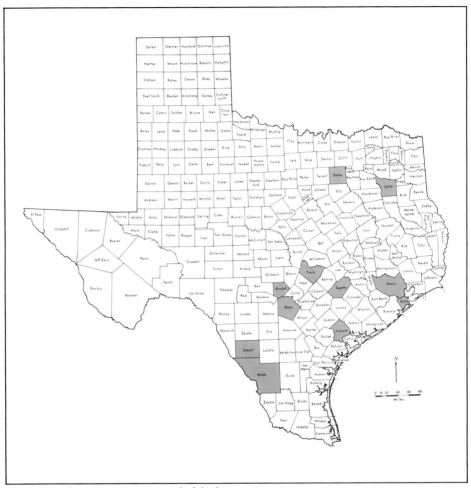

Counties where Hungarians settled before 1860

As Hungarian-American historian Bela Vassady Jr. has pointed out, the idea of a quiet, agricultural existence in the American West did not appeal to all of the exiles. Many had risen to prominence during the revolution and had illusions of exploiting their newly gained status in America. Fresh from the battlefields of Hungary, they anticipated a rapid resumption of the struggle and repatriation to their homeland. Soon, however, financial support for the Hungarians ceased to be offered in New York, and individuals were forced to seek their own livelihoods. Some followed Újházi to New Buda, perhaps sharing his dream of achieving personal satisfaction through "self-sufficient hard labor on free soil." But the great majority simply scattered across the North American continent in search of careers, while some returned to Europe.

The choice of Texas as the site for a Hungarian colony was mentioned soon after the arrival of the exiles in New York. In part because of factionalism among the émigrés, a plan for a Hungarian colony in Texas was proposed in 1850. Colonel John Prágay, a leader of the anti-Újházi group of "radical leftist elements" and a former adjutant to General György Klapka at Komárom, was the first to suggest such a colony, but why he chose that state as a site is not known. In the proposed colony Prágay and his friends wanted to distribute land according to military rank (Kossuth was to receive seven sections—640 acres to a section—former officers one section, and common soldiers one-half section). But the Texas scheme came to naught. Prágay and others joined the Narciso López filibustering expedition at New Orleans to free Cuba from Spanish rule and took part in the invasion of that island colony. When it failed, Prágay, López's chief of staff, committed suicide to avoid execution.[3]

László Újházi succeeded, in part, where Prágay failed. As with his first attempt at New Buda, Újházi hoped to form a Hungarian colony pending the revival of the Hungarian revolution against Austria. This goal continued to motivate his thinking, even after he learned in 1852 of Kossuth's refusal to permanently join the émigrés as head of a Hungarian colony (or even a Hungarian-populated state) in the American West. In 1853 Újházi moved to San Antonio, Texas, where he—vainly—clung to the hope of organizing a Hungarian settlement and finally accepted his exile as permanent.

Among the exiles was John Xantus (de Csiktapolcza, or de Vesey) (1825-1894), who typified the adventurous Hungarian 48ers who dispersed across America in the early 1850's. He was one of the few who reached remote Texas, where he thought of settling in 1853. Much has been written about him as a Hungarian naturalist in the American West, for he established his scientific reputation west of the Mississippi during the middle decades of the 19th century. It was said of him that he "came as a refugee, lived as an adventurer, and departed as a scientist."[4]

Xantus was born in Csokonya, Somogy County, to a family descended from Greek or Macedonian settlers. He worked in the Hungarian civil service and during the revolution served as an artillery sergeant in the Hungarian Honvéd Army at the Battle of Pákozd. Later he was made an infantry lieutenant in the 46th Battalion at Komárom, where he was captured in February 1849, imprisoned, and then impressed into the Austrian army. He later escaped and arrived in New York in May 1851.[5]

From that date until his final departure from the United States in 1864, Xantus rose to prominence as an explorer, naturalist, botanist, and collector of natural history for the Smithsonian Institution. Arriving in New York with seven dollars, seven languages, and a mastery of art and the piano, he started as a ditchdigger in New York and became a cartographer in St. Louis for the Pacific Railroad Company, which wanted to build a railway to California through Indian territory. He accompanied an exploring and surveying expedition westward through Kansas towards Fort Laramie, Wyoming, meeting various Indian tribes and collecting natural specimens.[6]

Xantus next visited yellow-fever-plagued New Orleans in the summer of 1853 and traveled along the Gulf Coast as far as San Antonio Bay in Texas. Moving inland along the Guadalupe River valley, he reportedly bought a 640-acre farm in October 1853. He planned to make it his permanent home in America and so invited his family to join him. Writing about his Texas trip to his mother from New Orleans on October 21, 1853, he said:

> There are plenty of fish and game there. One evening I shot seventeen turkeys from the giant sycamore palms along-side the river. I weighed one of them; it came to twenty-eight pounds, plucked and cleaned.
>
> Antelope, deer, grouse, and pheasants are in such abundance that it is difficult to protect the crops from them. The region is one of the healthiest in all Texas.
>
> When I was there in October, the oranges were ripening. In the mornings the aroma is unimaginably pleasant. There are no other trees but palms, live oak, orange, walnut, chestnut, and sky-scraping oleanders with yellow, red, and blue flowers; . . . if you want to see something beautiful, Texas is the place to go, the sooner the better."[7]

Before leaving Texas Xantus made arrangements for a cottage to be built, expecting to return the next May. He described the neighborhood of his proposed new home: a German pharmacist from Regensburg was the nearest neighbor (nine miles away), a Mexican colonel and his sons lived eleven miles to the west, and next door lived "an honest Swede." Other neighbors included a Frenchman from Marseilles, three American families, and a German from Braunschweig. The nearest town was 15 miles away and had three doctors, a pharmacy, two newspapers, and other stores. Xantus never returned to Texas, however. Perhaps, unable to settle immediately, he accepted opportunity as he encountered it elsewhere.[7]

Xantus later joined the U.S. Army as a private and was stationed at Fort Riley, Kansas. There he began visiting nearby Indians and collecting specimens of birds and animals as well as flora and fauna. In 1857 he went to Southern California to continue his collecting and was later assigned to conduct a geographic and ethnographic survey of Southern California. Some of his botanical and zoological samples were sent to the Hungarian National Museum, and he initiated a program in which natural history and scientific information was exchanged by America and Hungary.[8]

With his reputation as a naturalist established, he visited Hungary, but when no position was offered him at the National Museum, he returned to the United States in 1862. He was appointed as acting assistant surgeon in the Union army but was almost immediately sent as the American consul to Manzanillo and Colima, Mexico, where he remained for a year. In 1864 he returned permanently to Hungary and became director of the Budapest Zoological and Botanical Garden and the Ethnographical Section of the Hungarian National Museum, as well as president of the Hungarian Geographical Society. He died in Budapest in 1894.[9]

George Pomutz (1828-1882) also visited Texas briefly during the 1850's. A native of Gyula in Békés County, Hungary, he studied in a military school before joining the Hungarian army in 1848. Appointed to the rank of captain by General György Klapka, Pomutz also served as secretary to László Újházi, then the civilian commissioner of the fortress of Komárom, and Újházi later appointed him Chief of Police. Following the surrender of Komárom, Pomutz chose exile and, with 50 others, formed the Komárom American society to emigrate. He was present at the founding of New Buda, Iowa, in 1850 and helped Újházi build his log house. He had his own farm nearby.[10]

Personal glimpses of the 48ers are rare. While Pomutz was living temporarily with the Újházis and other émigrés at Hungarian House in New York early in 1850, Újházi's daughter Klára described him in her diary:

He is a cultured, fine gentleman with whom one can converse with the greatest delight for hours. . . . In the city [New York] one could trust him to haul the water and go to the market to shop, but he is not made for heavier work. His occupation is lawyer. During the war he was a revolutionary police commissioner; that is how he got to Komárom. Our father likes him very much and trusts him.[11]

From New Buda Pomutz accompanied Újházi to meet Louis Kossuth in St. Louis in March 1852 and then on to Texas to inspect land offered the Hungarian leader near Corpus Christi. When Újházi returned to San Antonio in 1853, however, Pomutz remained in Iowa. During the Civil War he helped organize the 15th Iowa Volunteer Infantry Regiment and rose to the rank of colonel (some sources say he was made brigadier general upon his retirement). Later Pomutz was appointed American consul general at St. Petersburg, Russia, by President Andrew Johnson and, like Xantus and Újházi, served his new homeland as a diplomat. After his recall in 1878 Pomutz remained in Russia, where he died in poverty in 1882.[12]

The romantic poet Frigyes Kerényi was perhaps the most tragic figure among the exiles. Of German ethnic background, he was born Friedrich Christmann in Eperjes, Sáros County, in northern Hungary on January 1, 1822. His father was a wealthy iron foundry owner, and his mother wrote poetry, thereby influencing her son. As a young university student Kerényi was swept up in Hungarian nationalism and the magyarization process current during the first part of the 19th century. By the age of 18 he had dropped his native German and begun writing poetry in Hungarian, using the assumed name of Emil Vidor. At the age of 20 he magyarized his name to Kerényi and moved to Pest, where he became a lawyer.[13]

Kerényi became friends with Hungary's romantic nationalist poets, including Sándor Petőfi, Mihály Tompa, and others. Petőfi, the most famous and one of world's greatest lyric poets, became a popular leader in the Hungarian nationalist movement which led to the Revolution of 1848-1849. It was said that his poetry was able to incite mob action. On March 15, 1848, he read his *Nemzeti dal,* or *National Song* (known to most Americans as *Talpra magyar!, Rise, O Hungarians!*) in front of the Hungarian National Museum, thus inspiring the freeing of political prisoners in Buda, and his name became synonymous with Hungarian resistance to foreign oppression. Kerényi served as a lieutenant during the revolution. His friend Petőfi was killed at the Battle of Segesvár in 1849. With Hungary's defeat, Kerényi chose exile and reached America in 1850.[14]

Ill when he arrived in New York, Kerényi spent weeks recovering before setting out for New Buda in the spring of 1851 to join Újházi. In Iowa the young poet attempted to farm, but failed because of his poor health. Later Újházi invited him to Texas to become his "perpetual guest and house poet" and supplied money for the trip. Kerényi's health soon made him a romantic victim, however. Upon reaching San Antonio during the winter of 1853-1854, he decided to walk the four miles to Sírmező. Along the way he collapsed and died. The next day farmers found his body in a ditch along the road. Kerényi was identified by documents in his pockets, although the locals ". . . had a hard time reading his name and thought he was a tramp, a foreigner." [15]

Another Hungarian 48er who briefly lived near San Antonio during the mid-1850's was Márton Koszta (1819-1858). Before arriving in Texas he was involved in an international incident which later came to bear his name in international diplomacy. Having fled to Turkey after the Hungarian surrender in 1849, Koszta came to the United States in 1851 and declared his intent to become a citizen. Thereafter, in 1853, he visited Turkey on personal business. Although not yet a U.S. citizen, he placed himself under the protection of the American consul at Smyrna. He was seized on June 23, 1853, by Austrians who considered him a war criminal and placed him in irons on board the warship *Huszár* in Smyrna harbor to await transportation to Austria for trial as a traitor.[16]

Captain Duncan Nathan Ingraham, commander of the U.S. sloop-of-war *St. Louis* in Smyrna, was ordered to reclaim Koszta, who was under American protection. On July 2, 1853, Ingraham maneuvered his vessel broadside to the *Huszár* and demanded the release of Koszta. When his demand was ignored the American vessel sounded battle stations and cleared for action. A military incident was narrowly avoided when the Austrians agreed to place Koszta under the care of the French consul in Smyrna while the matter was being adjusted between the American and Austrian governments. There Koszta remained until October 25, when Austria recognized that he had "nationality rights" as a legally admitted resident of the United States. The American secretary of state maintained that Koszta was the victim of injustice and trickery on the part of the Austrians. Immediately upon his release Koszta left by steamer for Boston.[17]

The "Koszta Case" set a precedent in international law. President Franklin Pierce declared that America would adhere to this interpretation of protection afforded not only American citizens but also those who had declared their intent to become citizens. The Koszta Case became part of American diplomatic history.[18]

Koszta later became noteworthy in a more local and personal sense. In San Antonio by 1855, he publicly embarrassed Újházi, with whose hospitality and help he and his wife, Lucinda, located a farm. On January 3, 1856, they bought a 1,350-acre farm on the Medina River, 13 miles southwest of San Antonio. Along with the land, the purchase price of $9,000 included a frame house, kitchen and smokehouse, 48 cattle, 15 hogs, a yoke of oxen and a wagon, household and kitchen furniture, carpentering and farming tools, and "other products and all materials pertaining to the farm." In the transaction they also acquired a 40-year-old female slave and her ten-year-old son! Thus Koszta became the first known Hungarian slave owner in Texas, much to Újházi's consternation and shame, for he and other Hungarians steadfastly opposed slavery.[19]

It is uncertain whether Koszta actually farmed his Texas land or how long he kept the slaves. Perhaps because of drought conditions, he leased the farm in January 1857, but the slaves were not listed in the agreement. Nor were they listed in the order of sale issued by the District Court of Bexar County (in favor of the lien holder) among the "goods and chattles, lands and tenements of Martin Kozta [*sic*] and Lucinda Kosta [*sic*]." Seized by the Bexar County sheriff in November 1859, the property was sold from the courthouse door the next month.[20]

Koszta apparently left Texas for Central America. Supposedly a lady who owned a plantation in Guatemala saw his portrait in the American newspapers and came to New York to meet and marry him. The San Antonio *Herald* reported on July 17, 1858, that Koszta, "the Hungarian refugee who was rescued from the Austrian authorities in 1853" had recently died in "very indigent circumstances on a sugar plantation, near the city of Guatemala."[21]

László Újházi's hope for "companionship, for friends and community" in his new Texas location was only partially fulfilled. Within a few years of his arrival in 1853, other Hungarians came, including Gabriel and Terus (Teréz) Katona, Francis and Julia Böröndi, Benjamin Varga and his four sons, Anton and Julia Lorenz, and others.

"San Antonio de Béxar" by Hermann Lungkwitz

These émigrés remained permanently in or near San Antonio as craftsmen, farmers, and ranchers, and had business and social contacts with the Újházi family. The old "Governor" (the honorific title which his Texas contemporaries bestowed on him) initially hosted the new arrivals, but Sírmező lacked adequate sleeping accommodations and food for all his visitors, and he soon complained that "the good Hungarians often took advantage of my good will." But he helped them locate nearby farms. The result was that approximately 20 Hungarians formed a small ethnic community in Bexar County prior to the Civil War.[22]

Gabriel (Gábor) Katona was perhaps more closely associated with László Újházi and his family than others in the exile group. A native of Balmazújváros, Hungary, he had been a major in the National Guard from Szabolcs County during the revolution. Afterwards he was impressed into the Austrian army, but escaped to Italy before coming to America. He arrived on the *Hermann* with Újházi and other exiles in December 1849, settled temporarily at New Buda, and came to Texas in 1855. In 1860 Katona bought a farm on Mud Creek in Bexar County eight miles north of Sírmező.[23]

The Katonas worked for the Újházis, building fences and plowing fields for $14 a month. While living at Sírmező in a borrowed tent, Katona, with Újházi's sons and a few other émigrés, also engaged in a cooperative effort to earn money: they cut hay to sell in San Antonio or to the U.S. Army post. What they could not sell, Újházi, probably the wealthiest of the immigrants, bought for three dollars a wagon and stored until the winter, when he could make a good profit. After moving to his own farm on Mud Creek in the early 1860's, Gabriel Katona remained a near neighbor and friend to the Újházi family and assisted them periodically, including hauling water during the years of severe drought. He also was a guest in some of Újházi's rabbit hunts. Újházi remarked of Katona that he "drank more coffee . . . in America than the whole county at home in many, many years." [24]

A contemporary of Katona at Sírmező, Mihály Eötvös, a former county judge from Szatmár, rented a portion of Sírmező from Újházi during the mid-1850's. At first Újházi helped Eötvös rent a farm 18 miles away on Cibolo Creek, but, because he enjoyed Eötvös's company, he soon regretted the distance, which prevented more frequent visiting. Thereafter Újházi rented him 12½ acres and a little hut at Sírmező for $80 a year. Although Eötvös worked with Katona and other Hungarians gathering hay for the San Antonio market in 1855, he soon left Texas. [25]

Francis Böröndi (also Borondy, Boeroendi, Boeroendy, Brandi, Brandy, and Bernady), was also a friend and associate of Újházi and other 48ers in San Antonio. He arrived in America in the early 1850's, stayed for a short time at New Buda, Iowa, and, with his Hungarian-born wife, Julia, came to Texas in 1855. Five years later he purchased 160 acres near Salado Creek eleven miles northeast of San Antonio and took part in Újházi's hunts during the Reconstruction years. In 1875 he loaned $2,000 in gold to Farkas Újházy but lost his money when Farkas lost Sírmező and "took off with his wife and children." [26]

Little else is known of the Böröndis' activities in San Antonio. They operated an early San Antonio cafe, the Globe Restaurant, in the rear of Bosshart's Saloon at the busy intersection of Commerce and Navarro streets. During the early 1880's, perhaps unable to recover financially from the loss of his loan to Farkas Újházy, Böröndi went to work on a railroad construction crew outside town. There he contracted scurvy and died on March 1, 1883. Before his death he had deeded the contents of the Globe Restaurant to his wife, including all kitchen and dining room fixtures and utensils. [27]

Of all the Hungarian immigrant families who settled around San Antonio in the 1850's, only the Vargas were equipped with skills to meet consumers' demands on the Texas frontier. Benjamin Varga and his four sons, John, Alexander, Joseph, and Paul, had been saddlemakers in Hungary. They followed their ancestral craft on the Texas frontier, where the horse was the most important means of transportation, and saddlemakers could rapidly and easily assimilate into the local economy. They were the largest immigrant Hungarian family, next to the Újházis, in San Antonio prior to the Civil War.

In 1954 the San Antonio Chamber of Commerce saluted the Ben Varga Saddlery as one of a handful of century-old businesses in the city, and Milton C. Varga, representing the fourth generation of his family, accepted the award. The history of the Varga Saddlery was traced back to its founder, Benjamin Varga, who arrived in San Antonio about 1853 and opened his business in an adobe house on the present site of the Bexar County Courthouse on Main Plaza. He was followed in business by his sons Alex and Joseph, his grandson Ben J., and his great-grandson Edwin, brother of Milton C. Other members of the family were also saddlemakers, working in other shops and in various Texas towns.[28]

By the end of its first century of operation, the family company was making everything from pigging rope to chaps to saddles which "generations of cow ponies wore with pride." It was said that the original Varga "set to making cayuse fashions, custom-designed and ready to wear, thereby burning the Varga name across the harness-shop history and the levis of legions of customers." Benjamin Varga's great-grandsons continued making saddles in much the same manner as he had, all marked with the "VARGA" emblem.[29]

Benjamin Varga was born August 8, 1805, in Szerdahely (one source said "Boesh"; in original Hungarian, Bős), Hungary, and was trained as a master saddle and harness maker. Little is known of his early life other than that he lived for various lengths of time in Patas, Szerdahely, and Bős. A Calvinist, Varga married Magdalene Vita (Vida) and was the father of at least five sons and a daughter. According to a family legend, he fought in the Revolution of 1848-1849, left Hungary alone (his wife had died), and came to America with other refugees. He reportedly came to Texas by way of Iowa in 1853 and established his saddlery on San Antonio's Main Plaza. Once in business, he sent for his sons to join him in Texas. Four years later John, Alexander, Joseph, and Paul arrived at the port of Galveston on their way to San Antonio to join their father.[30]

Little is known of Varga's early years in San Antonio. He bought a city lot on the east side of the San Antonio River near the Acequia de las Pajalaches in the old La Villita neighborhood near the Alamo in June 1858. There he established his permanent home in San Antonio. (In the 1860 census the five Varga men were listed as saddlers: Ben, 54; John, 26, a saddletree maker; Alexander, 24; Joseph, 21; and Paul, 17. In San Antonio Benjamin Varga and László Újházi became acquainted as early as 1853, when the latter considered sending his youngest son, László Jr., to apprentice in the saddle trade. In 1857 Újházi remarked that Benjamin Varga was one of his visitors at Sírmező. A close association between the families continued for the duration of the Újházi family's life in San Antonio, and two of the Varga sons, Joseph and Alexander, made real estate investments with and witnessed legal documents for the Újházis.[31]

● ───────────── ●

Four Hungarian Brothers Serve the Confederacy

During the Civil War all four of Varga's sons saw Confederate service. The oldest, John, who was born on December 6, 1833, in Patas, enlisted for the duration of the war on May 7, 1862, and was a private in Co. H, 3rd Texas Infantry (1st Regiment, Luckett's Regiment). He was placed on detached duty on October 1, 1862, and sent to the Ordnance Depot at San Antonio, where he served as a saddler in 1863 and 1864. Early in 1865 he was listed as having "Rheumat" in the Confederate General Hospital at Shreveport, Louisiana, and was paroled on June 8, 1865.[32]

After the war John worked in the family saddlery in San Antonio and married Roselia Deák, a Catholic Hungarian chambermaid from Transylvania, on April 14, 1866. Unfortunately, she died in six months. He later married Katherine Keuppers, a native of Critz, Hinsburg, Germany, and had a family of six children, including a son, Ludwig, who later had a saddlery in Cuero, Texas. John also attempted farming during the late 1870's and early 1880's in San Saba County, where he was identified as a saddler in 1880. Then he returned with his family to San Antonio and worked in his brother Alex's shop until 1889, when he was employed by another saddler, C.J. Langholz, during the nineties. In 1900 he listed his occupation as "carriage trimmer." John Varga died at his home in San Antonio in 1915 and was buried in the local Confederate Cemetery.[33]

Alexander Varga had worked in his father's San Antonio shop since arriving from Hungary in 1858 and also fought for the Confederacy. He enrolled in the 3rd Texas Infantry (1st Regiment, Luckett's Regiment) as a private in Co. I and was paroled in San Antonio on August 7, 1865. No other details of his service are available, although it is most likely that he too was a saddler for the San Antonio Ordnance Depot. He married Natalie Kleabe, a Prussian immigrant, on May 30, 1867.[34]

In 1876 Alexander separated his business from that of his brother Joseph, who had joined him after the war, and opened his own harness and saddle company, advertising himself as a manufacturer of harnesses, saddles, bridles, collars, hames, saddletrees, and saddle hardware. His store was on Military Plaza until the mid-1880's and then moved to Dolorosa Street between Main and Military plazas. After 1891 he managed the Lone Star Saddlery Company. His family's business was carried on by a son, Lionel J. Varga, through the end of the century. Alexander died in San Antonio on September 24, 1921, and was buried in City Cemetery #4.[35]

Joseph H. Varga, the third son of Benjamin Varga to serve the South, enlisted on March 27, 1862, as a private in Captain R.B. Maclin's Company, 1st Regiment of Light Artillery, for the duration of the war (with a $50 bounty). He was assigned extra duty as the company's saddler. His company was later part of Willke's Battalion of Light Artillery, and by the war's end he was a sergeant in Co. C, 8th Texas Field Battery. He was paroled in San Antonio on August 9, 1865. After the war he and Alexander operated the family's business until their split in 1876. Thereafter their saddleries were located on opposite sides of San Antonio's Military Plaza—Joseph's shop on the south side, and Alexander's on the north.[36]

Joseph married Josephine Scheke in Galveston in 1865. A native of Oldenburg, Germany, she reportedly had nursed him to health after a yellow fever attack. They eventually had six children. In addition to operating his own saddlery, Joseph worked for Lazarus Frank's company as a saddlemaker and leather cutter during the 1890's. His elder son, Ben J., took over his father's business when Joseph died in 1898 and continued its operation until his own death in 1944. Ben J. Varga was a director of the Finance Committee of the Retail Merchants Association, the Chamber of Commerce, and the Belknap Rifles. He was also president of the Southwestern Retail Saddle and Harness Manufacturers' Association (1914). His son Edwin continued the Ben Varga Saddle Company, located after 1904 on South Flores Street, for another generation after becoming a partner in 1940. The company received its 100-year award in 1954 and was sold in 1959 upon Edwin's retirement.[37]

Paul, the youngest of the Varga brothers in Confederate service, enlisted at age 19 as a private in Captain Daniel H. Ragsdale's Company, Texas Mounted Volunteers, 5th Texas Cavalry, which subsequently became known as Sibley's Brigade Texas Mounted Volunteers. Paul's military service proved more adventurous than that of his brothers. His unit was part of the Confederate force sent to occupy New Mexico in 1862, and he took part in the battles at Valverde, Glorietta, Apache Canyon, and Peralta. Following the disastrous defeat of Sibley's forces, Varga was left to care for the wounded at Santa Fe and was captured. He was exchanged at Vicksburg, Mississippi, and became his company's saddler.[38]

Paul married Blanche Russell on September 6, 1866, and soon moved to Bell County, Texas, where he took up farming. In 1876 he bought a 160-acre farm on Wilbarger Creek in San Saba County from his father and moved to the site in an ox-drawn wagon. Although Paul and his family lived in a log cabin at first, he later built a two-story farmhouse in what became known as the Bowser community near Richland Springs. Recognizing the need for a church and cemetery in this rural community, Paul gave land in 1888 to the Methodist Episcopal Church South for the Richland Mission church, later known as the Varga Chapel. He also gave land for a cemetery, which was named for him. Paul Varga died on August 15, 1912, and was buried with Masonic Rites in the Varga Chapel Cemetery.[39]

John and Katherine Varga   *Ludwig Varga, son of John*

The Ludwig Varga Saddle Shop in Cuero

Joseph Varga

Joseph Varga's Saddles & Harness shop (second from left)
on San Antonio's Military Plaza

126

127

Blanche and Paul Varga

The Paul Varga House, c. 1890 — standing, from left, *Paul Varga, Will Varga, Warren Abraham;* seated, *Blanche Varga with Willie Abraham, Ernest Varga, Sadie Varga with Terry Varga, Elvira Abraham with Ethel Abraham*

Ben J. Varga

Varga Saddle Company, San Antonio

The story of the Varga family would not be complete without mention of its patriarch's life in San Antonio after the Civil War. In the city's 1865 business directory, Benjamin Varga & Company was listed on Commerce Street. A personal glimpse of his life was revealed in a few surviving letters to his sons during the 1870's and early 1880's. Because of his efforts to help his sons become established, he wrote that he was "mixed up in bitter troubles" in 1878 and had sold his tools and materials of his trade to meet obligations. In writing to John in July 1879, Varga described his city property: "I have my land in the city. I fenced it. . . . I still need some 2,000 feet of lumber" to complete the fence. His house stood in the middle of three acres, which included a well, a small utility yard behind the house, and a barn. In that year he also gave his son Alexander $300 of his "handiwork" to sell in the saddlery shop.[40]

In an unusual bit of gossip about local Hungarians, Benjamin Varga wrote to John that the "wise" Farkas Újházy had married and departed with his wife and children, leaving lots of debts, including those on his land. Újházy had borrowed $2,000 in gold from Francis Böröndi against a lien on his land, but had overmortgaged his farm, and Böröndi lost his money. Varga went on to say that Újházy owed money to "doctors and lawyers who took the value of his land."[41]

By February 1880 the 75-year-old saddler was ill and staying with his son Joseph in San Antonio. A drought left him without feed for his horse, and he had no roof on his barn and utility shed. In addition, his 60-foot well was dry, and he was forced to carry water from the San Antonio River. In a depressed spirit, he lamented, "I am old and sick, not able to work anymore." Varga informed John the next month that "I spent $200 for tools for you to have your own leather business." Then, in August 1881, he said that he had plowed two or three acres, then a freeze and a rainstorm had destroyed his crops, but he had worked "in my profession" for his sons Alexander and Joseph for a time thereafter.[42]

In the fall of 1881 he strongly advised John against moving back to San Antonio from San Saba, saying that "People here are corrupt. . . . You would have problems with your children, and the food is very expensive." He also reported that corn was $1 a bushel, sweet potatoes $1.50, beef 6¢ a pound, pork 10¢ a pound, and a dozen eggs 30¢. Varga went on to observe that rents were rising, and Alexander had been forced to move his saddlery shop from the Plaza to the office building of the *Herald* newspaper, where he paid $30 a month for two rooms. Joseph still had his saddlery shop on Military Plaza. He also observed that "For the poor, it is very hard to make a living, and food is sky high." Varga lived in his little cottage or with his sons for the remainder of his life. He died on November 20, 1889, and was buried in the city cemetery.[43]

Personal stories of pioneer Hungarian women in Texas are rare. According to a family tradition, one of San Antonio's early Magyar women arrived alone at the port of Galveston at the age of 16, having refused to marry a man many years her senior according to the wishes of her noble Catholic family. Julia Michika (or Missesska) convinced a family friend, a ship captain, to bring her to America. Friend or no, the captain dumped her on a Galveston dock with her trunk. Hearing of Hungarians in San Antonio, Julia then made her way there.[44]

Other evidence contradicted this tale, however. Born on January 17, 1839, Julia was employed in her teens as an outdoor maid at Nyustya, the Hungarian estate of Klementine Fáy, Helen Madarász's sister. Quickly deciding to emigrate to America with Helen, Julia packed her bags in half a day, bade farewell to her relatives, and accompanied her new employer to Hamburg, whence they sailed on June 15, 1858. During the Atlantic crossing Julia was seasick much of the time. She arrived at Sírmező in August of that year. Through Helen's letters to relatives in Hungary, Julia asked her mother to send her two or three pairs of cordovan boots and slippers for summer wear, using money she had previously earned from a flax sale. She also asked her mother to insure a $60 inheritance from her father.[45]

Once in Texas, the attractive Hungarian girl's desire to lead her own life conflicted with her employer's need for help. Helen Madarász drove away one of Julia's first suitors and then moved to a remote farm on Cibolo Creek in northeastern Bexar County, but Julia was fired suddenly in November 1859. Helen wrote to her sister Pauline that, "In this America, it is as if a devil has gotten into the housemaids. Anybody who brings a maid here is insane. It is the same as if one would throw one's money out the window. She [Julia] was here only a few months, and she wanted to become the lady of the house." [46]

Julia married Anton Lorenz (Loránt) on December 10, 1861. Born in Hungary on February 20, 1829, he fled to America after the revolution to avoid impressment into the Austrian army and came to Texas during the 1850's. Although he was conscripted into the Confederate army during the Civil War, family stories held that he tried to avoid service and spent most of his time in the stockade in San Antonio. Anton acquired a farm on the Dry Salado Creek about twelve miles north of San Antonio. There Julia and Anton became the parents of ten children, who ranged in age from two to 15, by 1880. Some of their sons bore distinctive Hungarian heroes' names—Árpád, Attila, and Ladislaus (László).[47]

According to family memories, one small son was carried away from the Lorenz's farm near Bulverde by the Indians. A determined Julia, only four feet, nine inches tall, thereupon mounted her horse and swore to follow the Indians all the way to Colorado if necessary. But the Texas Rangers trailed the band to the Mexican border, where, during an attack on the Indians' camp, the little Lorenz son was thrown into the fire and killed. Julia never accepted the fact that he would not be coming home and pledged her other sons to share their inheritance with him when he did.[48]

Another family story recalled an equally tragic event. During the early 1880's the Lorenz children rode to school on horseback. One day, while passing an isolated house, they heard cries for help. Investigating, they found the inhabitants sick and fetched water for them. As a result, all five of the Lorenz daughters caught smallpox and died. The sons survived by avoiding water and baths until the disease ran its course. Anton and Julia sold their Bulverde farm and moved to School House Creek, a tributary of Olmos Creek, near Sírmező. At their "Sunday Farm" they reared their surviving sons, none of whom married before their mother's death on August 4, 1916. Julia was buried in the family cemetery on the "Sunday Farm" next to Anton who had died on May 22, 1911.[49]

In addition to the Újházis, Vargas, Lorenzes, Katonas, and Böröndis, two other immigrants became part of the small Hungarian community, and both became lifelong farmers and ranchers near San Antonio. Alexander Benke (Benkő) (1824-1906) and John Finto (Finta) (1831-1905) were both veterans of the Hungarian Revolution. Once in Bexar County, both married (Benke to Elise Schmidt from Hesse, Germany, in 1858, and Finto to Lurinda Brown in 1866) and had large families. Benke acquired a ranch in northwest Bexar County near the community of Helotes, and Finto farmed on Cibolo Creek 12½ miles north of San Antonio in the Wetmore community. It was said that Benke was the first in his area to acquire a horse and buggy and to

The Benkes—from left, *unknown, A.J., Louis, unknown, Alex Jr.,
unknown child, Alexander Sr. [Identifications are not certain,
except for "Grandpa."]*

raise cotton, and Finto supplemented his farm earnings by cutting and
hauling wood to the city.[50]

Alexander Benke's arrival in Texas was unique among his
contemporaries. After arriving in America he enlisted in the U.S. Army
at New Orleans on June 3, 1852, and was posted to the Texas frontier
in Captain John H. King's Company I, 1st Regiment, U.S. Infantry,
to guard against Indians. During his military service Benke fought in
two Indian battles, against the Comanches ten miles north of Fort
McKavett in Menard County in 1852 and later on the Devil's River
in 1854. During part of the time he was stationed at Fort Clark.
Although Benke survived the Indians the army's diet almost killed him.
He was discharged at Fort Belknap on November 22, 1856, because
of incapacity brought on by "chronic scurvey" caused by exposure and
salted provisions. Perhaps hearing of Hungarians in San Antonio, he
made his way there to recover.[51]

John Finto also saw military service after coming to the United
States in 1854. When the Civil War began he enlisted at San Antonio
as a private in Company D, 5th Texas Regiment (Captain Daniel

Ragsdale). Finto's unit participated in the 1862 New Mexico campaign, during which he was wounded and left in the hospital in Santa Fe. Captured by Union forces, he was sent to Camp Douglas, Illinois, and exchanged at Vicksburg in September 1862. He was paroled at San Antonio at the end of the conflict.[52]

Other Hungarians may also have attempted to settle near László Újházi during the 1850's, but very little is known of them. Bexar County's census takers in 1860 recorded (and misspelled) the names of such Hungarian-born persons as Drat Vigarnardity, Andrew and Gustav Florent, Francisco and Rosilia Broderick, and Francis and Christine Brandel. There is no information to explain the presence of Ferenc Badalik (Badalek, Budalik), a journeyman born in Szeged in 1826, who worked in Hungary, Turkey, and Wallachia (Rumania) during the 1840's. His death in San Antonio at the age of 36 was witnessed by another Hungarian, John Varga, on April 23, 1863.[53]

After László Újházi's death in 1870, the little San Antonio Hungarian community lost what small focus it might have had. There, and elsewhere in Texas, the immigrants and their families went their own ways, and no ethnic Hungarian organizations from that period can be identified. The 48ers were too few and scattered to accomplish any sort of cohesive community action in their own behalf (other than the short-lived hay marketing scheme of the mid-1850's). Within a generation they and their American-born children assimilated into the general community.

CHAPTER SIX

Other 48ers in Texas

San Antonio was not the only Texas destination for Hungarian 48ers, and those who settled elsewhere may have had little or no contact with László Újházi and the Magyars in Bexar County. Large towns and port cities such as Galveston, Houston, Indianola, Dallas, Austin, La Grange, and others in more settled, eastern parts of Texas provided hospitable surroundings for individuals who became craftsmen, businessmen, and professionals in their adopted homeland. A few also served as public officials at the local level, and many of military age joined Texas and Confederate units during the Civil War. Their numbers were soon augmented by others, fortune-seeking 48ers who fought for the Union and came to Texas following the restoration of peace in 1865.

One founder of a Texas dynasty was Charles Vidor, who arrived in Galveston, Texas' main port city, during the 1850's. Born in the Hungarian capital on October 16, 1834, Vidor reportedly studied for the priesthood during his youth. Facts about his emigration to America are confused. Although his obituary in 1904 stated that he arrived in New York with his parents during the late 1840's, a family story said that he came to America as a press representative and business manager for his cousin, Edward (Ede) Reményi (1829-1898). A famous Hungarian violin virtuoso and a veteran of the Revolution of 1848-1849,

Charles Vidor

Reményi toured the United States in 1849. Still another source stated that Vidor came to New York in 1853 at the age of 19 and worked for the New York *Herald.*[1]

Perhaps the only Hungarian in Galveston in 1855, Vidor worked as a clerk for Lent Munson Hitchcock, a successful merchant and landowner. He married Hitchcock's daughter, Emily, in Christ Episcopal Church on October 20, 1858. Charles and Emily lived with her parents until the outbreak of the Civil War, but tragedy stalked the young family: their two children died in infancy, and Emily died shortly thereafter, in 1860 or 1861.[2]

Vidor may have been seeking escape from his grief by volunteering for service when the Civil War loomed. In the late fall of 1860, Galveston's volunteer companies were brought up to maximum strength, and on December 3, 1860, Vidor was elected fourth sergeant of the Galveston Lone Star Rifles (which selected uniforms of gray cloth with red trimmings), a popular unit attracting Galveston's "best citizens." Thereafter he enrolled as a private in the 1st Regiment Texas Infantry (later the 2nd Battalion under Louis Wigfall) at Galveston for the duration of the war. In November 1862 Vidor worked as a clerk for the brigade and division quartermaster, a position he held throughout 1863. On February 19, 1864, he was promoted to the rank of captain in the Confederate Quartermaster Department.

Many years later Vidor's obituary stated that he saw service with the Army of Northern Virginia in Hood's Brigade, Longstreet's Corps, as well as under Generals Albert Sidney Johnston and Stonewall Jackson. He was paroled at Greensboro, North Carolina, on May 1, 1865.[3]

As historian David G. McComb has observed, the main thrust of Galveston's economy after the Civil War involved port activities — exporting raw materials such as cotton, sugar, grain, cattle, and other produce, and importing finished consumer goods and machinery for Texas' farmers. "The city served as a storage and shipping point, with the Galveston merchants providing some services and arranging for transportation." Its population of almost 14,000 in 1870 increased to nearly 40,000 at the turn of the century. In 1900 more than 2.5 million bales of cotton were exported through Galveston to East Coast and European markets.[4]

Returning to Galveston after the war, Vidor quickly involved himself in the business life of the city. By June 1865 he was a partner in the cotton factor and general commission merchant firm of (John) Wolston, (C.G.) Wells and Vidor, a position which he held until 1885, when he became a partner in the insurance agency of Hughes, Stowe, and Company, where he remained until 1901. He was also a charter

Cotton awaiting shipment on a Galveston wharf

Galveston Cotton Exchange and News *Building*

member of the Galveston Cotton Exchange. In 1868 Vidor joined the Galveston Hook and Ladder Company #1 and was a junior warden of Harmony Lodge No. 6, A.F. and A.M. of the Masons. His community service also included a stint as Galveston County treasurer. An eye-witness in 1880 stated that the city was operating on a cash basis and "To Mr. Charles Vidor, the efficient county treasurer, may perhaps be due these pleasing results." He was also a Galveston County commissioner in 1892.[5]

Charles Vidor married 16-year-old Anna Walter in Trinity Episcopal Church on January 23, 1866. Of the ten children born to them, the first five died in infancy or early childhood. Of the five who survived to adulthood, Vidor's eldest son, Charles Shelton, became a Texas lumber baron, and his grandson, King, became a pioneer moviemaker in Hollywood. Charles Vidor's home was destroyed in Galveston's Great Fire of 1885, but he built a large house in 1886 which was still standing a century later. Charles died on September 14, 1904, at the age of 70. The flag on the Cotton Exchange building was flown at half mast during his funeral. He was buried in the Episcopal cemetery.[6]

Charles Shelton Vidor played a major role as a partner in the firm of Miller and Vidor Lumber Company, one of the largest producers and wholesalers of lumber products in the southeast Texas lumber region during the first two decades of the 20th century. As a result, two of the few Texas towns named for Hungarians were named in his honor — Milvid (for Miller and Vidor) and Vidor.

Born on November 12, 1866, in Galveston, Vidor followed in his father's footsteps, entering the frenetic business world of late 19th century Galveston after obtaining his education at Southwestern University in Georgetown, Texas, and doing postgraduate studies in Brooklyn. At the age of 16 he began clerking in the offices of the Gulf, Colorado, and Santa Fe Railroad Company, thus engendering his interest in railroads in Texas. In 1884 he was a shipping clerk for the firm of Block, Oppenheimer and Company and later was a clerk in the claims department of Leon and H. Blum wholesale dry goods company. Following the failure of the latter, Vidor became the assistant secretary, then cashier, of the Galveston Bagging and Cordage Mills. But disaster struck Galveston in September 1900 with the Great Hurricane, and the bagging mills lost many skilled workers. As a result, the mills were closed, and Vidor began a new career in the lumber industry.[7]

Charles Shelton Vidor with King and Cassie

ALL CONTRACTS SUBJECT TO CAUSES BEYOND OUR CONTROL.

A. W. MILLER, President
C. H. MOORE, Vice-Pres't
C. S. VIDOR, Sec'y and Treas.

Miller & Vidor Lumber Co.

INCORPORATED 1890

MANUFACTURERS AND WHOLESALE DEALERS
ROUGH AND DRESSED
YELLOW PINE LUMBER,
Timber, Ties, Piling and Railway Material.

PEACH RIVER PINE AND RED
CYPRESS, LUMBER AND SHINGLES,

GALVESTON, TEXAS.   11/21/08

Company letterhead

Charles S. Vidor married Katie Lee Wallis (also spelled Wallace) on February 9, 1893, at the First Presbyterian Church in Galveston, and they became the parents of two children, King Wallis Vidor and Catherine (Cassie). The Vidors, who later joined the Episcopal Church, were active in the business as well as the social life of the city. Vidor was a member of the Chamber of Commerce and the Galveston Business League, and he served as the last commanding officer of the old Galveston Artillery Company.[8]

Vidor's involvement with the East Texas lumber industry began in 1902. His investments in sawmills and logging railroads made him a stockholder and officer in a number of interrelated businesses; Darlington-Miller Lumber Company (after 1905 named the Miller-Vidor Lumber Company), Peach River Lumber Company, Peach River and Gulf Railroad Company, and Seaboard Oil Company. The Miller-Vidor Company, whose timberlands lay in East Texas (in Orange, Jefferson, Jasper, Hardin, Liberty, Polk, Montgomery, San Jacinto, Grimes, and Waller counties), began manufacturing and wholesaling rough and dressed yellow pine lumber for domestic and export markets. By 1910 it controlled about 130,000 acres of timberland, and the capitalization of the mills stood at $1,500,000. The combined mills at Orange, Milvid, Timber, and Beaumont produced about half a million feet of lumber. Employing almost a thousand men, the Miller-Vidor mills were well equipped with logging railroad lines which transported the company's raw and finished materials and supplies.[9]

The Peach River Lines

Together with many young men of the late 19th century, Charles Shelton Vidor was interested in railroads. He became active in the Miller-Vidor empire by developing transportation for logs, lumber, and other products of the mills and forests to shipping points. The Peach River Lines (named for a tributary of the East San Jacinto River in Montgomery County) was the result and consisted of the Peach River and Gulf, the Galveston, Beaumont, and Northeastern, and the Riverside and Gulf railways. Vidor served as president.

The Peach River and Gulf Railroad Company was chartered on October 31, 1904, with its headquarters and shop at Timber, Texas. Although considered a common carrier, it was a 16-mile tram road which employed ten workers. It ran from the Sante Fe lines at Timber in Montgomery County southeastward to Midline and a connection on the Houston East and West Texas Railroad. It also had a branch line of five miles to Lincoln, Texas. Its sole purpose was to bring logs to the mill at Timber and to transport finished lumber and products to the sidings on the large common carriers such as the Santa Fe. Later it was abandoned.

The Galveston, Beaumont, and Northeastern was chartered March 14, 1906, with its headquarters at Beaumont and its machine shop at Vidor. It employed 35 men and ran from the Beaumont mill three miles to the junction with the Kansas City Southern and from there another eight miles into Orange County. It was equipped with three locomotives, a passenger car to carry workers into the forests, three boxcars, 40 regular flatcars, and 20 regular log cars. In all, it had 17 miles of track, including spurs and sidetracks. Although chartered to extend into northern Newton County, it never achieved its goal, and its charter later lapsed.

The Riverside and Gulf Railroad was chartered on April 30, 1907, with headquarters at Milvid in northeastern Liberty County, a station on the main line of the Santa Fe system. The Riverside and Gulf had twelve miles of main line, with three collateral spurs, although it was intended to extend eastward to the Trinity River with a total of 28 miles of track. Three locomotives, a passenger coach, a caboose, and 62 log cars completed its stock. Fifty-two men were employed (three engineers, three firemen, twelve section men, ten steel-gang men, two track walkers, two night watchmen, ten shop men, one brakeman, and nine men in the grading crew). The line was intended to extend to Wallisville on Galveston Bay from Livingston in Polk County, but it failed to do so and went out of business.

In 1910 the combined units of the "Peach River Lines" carried 384,492 tons. All were later abandoned.[10]

Vidor's career in the Miller-Vidor lumber empire reached its apex in 1910 when he was the secretary-treasurer of the Miller-Vidor Lumber Company, the Peach River Lumber Company, and the Orange Saw Mill Company. In that year he was also president of the Peach River and Gulf Railroad Company and vice-president of the Beaumont Saw Mill Company, the Galveston, Beaumont, and Northeastern Railroad Company, the Riverside and Gulf Railroad Company, and the Miller-Vidor Saw Mill Company. Vidor remained a part of the combine, which was headquartered in Galveston, until 1912. For the next two

Engine of the Peach River Railroad

years he remained president of the Miller-Vidor Lumber Company and the Peach River Lines. In 1915 he also became vice-president of his son's Hotex Motion Picture Company in Houston.[11]

Miller and Vidor Lumber Company, Galveston, Texas, 1910[12]
(Timber holding listed in board feet)

Total timber owned	611,480,000
Other timber available	725,000,000
Timber owned and available	1,336,480,000
Present car side value of possible product	$18,710,720
Total annual sawmill cut	$74,000,000
Contract lumber handled annually	$15,000,000
Grand total annual amount of sales	$89,000,000
Total number of persons operations support	2,660

"Peach River Lines" of Railway of Texas

Total number of miles equipped	60.62
Total number of miles chartered	340
Total number of locomotives in use	8
Total number of persons operations support	365
Total number of tons carried last year	384,492

Thereafter Vidor's involvement with the Miller-Vidor Lumber Company decreased, and he continued only as a stockholder for several years. In 1916 he moved to Morrilton, Arkansas, where he was associated in business with relatives in the Rainwater Bank and Trust Company (Wood Rainwater, president; Cloudy Night Rainwater, vice-president; and Night Rainwater, secretary and treasurer). Vidor was active in the insurance business and sat on the Board of Directors of Bankers and Planters Mutual Insurance Association, but resigned in 1919 to devote his time to his extensive lumber and financial interests, including the Dominican Corporation.[13]

Vidor's business interests as early as 1914 included exploitation and development of hardwood forests and mines in the northern provinces of Montechristi and Santiago in the Dominican Republic.

143

He estimated that he owned or controlled between 200,000 and 300,000 acres of virgin mahogany, walnut, boxwood, rosewood, and cedar. The valleys contained deep, rich, alluvial soil, equal to that of Cuba, which he believed would produce sugarcane, coffee, cocoa, pineapples, and the purest of leaf tobacco. In 1923 he moved temporarily to New York City to supervise his enterprises.[14]

Charles S. Vidor followed his talented son, King, to Los Angeles, California, in 1919. Thereafter, until his death on January 17, 1931, he pursued interests in motion picture production, beginning with the Vidor Village Studio in Hollywood.[15]

King Wallis Vidor was born in the family home in Galveston on February 8, 1894. His first two decades in Texas foreshadowed his brilliant career in Hollywood, which earned him a permanent place in American film history. While a student in the local high school, he took a summer job as a ticket taker in Galveston's first nickelodeon theater, having been interested since the age of ten in preserving "the phantasmagoric scenes of friends diving in a pool." While earning $3.50 a week for twelve-hour days in the local theater, Vidor also learned how to run the projector and so viewed *Ben Hur* 147 times. Thus he learned the basics of film, acting, and direction.[16]

At the age of 15, while on vacation from Peacock Military Academy in San Antonio, Vidor and a friend made a crude movie camera with which they filmed giant waves washing across Galveston's seawall during the hurricane of 1909. King Vidor must have recalled his own family's experiences during the devastating hurricane nine years earlier. He and his mother had survived in the home of friends, while his father had clung to the rafters in the factory where he worked. Fortunately, the rest of the Vidor family survived that hurricane as well.[17]

Following the showing of his first film, the 1909 storm, in local theaters, Vidor's future as a filmmaker and director was certain. When he was 18 he filmed a movement of massed U.S. Army troops between Houston and Galveston for a film distribution firm, Mutual Weekly, which paid him 60 cents per foot of usable film and appointed him as its representative in Texas. His film of the troops was distributed throughout the world. Vidor made two-reel pictures for his newly organized film company, Hotex, in Houston and Galveston until 1915. But Hotex was short-lived, for Vidor and his new bride, Florence Arto, went to Hollywood. There he pioneered in film producing and directing for the next four decades.[18]

The young King Vidor in Galveston; inset, *King Vidor, c. 1960*

King Vidor (in straw hat) *in a scene from the film* My Hero

Described later as a "trailblazer and often a rebel, widely respected for his independence, individualism, and humanism in a notable directorial career," Vidor made more than 50 feature movies in Hollywood. Among them were his hits *The Big Parade* (1925), *The Champ* (1931), *The Citadel* (1938), and *Duel in the Sun* (1947). His *Hallelujah* (1929) was a musical drama with an all-Black cast, and *Our Daily Bread* (1934) "depicted the plight of the Depression's unemployed." It was said that his movies were "characterized by this honest simplicity and a visual tension not only between people but also between man and the elements." Using a metronome and drum, Vidor paced the rhythms of his movies to a crescendo through his "silent music" technique in directing. His philosophical motivation in directing indicated that a movie "should say something meaningful" through simplicity, clarity, and sincerity.[19]

Previously nominated for five Oscars, Vidor won a special Oscar in 1979 for his achievements over four decades. He won many other awards from film festivals, the Christophers, and the Screen Directors Guild, which included two of his films, *The Big Parade* and *The Crowd*, among the ten best directorial achievements of the first half of the 20th century. In 1953 Vidor retired to his ranch at Paso Robles in California and devoted himself to writing his autobiography, *A Tree Is a Tree*, teaching film directing at a number of colleges including the University of Southern California, making short documentaries, and chronicling his family's history.

King Vidor's reputation and contribution to filmmaking was internationally recognized. His films were noted for their realistic portrayal of social themes dealing with the ideals and disillusionment in American life during the first half of the 20th century. Vidor died at his ranch on the California coast on November 1, 1982.[20]

Other exiles scattered into the hinterland of Texas. A lone 48er was attracted to the rich farmland of the Colorado River valley with its rapidly growing population of immigrants. John Henry Újffy established himself as a pharmacist and merchant in the Fayette County town of Fayetteville, a lone Hungarian among the American, German, and Czech immigrants. Born in Hungary March 14, 1820, family stories reported that he fought for Hungarian independence as an officer in the Revolution of 1848-1849. With its failure, and because his father and brothers had supported the Austrian cause, Újffy emigrated to the United States in 1850 and settled in Fayette County within a year.

John Henry Újffy   *Ida Hermine Újffy*

He married Ida Hermine Walz (1833-1900), a native of Liegnitz, Germany, on October 14, 1855, and they eventually became the parents of five children. Two years after their marriage the Újffys moved to the county seat, La Grange, where he opened a pharmacy. He became a charter member of the Fayetteville Masonic Lodge.[21]

With the outbreak of the Civil War, Újffy sought military service near his home and enlisted in units which never left Texas. First he enrolled as a private in the La Grange German Company, Texas State Reserve Troops of Fayette County, on July 1, 1861. Then, in January 1863, he again enlisted for three months as third sergeant in the 22nd Brigade, CSA, at La Grange and served in Columbus and Houston (his unattached company was undrilled, had no uniforms, and was armed with hunting rifles and shotguns). In August 1863 he mustered for six months as a private in the 1st Regiment Infantry, 22nd Brigade, Texas State Troops, at Camp Columbus, Texas.[22]

Upon his return from military service, Újffy resumed his profession in La Grange. Tragically, however, his life was cut short. During the summer of 1867 yellow fever broke out along the Texas coast and by August had been brought to inland towns by travelers. It was reported that "During the epidemic the town resembled a huge mortuary, as death ran rampant through the streets. Chaos touched every nook and cranny; many deaths went unreported." When the sexton also died of the fever, volunteers began burying the bodies in mass graves. The yellow fever epidemic left 204 dead in La Grange. The Ujffys' younger daughter died on September 10, and John H. Ujffy fell victim on September 29, 1867.[23]

Maurice Sidney Újffy, the oldest son of John H. Újffy, became a successful Galveston businessman. He was born in Fayetteville on November 12, 1857, and completed his education in La Grange. He moved to Galveston in 1876, where he began working in the mercantile firm of LeGierse and Company. Later he clerked for T. Ratto and Company, beginning in 1880. His brother, Arthur Újffy, also clerked in the same business during the early 1880's. Maurice Újffy became partner in 1886 in his own business, Conklin and Újffy, wholesale merchandise brokers. He later prospered as an independent merchandise broker and invested in stocks and bonds.[24]

On June 6, 1883, Újffy married Clara Jockusch, the daughter of John William Jockusch of a leading German immigrant family in Galveston which provided honorary consuls for Prussia and, later, Germany. They had five children. The Újffys moved from their first home to an opulent Victorian mansion which stood at 1026 Avenue I. As his business flourished Újffy's interests broadened to include civic and cultural affairs such as amateur theatricals in which he acted. In 1889 he became a member of the Galveston Cotton Exchange and took offices in its building.[25]

• ——————— •

Elise Újffy von Johnson Recalled the 1900 Hurricane

Late in life Elise, the daughter of Maurice and Clara Újffy, recorded her memories of the storm as a birthday message to her sister, Loula Újffy Harris of Austin:

> Let me tell you about the storm, 1900, in Galveston. It was one of the biggest catastrophes at that time that had probably ever visited any country. It began the evening before with a wonderful moonlight night and the waves coming in full strong that [sic] we knew that it was going to be a storm. The next morning the waves had already entered the city. We went out to see what was happening. . . . Loula . . . you were only two

Maurice Újffy

Clara Jockusch Újffy

The Maurice Újffy House in Galveston

149

weeks old. Of course, my mother was very much afraid for us to be lost in that storm. She did not know where to reach us. But we got home in time to be there when the worst of the flood struck the city.

The people passed our home on the roofs. Our eighteen wonderful oak trees bent to the storm, the horses were swimming, the people were screaming. And then, everything was dark. We had no lights. Only the Negroes were there. Everything was quiet because the water rose inch by inch, and there was no running away from it because we were [on] an island, and there isn't anything around an island but water. The Negroes sang their spirituals in between times. And then, after a night of horror, the people screaming, the darkness, the waves, the next morning [brought] wonderful sunshine.

And eight thousand people had been drowned. . . . No water [was to be had] because we were cut off from the mainland. It was the most awful experience. Because I was sixteen at that time, I can remember perfectly everything that went on. Then people began to loot. [There were] no windows, no roofs. But every man who had a revolver was allowed to use it in case they looted the dead people. Then, gradually, the Red Cross started [operating]. Clara Barton was the first to start that. She came to take care of us with her retinue with water. Until the city could be built up again, of course, many left Galveston, for they were afraid of that storm.[26]

· ———————— ·

The hurricane of 1900 devastated the city of Galveston and took more than 6,000 lives, but the Újffys survived intact. Their home, sitting on pillars one floor above the ground, was not damaged by the waters which streamed beneath it and through the open floor-to-ceiling windows of the first floor. During the height of the flooding, Maurice Újffy rescued one of Judge Kleberg's sons, who was floating by on a board, by pulling him through the dining room window. The family also recalled that a Black family was saved by huddling beneath a dining room table. Afterwards, the Újffys were indeed fortunate to still have fresh water in their cistern. Following the disaster, Újffy joined other civil leaders in the formation of Galveston's Commission Plan of city government to aid the city's recovery. He also served as a Galveston County commissioner, 1904-1906, and advocated brick pavement behind the new seawall, which had been built to protect the city from future storms. He was a member of the citizens' committee to build the new causeway to the mainland in 1916 and gave funds to beautify the highway to Houston. Újffy, orphaned himself at an early age, also served on the board of directors of Galveston's Orphans' Home.[27]

Maurice Újffy died in New Orleans, Louisiana, December 18, 1930. In addition to generously providing for his family and the education of his grandchildren, he remembered his old hometown of La Grange with funds for the local public school (two water fountains and a stage curtain were purchased) and Mothers' Club. Maurice Újffy succeeded in his enterprises and provided sorely needed leadership after Galveston's greatest natural disaster.[28]

The growing city of Houston also attracted Hungarian exiles. A handful of immigrants already lived there by 1860, including J. Veith, a wealthy Hungarian-born grocery merchant, and Maximilian F. de Bajligethy, who served as the deputy city assessor and collector during the 1880's. Another, Adolf Alexander Szabó, served as a public official in Texas longer than any other Hungarian immigrant of the 19th century. At the time of his death in 1905, he had been city treasurer of Houston for 15 years. Szabó was recognized as being closely associated with Houston's development from a village in the 1850's to one of Texas' leading cities at the turn of the century. The son of István and Eleanor Szabó, he was born in Kis-Szombat near Pest, on July 13, 1831. At the age of 17 he joined the Honvéd Army to fight for the freedom of his homeland. With the revolution's failure, Szabó fled to Switzerland and then came to New York on July 4, 1849.[29]

Alex Szabó arrived in Texas in 1853 after short stops in Massachusetts, South Carolina, and Mississippi, during which time he learned English. Although he briefly worked to install telegraph lines between Dallas and Houston, he settled permanently in Houston in 1855. There he reportedly became superintendent of the first cotton compress in the city and later ran a cotton gin. He married Kate Kelley, a native of Connecticut, on June 5, 1860, and was identified in that year's census as a clerk, probably for a cotton gin.[30]

During the Civil War Szabó ran a powder mill in Houston. Then, for the remainder of his life, he made his career in the cotton businesses in that city, where he worked successively as a public weigher at the cotton factor and planters' commission firm of T.M. Bagby, as a cotton factor and agent for the Cotton Press Company, and as superintendent of the Houston City Compress (1877-1878). By the early 1880's Szabó was an independent cotton merchant and buyer, then

Alexander Szabó

worked for a cotton gin and pickery in the latter 1880's. In 1890 he began a 15-year term as Houston City treasurer, his final employment in Texas.[31]

Szabó died August 6, 1905, and was buried in the rites of the Presbyterian Church in Houston. Among the wreaths placed at his grave was one recalling his Hungarian nativity—"A pillow and a heart were sent in recognition of the land of nativity of Mr. Szabó and bore broad streamers in Hungarian colors of red, green and white." The city council of Houston honored him with a resolution, and the 61st District Court adjourned for his funeral. Szabó's role as a business and civil official in Houston for a half century was recognized by his fellow citizens, and a street was named in his honor.[32]

A Hungarian Cobbler in Dallas

John M. Bartay was one of Dallas's earliest Hungarian settlers. Born in Pest on March 21, 1828, Bartay, a lieutenant of the Huszárs in the Hungarian army during the revolution, accompanied his parents into exile in France and Germany. In 1855 he emigrated to the United States and worked for several years in New York. He moved to Dallas in 1858 and established a shoe and leather emporium, which he operated until 1863. In the Dallas *Morning Herald*, he advertised a wide variety of leathers, including French calf and kips (untanned hides), Philadelphia calf and common kips, and a variety of lining skins for boots and shoes.[33]

John Bartay married Katharina (Katalin) Hügel, a native of Lörrach, Baden, Germany, on September 15, 1859, and they became the parents of five children. She died in New Wehdem, Austin County, on February 2, 1870, and John married Lena Rothermel in Bellville, Texas, on June 22, 1871. By his second

John M. Bartay in Mobile, Alabama, c. 1862   *Katharina Hügel Bartay*

wife he also fathered five children. Having moved from Dallas to Cameron in 1863 and then to New Wehdem about 1866, John Bartay pursued a career as a farmer and rancher until his death on December 21, 1885. In 1869 he helped found the St. James Lutheran Church in New Wehdem.[34]

•   ————————   •

J.R. Holmy, an Indianola Artillery Guard

Little is known of J.R. Holmy (or Halmy), who enlisted as first sergeant in Company B, 8th Texas Infantry, at Indianola, Texas, on October 5, 1861. The Hungarian native was described as five feet, six inches tall, a 28-year-old with brown eyes and hair, who was farming in Victoria County.[35]

Holmy served as first sergeant in the Indianola Artillery Guards until July 1863, when he was elected second lieutenant. Thereafter his unit was assigned to Galveston's defenses, including Virginia Point and Point Bolivar. Early in 1865 he was the post quartermaster and acting adjutant. Holmy remained at the post of Battery Green guarding the approaches to Galveston harbor until the end of the war. He was paroled at Victoria, Texas. Unfortunately, nothing further is known of this Hungarian-born Confederate officer.[36]

•   ————————   •

Other talented 48ers included Anton R. Rössler, one of Austin's first Hungarians, who was variously described as "perhaps the most competent geologist of the period," young, ambitious, well-trained, and an excellent cartographer, as well as an accomplished violinist. He also was called the "sometime State Geologist of Texas, and the most thorough and ideal crank of any age." An acquaintance who found his Hungarian-accented English difficult to understand, said that he was dark as an Indian.[37]

He was born in Bős in 1826; otherwise, little is known of his early life other than that he was "brought up" in the Austrian Imperial Artillery School, where he gained a thorough knowledge of all branches of ordnance. No comment survives concerning his participation in the Hungarian Revolution, but he was in Austin by the late 1850's and married Octavia Baker (1832-1899) in October 1860. They had four children, two of whom lived to maturity. Rössler lived in Austin for the remainder of his life except for brief periods spent in New York, Washington, D.C., and New Orleans. He died on October 20, 1891, in Washington.[38]

Rössler's first service in Texas was as an assistant and draftsman to Benjamin F. Shumard, chief geologist of Texas, in the first Geological and Agricultural Survey of Texas (called the Shumard Survey) in 1859. When the Civil War began he became a draftsman and clerk in charge of the Texas State Military Board's foundry. He was instrumental in saving some fossils and maps from the Shumard Survey when the geological survey rooms were turned into a percussion cap factory. After the war he sent some of the fossils to Vienna, where they were mistakenly mixed with similar fossils from Nebraska. This caused confusion in the paleontology world for years. Other fossils were also given to the United States National Museum and Columbia University.[39]

Rössler worked in the state cannon foundry in Austin throughout most of the war years, attempting to cast twelve-pound howitzers and six-pound cannons. Although he claimed experience and knowledge of ordnance and metallurgy, his "defective understanding of cannon-founding" was due to his failure to recognize the "critical importance of iron in Mexican copper" which was being used. "The traces of iron in the Mexican copper caused brittleness of the metal," and "when the cannons were test fired, they mostly exploded." His efforts to cast two six-pound guns and two twelve-pound howitzers for a field battery ended in failure, for the most part. Furthermore, Rössler spent much time attempting to discredit William DeRyee, the state chemist and head of the percussion cap factory. Although Rössler resigned his position on May 18, 1863, he was rehired in July of that year and continued his dispute with DeRyee until he was captured by federal forces in Louisiana in February 1865.[40]

Confederate war secrets apparently meant little to Rössler, for he informed his Union interrogators about the Texas Military Board and all ordnance sites in Texas, including the foundry and percussion cap factory in Austin. He also detailed the disposition of Confederate and Texas State Troops as of February 20, 1865. Soon thereafter Rössler entered federal service as an assistant engineer in the Engineering Department of the Military Division of the Gulf and proceeded to use his cartographical skills in making maps for the movement of Union forces into Texas in 1865. These included routes for the movement of occupation troops from Laredo to Ringgold Barracks, from Indianola to San Antonio, from San Antonio to Laredo, from San Antonio to El Paso, and from San Antonio to Brownsville.[41]

During the late 1860's Rössler worked in Washington, D.C., as a geologist for the United States Land Office but returned to Austin during the Radical Republican regime of Governor E.J. Davis. Rössler's article on "Texas Minerals" was published in the June 8, 1872, Dallas *Herald*, setting off a controversy, since it was largely taken from William DeRyee's report of 1868 concerning copper ore in Archer and surrounding counties made to the Texas Copper Mining and Manufacturing Company organized in 1864. Rössler was also chided for taking the results of S.B. Buckley's *First Annual Report of the Geological and Agricultural Survey* in 1874. He wrote his *Reply to the charges made by S.B. Buckley, State Geologist of Texas*, in the *Official Report of 1874 against Dr. B.F. Shumard and A.R. Roessler*. Buckley accused Rössler of stealing information on the copper ores of Archer County from the state geologist's office. Each accused the other of lying.[42]

"A.R. Roessler's Latest Map of the State of Texas" (1874) included information on mineral and agricultural districts. In addition, Rössler made 16 county maps during the 1870's. In 1876 his "New Map of the State of Texas Compiled from the Latest Authorities" identified him as a civil and mining engineer in New York.[43]

During his later career Rössler was secretary to the Texas Land and Immigration Company of New York and was also employed by the Texas Land and Copper Association. In 1872 he accompanied the latter's mineral exploring expedition to the areas including the Big and Little Wichita rivers, the Salt and Double mountains, and the upper reaches of the Brazos River in Texas. The route extended from Grayson County westward to Haskell County. Ill during much of the exploration, he submitted his observations on the value of the lands covered in his *Geological Report of the Property of the Texas Land and Copper Association* in December 1872. It was said that although he earned a reputation among the men as the "most thorough and ideal crank of any age," Rössler provided the exploration party with some "nice music in the quiet moonlight" with his violin.[44]

Family lore as well as contemporary sources often embellished the lives of Texas' Hungarian 48ers. Perhaps there is no more unlikely story than that of a self-proclaimed Hungarian nobleman who became an Episcopal priest in a small East Texas town. In fact, Imre Hamvasy (Emeric Hamvassy, Emir Hamvasy) was born in Székesfehérvár, Hungary, on April 19, 1820, to a middle-class Protestant family. Stories and accounts published about him in later life reported that he was educated by private tutors at his "noble" father's large estate and could read and write and was studying music by the age of five. Other tales added to his background: at twelve he played the organ for a Catholic service and four years later played a piano duet with composer Franz Liszt; he studied Italian in Venice, then entered the university in Buda, where he received his doctoral and legal degrees. The master of seven languages, natural sciences, and mathematics, Hamvasy had great taste and skill in music, drawing, and painting.[45]

A captain in his native city's police force, Hamvasy supposedly entered the Hungarian Diet at the age of 21 and was sent to Western Europe by Kossuth's Ministry of Finance to study different systems of banking and life insurance. This resulted in the establishment of a system of agricultural insurance as well as one ensuring a dowry for every child. Hamvasy, said to have been a radical republican, was swept into the national war for independence in 1848. Available sources reported that he joined a volunteer unit, quickly rose to the rank of major, and was wounded twice in battle. With the fall of the last Hungarian fortress, Komárom, in October 1849, Hamvasy found that he was wanted by the Austrian authorities, who had condemned him to death. Appealing to a fellow Mason for help, he slipped out of the country in a borrowed uniform and went to England.[46]

Hamvasy arrived in the United States late in 1849. He was one of the seven leading exiles invited by Congress to visit Washington, where they dined with President Zachary Taylor and were lauded in Congress in March 1850. Hamvasy and others also signed a "proclamation" deposing the Habsburgs as rulers of Hungary "in the name of the Hungarian people." The same year he replaced László Újházi as president of a Hungarian association which sought to raise funds for the immigrants in New York City. Hamvasy reportedly was chairman of the executive committee of exiles which welcomed Louis Kossuth on his American Grand Tour, 1851-1852. But making a living soon became a problem for the penniless exile. Family stories may have exaggerated his later activities. Although Hamvasy tried farming at the Hungarian colony at New Buda, Iowa, he returned to New York, where he operated a cigar store for a time and taught music and astronomy in Troy, New York. He later joined Albert Kayser, a fellow refugee, in establishing a boarding school for girls at Maysville, Kentucky, and then toured the nation with an opera troupe. Later Hamvasy and Kayser became private tutors and taught music in Louisiana. It was said that Hamvasy had accumulated $30,000 in gold, which he lost at the beginning of the Civil War by loaning it to a slaveowner who wished to move his property to Texas.[47]

Facts about the Texas career of the former soldier-of-fortune prove more reliable. Hamvasy tried grape growing in Smith County, Texas, and sheep ranching on the Brazos River before moving to Austin, where he taught music at Reverend R.J. Swancoat's Academy and also sold pianos. There he became the organist and choir director for St. David's Episcopal Church. In addition, he directed a "Grand Vocal and Instrumental Concert" in benefit of that parish on April 12, 1869, at Austin's City Hall. Hamvasy was converted to the Episcopal faith while boarding with the local rector, the Reverend Benjamin A. Rogers, and began studying for the ministry. He felt that "after all the adventures [he had] experienced, [he] was destined to become a man of God." He was licensed as a deacon and lay reader in 1870, was a candidate for Holy Orders in 1871, and was ordained as a priest in 1872 at the age of 52.[48]

The Reverend Hamvasy became the vicar of the Episcopal mission and the founding rector of Tyler's Christ Church parish in 1872. He built its first church and served the congregation until 1876. He also married Laura Paulson Haden, a widow 30 years his junior, and they had three children. The Hamvasys later served parishes in Palestine and Huntsville, Texas, and in Como, Mississippi, where Hamvasy retired in 1885. The family then returned to their small farm in Tyler, where they struggled to make a living during the last 15 years of his life. Hamvasy died on January 17, 1901, and was buried in Oakwood Cemetery. A street, Hamvasy Lane, was named in his honor, and a stained-glass window in Christ Church in Tyler also commemorated his role as its founder.[49]

Described as a "quiet, unassuming man of God, whose influence in the fields of music, statesmanship, education, and religion touched the lives of countless thousands on two continents," Hamvasy was remembered as "one of the best preachers in Texas." He drew upon his classical studies for sermons such as "Antiquity in Forms of Prayer," "Gate of Heaven," "God, Father of Us All," and "State and Free

Imre Hamvasy

Church." Admirers, including a U.S. senator, a judge, and a bishop, commented on the beauty of his sermons. A contemporary biographer wrote, "His sermons showed unmistakable evidences of a giant intellect having been subjected to the best and most refining influences." [50]

Albert Kayser of Tyler, a longtime friend and business associate of Imre Hamvasy in the United States, likewise fled his native land after the failure of the Revolution of 1848-1849. Born on August 11, 1827, at Versecz, he was educated in Temesvár and Vienna and became fluent in at least nine languages. As an exile in America he was recommended as "a patriotic citizen but an exile from Hungary" by Louis Kossuth on June 20, 1852, during the latter's tour of the United States. [51]

Whether Kayser knew Hamvasy before arriving in New York is unknown. Once there he made a living teaching music and languages, and formed a lifetime friendship with the future priest. During the 1850's they were associated in a variety of ventures before arriving in Texas. Kayser first visited Smith County in 1856 and settled there about the time of the Civil War. He married Mary L. Lawrence on November 23, 1868, and they raised a large family. He also established a private school and later taught in the Tyler public schools. Proficient in horticulture and known as a vintner, Kayser also opened a nursery. In 1875 he was elected president of the Patrons of Husbandry and met with the East Texas Fruit Growers Association in Tyler. [52]

Albert Kayser

Christ Church in Tyler, built by Reverend Imre Hamvasy

When the Reverend Hamvasy arrived in Tyler in 1872, Kayser resumed the close friendship, assisting in the founding of Christ Church parish and the building of the first church. Talented musically, he was a member of the first choir, was licensed as a lay reader on May 26, 1874, and served until 1880. With Hamvasy he shared a "love for home and dear ones across the sea" in Hungary. Albert Kayser died in Mineola, Texas, on November 8, 1890, and was buried in Tyler.[53]

One immigrant was noteworthy because of his familial association with Hungary's great leader, Louis Kossuth. The Civil War was barely over when Albert Ruttkay, described as "the sole surviving nephew of Kossuth, the renowned Hungarian patriot," opened a branch office of his New Orleans cotton brokerage firm in Galveston, Texas. There, and later in Houston, he was to continue doing business for nearly two decades. Identified as "a prominent cotton buyer and former director of the Houston Cotton Exchange," Ruttkay participated in the economic recovery of Texas after the collapse of the Confederacy. In the fall of 1865 his advertisement in a Galveston paper announced that A. Ruttkay and Company, general commission merchants, sought consignments of cotton, wool, and other produce for corresponding firms in New Orleans, New York, and Liverpool.[54]

Albert, the youngest of three sons of Louise (Lujza) Kossuth and Joseph Ruttkay, was born in Pest, Hungary, in 1841. Little of his childhood is known other than that he left his homeland with other members of the Kossuth family who sought safety in exile following the defeat of the Hungarian army in 1849. His mother and other relatives went first to Brussels, where she took care of her mother before following two sisters to the United States in 1853. To support her sons, she supposedly first ran a rural boardinghouse on the Hudson River and later moved to Brooklyn. It was at her farm on the Hudson that László Újházi and his family rested upon returning from Switzerland during the summer of 1858.[55]

All of Kossuth's nephews in America saw service during the Civil War. Ruttkay, along with his two brothers, Gábor and Louis, and his four Zsulavszky (Zulavsky) cousins, Ladislaus, Emil, Sigismund, and Casimir, the sons of Emilia Kossuth and Zsigmond Zsulavszky, joined the Union army with the outbreak of hostilities. Only Casimir was a disappointment to his family and adopted country. Having enrolled at Mound City, Kansas, on July 24, 1861, he served as adjutant in the 3rd and later the 10th Regiment of Kansas Infantry. Then, in

1862, Casimir B. Zsulavszky robbed an express office and was sentenced to the Kansas State Prison. He was later to become a partner in Albert's cotton commission firm in Texas.[56]

Albert Ruttkay's own military career apparently began in Tennessee, for by 1864 he was a captain in command of the 1st Battalion, 3rd U.S. Heavy Artillery Colored at Fort Quinby, Columbus, Kentucky. In March 1864, at age 22, he was promoted to the rank of major in the 1st Regiment of Florida Cavalry Colored stationed at Barrancas, Florida. There he was acting assistant signal officer of the District of West Florida in July and was detailed to collate important information concerning the movement of the enemy. In September 1864 Major Ruttkay served as assistant acting adjutant general at the headquarters of the District of West Florida. By April 1865 he was acting aide-de-camp to Major General Nathaniel P. Banks in New Orleans, where he resigned his commission and was discharged on May 31, 1865.[57]

Cotton was on Ruttkay's mind—the cotton held by planters and merchants in Texas during the war because of the blockade of the Gulf Coast. With money he inherited from someone in Hungary, Ruttkay started his business in New Orleans and included his discredited cousin, Casimir Zsulavszky, probably by family request. Ruttkay's agents toured eastern Texas to buy stored cotton, for he sent a telegram from Galveston to Major General C.C. Andrews, commanding the District of Houston, stating: "My agent Mr. DeLaunay bought cotton at Houston. Your Provost Marshal seized it on suspicion of its being Confederate Cotton. . . . Please have it released as I have freight engaged for it for New Orleans." He signed as "Late Major 1st Florida Cavalry, U.S."[58]

Although Ruttkay and Co. maintained an office in Galveston, none of the principals lived there. Galveston's 1870 business directory listed their office at 179 E. Strand. Later Ruttkay did move to Texas and was listed in the city directory of Houston beginning in 1882-1883, identified as a cotton buyer.

During the next few years he lived in boardinghouses and kept offices at Main and Commerce. He continued business as Ruttkay and Co. with G. Horton and Samuel McNeill as partners. When Ruttkay died on November 13, 1888, after a "protracted illness," his widow, Laura W., and possibly their three minor sons, Louis I., Gabriel, and Paul, were also in Houston. Ruttkay left little other than two insurance policies. After the estate was probated in Harris County, Laura and her sons returned to Greenwich, Connecticut, to live near her relatives. In 1896-1897 she was operating a millinery shop in Greenwich.[59]

With Ruttkay's death, the last of Kossuth's nephews in America was gone. The Houston Cotton Exchange and the Board of Trade passed a resolution of respect in honor of Albert Ruttkay, stating that he had been "a zealous, intelligent, and useful member." Further, he was remembered as "Always courteous, deferential and generous, open, honorable, and manly. He was the very embodiment of chivalrous manhood, and a refined and polished gentleman." Members of both groups attended Ruttkay's funeral as a body. In New York the aging members of the Hungarian and American Veterans of 1848 and 1861 took notice of his death, which was reported in the local Hungarian paper, the *Amerikai Nemzetőr* [American National Guardian], which called him "our beloved friend and highly respected soldier."[60]

· ——————— ·

A Gravestone for Imre Szabad

In Hungary Imre (Emeric, Emery) Szabad served as a secretary in the War Department during the revolution. He then fled to England, served in Philip Figyelmessy's Hungarian Legion in Italy, then came to the United States. On June 16, 1862, he was commissioned a captain in the New York Volunteers in the Army of the Potomac and was aide-de-camp as inspector of outposts. Szabad was captured by the Confederates at Licking Run, Virginia, on October 27, 1863, and sent to the infamous Libby Prison, but was later exchanged. In February 1865 he was adjutant to General G.K. Warren and was rapidly breveted to major, lieutenant colonel (March 13, 1865), and colonel (March 26, 1865) for bravery in the siege of Petersburg, Virginia. There he was wounded in the neck and right shoulder and was mustered out of the army on October 28, 1865.[61]

Born about 1828, Szabad, who gave his occupation as writer, wrote five books, including a history of Hungary, a biography of Ulysses S. Grant, and a discussion of war, all published prior to 1868 in Europe and the United States. In September 1864, while in the U.S. Army, he was initiated into the Continental Masonic Lodge in New York City and thereafter carried a Masonic traveling certificate for the remainder of his life. The wounds he received during the war prevented him from doing manual labor and even from writing. As late as 1885 two friends in Laredo, Texas, declared that Szabad could only write with a pencil a few minutes at a time.[62]

Because of his wounds, Szabad received a federal patronage position as assistant collector of customs at the Port of Galveston and was stationed at Laredo on the U.S.-Mexican border about 1880. During the 1880's he acquired property in Bexar, Kendall, Kerr, Webb, Wilson, and other counties. Later, he lived for a number of years in Boerne, where he died at the age of 69 on March 13, 1894, of a "dangerous and alarming malady." In a deathbed will Szabad directed that his executor erect a monument on his grave, pay his debts, and publish his manuscripts. Although it took 93 years, the Kendall Masonic Lodge joined with the local Veterans of Foreign Wars and the Boerne Area Historical Preservation Society in honoring part of his request. A gravestone was dedicated on August 14, 1987.[63]

• ──────────── •

Texas attracted other colorful characters, and Dr. Arthur Wadgymár fit the bill perfectly. According to stories handed down in his family, Wadgymár (Vadgymár?) lived a life of epic proportions. He was a veteran of the military services of four nations, and he practiced medicine on two continents, Europe and North America. Wadgymár was born in Debrecen (one source said Czackaturen) on May 26, 1824, the son of Belezar and Bianca von Wadgymár. Nothing is known of his early life other than that he received his education in Pest and his medical and surgical training in Vienna, Austria, 1839-1847. The next year he joined the Hungarian army as a surgeon in the 35th Battalion. With the end of the revolution, he left Hungary and enlisted as a surgeon in the Dutch navy, 1850-1852. Later Dr. Wadgymár was also a military surgeon in the Crimean War, 1854-1856.[64]

Arthur Wadgymár's departure from Hungary, according to family stories, was anything but usual. One reported that he was in love with a young ballerina whom his handsome father also loved. They fought a duel, and young Wadgymár killed his father. He then fled to America because his brother swore to avenge their father's death. By the mid-1850's he was practicing medicine in Louisville, Kentucky, when an epidemic broke out. A local convent was being used as a tem-

Some members of the Wadgymár family — seated, *Arthur and his wife, Maria Theresa Drewes;* standing, from left, *Angenor, Arthur Jr., and Louis, Carrizo Springs, 1880*

porary hospital. There Wadgymár met a young novice and fell in love. She climbed over the broken-glass-topped convent wall, and they eloped, married, and had one son. Tragedy soon struck, however, when his wife was washed overboard and drowned in the Ohio River while on a boating party. Their son supposedly was raised by his maternal grandparents, who directed him toward the priesthood. According to family legend, the son met his father in Galveston in 1873 and again in San Diego, Texas, when Wadgymár spent several months one summer attending a murder trial as an expert witness. They played chess for several days before Wadgymár's son identified himself.[65]

Wadgymár's second wife was Maria Theresa Drewes of Bredenborn, Prussia, who had come to America to visit a sister in Marietta, Ohio. Arthur married her there on September 2, 1858, but they quickly left for parts farther west, for he heard that his brother was in close pursuit. Tracing their movements for the next decade is possible by noting the places of birth of their eleven children (only four of whom lived to adulthood): Louisville, Kentucky; Chattanooga, Tennessee; and St. Louis, Missouri.[66]

Dr. Wadgymár was commissioned in Confederate service as second lieutenant of ordnance in the Provisional Army of Tennessee on September 21, 1861, and worked at the Confederate States Laboratory in Nashville. One biographer stated that he was also an army surgeon in the Memphis South Artillery in Chattanooga during 1862-1863. Nothing further is known of his military career, and the Civil War proved to have been his last war. Thereafter he devoted his life to medicine and teaching.[67]

In 1865 Wadgymár was practicing medicine in southern Illinois and in St. Louis, as well as teaching chemistry and botany at a local pharmaceutical college. He became a professor of chemistry and botany in 1866-1867 at St. Louis's Humboldt Medical College, where he published papers in medical journals. One such was on "Trichina spiralis," which described the parasite's origins and development in muscles and the disease trichinosis, in the St. Louis *Medical Reporter*.[68]

In 1873 the Wadgymár family suddenly left for Texas. An interesting family story gave the reason for Wadgymár's move. While in St. Louis he and one of his students "acquired" the body of a recently deceased young man in order to study anatomy. As their dissection began, the deceased suddenly came out of his coma. "Grateful for his resurrection, the young man agreed to postpone his reunion with his family until the Wadgymárs were safely embarked on the morning steamer for New Orleans." The story did not relate which direction Wadgymár's student and fellow graverobber took.[69]

Although Wadgymár considered practicing medicine in New Orleans, he decided that there were no satisfactory opportunities there and so came to Texas, where he settled at Five Mile Coleto Creek near Meyersville in DeWitt County. In 1877 he was living in Castroville, where he wrote a report on diseases of cattle and horses. He published an article on agriculture in Medina and surrounding counties in 1880 and was said to have been interested in the flora and entomology of southwest Texas, as well as botany, chemistry, and microscopy. During the late 1870's and early 1880's, Wadgymár was reported to have also lived in Cuero and San Antonio, before settling permanently in Carrizo Springs in 1882.[70]

Dr. Arthur Wadgymár made his home in South Texas for the remainder of his life and may have been the first physician in Carrizo Springs. He built the first drugstore and his home there in 1882. According to a family story, there was a built-in cabinet alongside the dining room which concealed a pump to supply artesian water for the dining table. Another story told of how Mrs. Wadgymár stood in the front doorway to prevent law officers from removing her piano to satisfy a judgment against her husband imposed by the local court for prescribing liberal amounts of alcoholic beverages in what was a dry county. Stories were told of how he, as the defendant, prevailed by causing the disappearance of the original complaint until the statute of limitations ran out. No one offered an explanation of what happened to the original complaint.[71]

Wadgymár and his wife died of influenza in February 1899, in San Antonio and Carrizo Springs, respectively. Critically ill, he had been taken to a San Antonio hospital (one family account said a mental institution) where he died. A terrible sleet, snow, and ice storm prevented the return of his body to Carrizo Springs, and he was buried in Cotulla. Since no minister was available because of the bad weather, Texas Ranger Captain Rodgers conducted his services, attended by the Commissioners' Court, which adjourned for the funeral. Thus ended the career of one of Texas' most colorful figures.[72]

Others of the approximately 4,000 exiled Hungarian 48ers in America may have lived in Texas. László Újházi's idea of keeping them together in a cohesive ethnic colony proved impractical in Texas as well as in Iowa. As Louis Kossuth foresaw during the early 1850's, the émigrés who scattered across America soon assimilated, and the former noblemen, government officials, and soldiers of the revolution were forced by necessity to adapt to new occupations.

Interestingly, their experiences in Texas were little different from those of other mid-19th century immigrants who succeeded after a few hard years in finding comfort and security. Together they helped civilize the state. With the death of the last of the 48ers in the early 20th century, the pioneer generation which had fled Austrian oppression of their homeland passed into history. Their Texas descendants maintained family heritages and the stories of their ancestors who came from Hungary.[73]

167

CHAPTER SEVEN

"A real adventure and challenge"

The Great Economic Immigration

The stories of individual 48ers and their children typified the first small wave of Hungarian migration to Texas. A much greater migration followed, beginning in the last two decades of the 19th century. No longer predominantly political refugees, the new emigrants arrived at a time when railroads reached throughout the state, including the Panhandle, South Plains, and Trans-Pecos regions, and opportunity for economic advancement existed everywhere. Choice of occupations was not limited to agriculture but covered a wide spectrum as Texas' economy and technology developed. Towns grew into cities where enterprising immigrants found employment in commerce and service industries, railroads, and the professions.

With the disappearance of the Indians and the buffalo from northwestern Texas and the closing of the frontier by 1890, the development of transportation was vital to the Texas economy. The state population numbered 212,592 in 1850, when exiles of the Hungarian Revolution began arriving, and no railroads existed in the state. By 1880 Texas had more than 1.5 million inhabitants and 3,244 miles of track. Within another decade 5,410 additional miles of track reached into all parts of the state, and the population had increased to almost 2.25 million. By the outbreak of World War I, Texas had over three million citizens.[1]

Steven Bela Vardy in *The Hungarian-Americans* emphasizes that the great mass migration of Eastern and Southern Europeans to America during the 34 years prior to 1914 included a group of Hungarians entirely different from those who had come earlier. The new emigrants, estimated at more than 1.5 million, were mainly peasants and workers who sought economic opportunity in the mines, factories, and bustling industrial and commercial cities of the American Northeast. Many wished to accumulate money in order to return to their native Hungary and resume farming, albeit on a larger scale than before. The great majority, however, settled permanently in the United States.

Although the Magyars represented about half of the population of Hungary, they made up only a little more than 30 percent of Hungarians emigrating to the United States. The remainder were Hungary's minorities: Croats, Germans, Rumanians, Ruthenians, Serbians, Slovaks, and a few other small groups. In addition to economic motivations, the minority peoples came seeking political and social freedoms forbidden them by the Magyar-dominated Hungarian government, which attempted to magyarize the minorities. The Magyars, in any case, were more reluctant to emigrate since "leaving their homeland . . . [was] a new and strange idea," whereas, "because of their different historical traditions, ways of life, and economy," some of the minorities were "more prone to periodic . . . migrations." Also, the Hungarian government sought to impede Magyar emigration in order to strengthen their small majority. Vardy gives a detailed picture of the numbers and motives of the emigrants in this period.[2]

Texas was not a prime destination for those who came to America during this time. Still largely agricultural, its small industrial base and low wages were not attractive to those who debarked in northeastern ports. It was farther away from ports of entry and from America's industrial heartland, where Hungarians concentrated. States such as Ohio, Pennsylvania, and New Jersey had factories, mills, and mines offering higher wages. A small percentage of Hungarians who entered America prior to World War I did, however, find homes in the Lone Star State. Census takers reported that 1,351 Texas residents claimed Hungarian nativity or ancestry in 1910.[3] Most, or 1,295, lived in 27 counties which reported ten or more Hungarian-born and children of Hungarian-born. The greatest concentrations were in the metropolitan counties of Bexar (San Antonio), Dallas, El Paso, Galveston, Harris (Houston), and Tarrant (Fort Worth). Ten or more lived in Anderson,

Bell, Cooke, DeWitt, Ellis, Erath, Falls, Fayette, Fort Bend, Goliad, Gonzales, Jack, Jefferson, Johnson, Navarro, Palo Pinto, Smith, Travis, Wharton, and Wheeler counties. Of the 1,295 in those 27 counties, 1,246 reported their Hungarian ethnic identification: Magyar (515), German (283), Slovak (157), Croatian (93), and Bohemian (66), although the latter, the Czechs, came from the Austrian portion of the Austro-Hungarian Empire. Other minorities, numbering less than 30, which were reported to the census takers included Moravians, Jews, Serbians, Rumanians, Poles, Russians, and even Bulgarians. The unfamiliarity of the various census takers with Eastern European minorities undoubtedly contributed to significant error in identification, especially in the case of Hungarian Jews who identified themselves as Hungarian

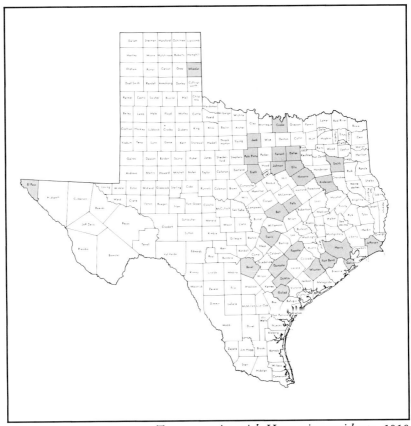

Texas counties with Hungarian residents, 1910

Magyars. They concentrated in Houston, San Antonio, and Dallas, as well as in smaller cities such as Austin and El Paso.

Only ten Hungarian Texans in 1910 could be identified as professionals: a geologist, an osteopath, a doctor of medicine, a lawyer, two civil engineers, an Orthodox church cantor, a veterinarian, and two publicly elected local officials. Others became businessmen, craftsmen, or day laborers in Texas' cities. The remainder lived in rural counties and reported a variety of occupations. For example, Slovak and Bohemian Hungarians farmed in Bell, Fayette, Fort Bend, Gonzales, Wharton, and Wheeler counties. German Hungarians concentrated in Goliad and Harris counties. Magyars clustered on farms in Ellis, Navarro, Jack, and Fort Bend counties. Two other interesting groups included Croatian coal miners at Thurber in Erath County and Croatian, Bulgarian, and Rumanian dockworkers in Galveston.

Although farming was the least-desired occupation of Hungarian immigrants, a suggestion was made to settle Hungarians as tenant cotton farmers in northwest Texas. In the Panhandle railroads and land developers vied for people to fill empty land along new railway lines. One plan involved the Wichita Valley Railway Company. Early in 1910 New York realtor A.C. Green initiated correspondence with the Great Northern Railway Company and the Chicago, Burlington, and Quincy Railroad Company, which eventually led him to the Fort Worth and Denver City Railroad Company and the Wichita Valley lines.

Green represented a "lady of noble Hungarian birth" who was "interested in the welfare of the many peasant Hungarians who emigrate to this country, who are good farmers." The unnamed lady felt that "from a moral, physical, and financial standpoint" it was better to settle them on farms in the West than in the manufacturing and mining centers of the Northeast. As a result, they would become better citizens. She wanted to buy 500 acres of good land in order to establish a colony of Hungarians as cotton farmers. Initially she wanted to settle ten immigrant families and to obtain the services of a practical farmer to teach them to grow cotton.

Green's inquiry was forwarded to the Wichita Valley Railway Company, which was opening a new line from Stanford to Spur, Texas, where S.M. Swenson and Sons and others in the Spur Syndicate were opening about 400,000 acres to settlement. The "lady of noble Hungarian birth" must have been disappointed, however, for her colonization plans in northwestern Texas came to naught.[4]

A more successful attempt to settle immigrants from Hungary, including its minorities, involved the Rock Island Railroad, which laid track across the Texas Panhandle during the early years of the 20th century. Prospective immigrants to fill the land were given free tickets by the company to inspect railroad property along its lines, and a group of Hungarian-born Slovaks from the Chicago area took up the offer. As a result, the immigrants decided to bring their families to the High Plains of Texas.

Sam and Kristina Pakan,
1897

Pakan has been proclaimed as the only Lutheran Slovak community in Texas and the last immigrant settlement in the state. Located in a rural area northwest of Shamrock in Wheeler County in the Panhandle, Pakan was named for one of its settlers. Sam Pakan attracted about 30 Hungarian Slovak families which had recently arrived in Chicago from their native Slovakia, then part of the kingdom of Hungary. There they composed 10.7 percent of the population (and formed 20.2 percent of those who left Hungary prior to 1914). Originally called Slavonia, the community was also briefly called Nitra. But, because Sam Pakan gave two acres of land for the community school, it became known as the Pakan Community.

Both Sam Pakan and his future wife, Kristina, were born in 1875 in Upper Hungary, and both were orphaned young. At age 13 Sam left his native Myjava for Vienna to learn a trade, and coincidentally

Kristina went there to become a maid. Sam emigrated to Chicago in 1892 to join friends, and Kristina joined the migration in search of a better life. They met in Chicago and were married November 22, 1897. After a series of jobs Sam and Kristina sought a new life away from the bustle of Chicago.[5]

* ———————— *

Why the Slovaks of Pakan Community Emigrated

Edward Pakan, the son of Sam Pakan, was born in the Pakan Community in 1913. He later explained why his family and other Slovaks had come to America. His story reflected the national aspirations which arose during the 19th century among the Slovaks who had been part of the Hungarian kingdom for a thousand years. Anti-Hungarian propaganda, passed on to the American-born generations, often ignored the economic motivation of Slovak emigration to America.

Most of the people in the Pakan Community, including the founder, were of Slovak origin. The Slovak people had lived in their European homeland for many centuries when the Magyars conquered them in the battle of Pressburg [Pozsony in Hungarian; Bratislava in Slovak] in A.D. 907. The Magyars bent their efforts towards the forcible conversion of all racial groups living in their conquered territory into one nation and one culture by enforcing a policy of denationalization of all non-Hungarian racial groups. In order to achieve this end, the Hungarians used a variety of means. One was to eliminate all languages except Hungarian. Once that language had achieved prominence, the pressure was immediately applied to suppress all other groups. Thus, little by little, the Slovak people lost their liberties until it became a prison offense even to whistle a Slovak melody on the streets of their native land.

Finally came the ultimate attempt to bring about the extinction of the Slovak people—the deportation of the Slovak children to the part of the empire known until recently as Yugoslavia, under the pretext that the lot of the children would be improved. The Slovak newspapers and libraries were destroyed. The people were forced off the land they cultivated and were heavily taxed until they were reduced to the level of slaves.

Under these conditions the people found it impossible to exist, and, in the middle of the 19th century, they began their exodus to the "Promised Land" of America.[6]

* ———————— *

174

Pakan Community residents, 1914

During his first trip to Texas in 1904, Sam Pakan bought land in Wheeler County for himself and some of his relatives. Though some families moved to the Panhandle that year, Pakan brought his wife and three children over a year later. They encouraged still other friends to join them in Texas to grow corn, kafir, cane, and cotton on the virgin prairie where grass had previously grown six feet high.[7]

Houses and farm buildings were built, wells dug, fences strung, fields plowed, orchards and vegetable gardens planted, and farm animals purchased. "None of these people knew anything about farming" on America's Great Plains, since most had come from towns or villages where tiny pieces of land were cultivated by hand. As a result, they found "plowing the prairies and getting their first crops in to be a real adventure and challenge." The women too faced new problems in the settlement; for example, cooking on wood stoves without a source of wood taught them to use cow chips and other fuel substitutes. Additional hardships they faced in the Panhandle included dust storms, droughts, and poor crops, as well as "illness, snake bite, black leg, shinnery poisoning, etc."[8]

By the Hit-and-Miss Method

Edward Pakan recalled the first farming efforts of his father and other immigrants in the Pakan Community:

> There were hardships, to be sure. None of these people were farmers by trade. Almost everything was done by hit-and-miss method. Many times there were misses. For instance, some of the people planted peanuts in their gardens, which produced a good crop. They then went into it on a larger scale. But, when they harvested, they had to dig up the soil in the fall time, leaving it loose and bare for the winter. The high winds then blew their soil away. Another example: Mr. Pakan shipped heavy draft horses from Chicago, thinking that such horses would get a lot of work done. But they were not used to the heavy work in the heat, and he soon lost them. Gradually, he learned to do his field work with mules, which even tho[ugh] much slower, were also much hardier. He kept a team of horses for faster purposes. He had a team named "Chiko and Peter." They were spirited. He liked to hitch those to his wagon, or buggy, when he had to run to town. They did this much faster than the mules would have. Often they had too much pep and nearly ran away with him and the wagon. They caused much excitement and were the talk of the community and the town.[9]

The families who followed Sam Pakan to Texas settled on nearby land, since he had not been able to obtain one solid block for them. In spite of their difficulties in the beginning, Pakan's settlers developed a sense of neighborliness, meeting each Sunday in private homes for Lutheran services as well as to exchange news, visit, eat, and sing folk songs. All had arrived in America between 1890 and 1905, and spoke Slovak at first.[10]

Helping each other at planting and harvesting time, the men exchanged labor to their mutual advantage, although an attempt by Pakan to organize the farmers into a cooperative for buying supplies wholesale and selling produce by boxcar loads failed. A community corn sheller was purchased, and the men worked together, while the women gathered to prepare meals for them. Wheat threshing and cattle branding also brought the men together each year.[11]

The Corn Cob a Great Blessing

Kristina Pakan waited in Chicago until the birth of her third child, refusing to move into the "wilderness" of the Texas Panhandle where no doctor was available. In May 1905 she and her sister-in-law, Elizabeth, with their four children, followed their husbands to Pakan:

> One can visualize the anxiety of these two women as they chugged along on that Rock Island train towards the unknown. With four children between them, they had their hands full. The journey seemed endless. Both women had learned to love their homes in Chicago [where] they had many friends. All this was left behind. Both women found flat-roofed cabins waiting [in Texas] for them. Kristina was somewhat prepared for this. She also had the advantage of having close neighbors. . . . But Elizabeth was separated by a distance of two miles . . . separated from view of everybody by the small hills that are typical of the locality. She found living there very lonely and had a hard time adjusting. . . . Here they found themselves out in the wide open spaces, not even a telephone to keep in touch with each other, no gas to cook with, no electricity. Even the wood which they

The Sam Pakan family, 1921—Kristina is holding their first grandchild.

[needed] to burn in their cook stoves was scarce. They followed the plows to pick out shinnery roots for burning. After the first crop they found the corn cob a great blessing. [12]

• ———————————————— •

Not all of these families stayed in Wheeler County. After World War I land prices rose, and some sold their land and moved back East, having found conditions on the farms too difficult for them. Others went to nearby towns, counties, or states. With the creation of the new state of Czechoslovakia in 1918, some returned to live in their newly independent homeland. It was said that those who remained were mainly relatives of the Pakan family. Sam Pakan died in 1939; Kristina lived until 1971. Pakan still exists as a farming and stock-raising community on the Texas High Plains. [13]

Thrashing crew on Paul Macina's farm, Pakan Community, c. 1911

Immigrant Children Go to School

One of the first goals of Pakan's immigrants was the establishment of a school for their children. The men obtained lumber, and money was raised for the purpose. Ed Pakan reported:

. . . the first teacher was hired. . . . She found herself with a group of children who did not speak a word of English, and she could not understand the Slovak. . . . Most of the teachers who followed seemed to enjoy this unique experience, even tho[ugh] there is no doubt that it must have been difficult. Those very first years every child was of Slovak parents. The older ones, . . . born in Chicago, had learned a few words of English, and they helped interpret for the teacher and the rest of the pupils. Later, Paul Stauffer entered and was the only non-Slovak child in school. It didn't seem to bother or puzzle him. He simple accepted it without a question. Still later, more and more non-Slovaks arrived, and they found it very strange to be among children who either didn't know any English, or spoke it laboriously.

All the Slovak children worshipped in the Lutheran faith, and this was another novelty to these "visitors." And they also thought it was strange how these foreign people enjoyed their community life. There were few Sundays when they didn't get together for a social hour. Many picnics were held during the summertime. Never a 4th of July [passed] without an elaborate celebration, with flags, singing, ice cream, and fried chicken. All this struck these "visitors" as very clannish, and they started referring to them as "a tribe," whose chief was Mr. [Sam] Pakan. All kinds of tales grew out of this, which aggravated the Slovak children, and many feuds developed.

No one knows how it came about, but it wasn't too long before the Slovak children felt snubbed because they still spoke with a distinct accent. . . . The Slovak children would irritate their non-Slovak schoolmates by speaking to each other in Slovak. This brought complaints to the teacher by the non-Slovaks, who quite understandably said they were purposely being left out of things because they didn't understand what was going on. . . . To try and solve this problem, the teachers would forbid the use of the Slovak language on the school grounds! . . . However, the Slovak children were not to be outdone. They simply walked out into the middle of the road and talked Slovak to their hearts' content.

When one teacher saw this development, he decreed that no students would leave the school grounds during school hours. . . . The Slovak children put their heads together and after lengthy deliberations concluded that even though they were forbidden to talk in Slovak on the school grounds, this in no way prohibited them from writing notes to each other in Slovak. . . . Intercepting one of these notes, . . . the teacher simply shook his head in obvious despair. Apparently he was concluding that he'd have to get up pretty early in the morning in order to outmaneuver these Slovak children.[14]

• ——————————— •

Pakan's Slovaks were not the only Hungarian immigrants to adapt themselves to farming in Texas. Others responded to word of mouth or to letters praising the fertile lands found in Texas. By the turn of the century, a score or more of Magyar families found their way directly from Hungary to the blackland farm belt of North Central Texas near Dallas.[15]

They settled in Ellis and Navarro counties and became cotton farmers, and, although cotton was a crop new to them, they learned its cultivation from their American neighbors. Some families bought land; others rented on the traditional third or fourth system (for one third of the corn and grain or one fourth of the cotton before deductions). By 1910 nine families were farming in Navarro County, and twelve worked in Ellis County. The Emory Pinters, who came in 1888, were the earliest to arrive. Other Catholic families followed almost yearly until the outbreak of World War I.[16]

Many children of the immigrants intermarried with other Magyar families in North Texas, yet no ethnic cohesion was evident. No churches, clubs, or mutual benefit societies were established. Some first-generation American Hungarians found local conditions unsatisfactory and moved to farms in other Texas counties or in Oklahoma. After the depression year of 1923, many went to Detroit to work in the automobile factories. A few repatriated to Hungary because they disliked the Texas climate and its accompanying hardships.[17]

The story of John and Christine Botka Nagy was typical of other Magyar couples who learned to grow cotton. John Nagy was born in Bácsföldvár, Hungary, March 5, 1845, and married Christine (Krisztina) Botka (born in 1853) on January 16, 1871. All of their nine children were born in Bácsföldvár, but the first three daughters died young. John completed twelve years of military service as a sergeant in the Emperor and King of Hungary's Royal Count Coronini 6th Hungarian Infantry Division and the Hungarian Royal Infantry Division in 1879.

John Nagy

Christine Botka Nagy

John and Christine Nagy at Millett, c. 1919

181

Then he became a postmaster. Three months later, on March 5, 1879, his first son, Joseph, was born. Eighteen years later Joseph was the first of the family to emigrate to Texas—he came to Ellis County in 1897 with the Frank Szénásy family (part of this family later spelled their name Szénási).[18]

John Nagy landed at the port of Galveston on October 14, 1900, with three of his children and was soon followed by his wife and the remaining children. The Nagys first settled at Telico and later near Rice, Texas, where they farmed cotton. John eventually retired and moved to Ennis, where he died in 1929. Christine lived until 1937.[19]

Many years later two of John and Christine Nagy's grandchildren recalled their grandparents. Their grandmother came from a noble Catholic family of flax farmers, who looked down on John as being beneath her social standing. As a result, he educated himself after the birth of his first three children and became a respected postmaster. In Texas John kept a small vineyard on his farm and made his own wine. Christine, a rather stern and humorless person, brought her hand-made linens and goosedown comforters and pillows to Texas. She did not allow her grandchildren to eat cookies and play in her clean house, which was decorated with fine carpets (covered with cotton-sack runners) and a large brass bed, which she touched only when wearing white gloves. Neither John nor Christine ever learned English but relied on their bachelor son, Mike, for translating and conducting business with their American neighbors.[20]

The oldest son, Joseph Nagy, met his future wife, Elizabeth Szénásy, in Hungary and accompanied her and her family to Texas. He arrived at the Port of New York on November 21, 1897, and made his declaration of intent to become a citizen in Ellis County in 1902. On April 21, 1898, he and Elizabeth were married in Ellis County and eventually had ten children, eight of whom lived to adulthood. Joe rented land and farmed cotton, first at Telico, Ellis County, and then for eight years on his own land near Corsicana in Navarro County. A son later recalled that Joe hired 110 cotton choppers at one time and leased prisoners from the Navarro County Farm to operate 20 walking cultivators. Elizabeth cooked the noon meal for the workers. For one cotton crop Joe received a check for $50,000 and used it to establish himself on land near Dilley in LaSalle County in 1918.[21]

There the Joe Nagy family settled on the 4,500-acre Nagy-Witherspoon Ranch, in which Joe owned part interest with C.L. Wither-

Elizabeth Szénásy Nagy (left) and her husband, Joe, in front of their house on the Ellis-Navarro county line, with Bessie Levay and unidentified children

The Szénási family in Török Bocse, Hungary—men standing, from left, *Frank Jr., George, Joe;* seated, *Frank and Ágnes Kormos Szénási*

Joe Nagy farm at Rice—front, from left, *three farmhands, Will, Joe Jr. with puppy, Joe Sr., Julia, Elizabeth, Christine, Mary, and Annie;* on horseback, center, *Jess Nagy and two other farm workers*

Joe Nagy family at Millett—front, from left, *Elizabeth, John, Louis, Frank, and Joe Sr.;* back, *Will, Joe Jr., Mary, and Annie*

Annie Nagy surrounded by onions drying for shipment, Millett, c. 1920

Crates of onions being loaded for shipment at the Nagy-Witherspoon Ranch near Dilley, c. 1920

spoon, a prominent San Antonio oil man. Nagy was manager of the development of this winter garden property as a ranch and for irrigated and dry-land farming of cotton, corn, feed, and vegetables such as onions and spinach, as well as plums and oranges. Twelve hundred acres were farmed. In addition, cattle, horses, sheep, and Poland China hogs were raised. Nagy also owned his own 500-acre irrigated farm and other ranch land near Dilley, and he served as a director of the Dilley State Bank. The Nagy-Witherspoon Ranch was considered a showplace. Then, at the height of his achievements, Joe Nagy was accidentally killed on March 26, 1929, when he was knocked from a 36-foot windmill tower by the rotating fan. Elizabeth lived with her children until her death on May 17, 1966.[22]

An Immigrant Views
Galveston's Devastation in 1900

Fifteen-year-old Annie Nagy arrived with her family at the Port of Galveston on October 14, following the disastrous hurricane of September 8, 1900, which destroyed much of the city and left more than 6,000 persons dead and missing. In 1961 she recalled her first experiences in Texas after leaving her native Bácsföldvár on the Tisza River in Hungary. The Nagys were on their way to Ellis County, where a brother, Joe, had rented a farm for them in the Telico community.

Because of news of the Galveston hurricane, their departure from Europe was delayed. Leaving the port of Bremen on September 13, they sailed for America. After unloading sugar at Baltimore the ship waited for the water to recede in Galveston. They arrived on October 14, 1900; once there, they could find nothing to eat but bananas, which they thought were some kind of long cantaloupes. Devastation was all around them — "on top of the railroad station there were bedsteads and other furniture that . . . had been washed there by the flood."

Later that day the Nagy family left for Ennis by train. "Between Galveston and Houston on each side of the train tracks, which were higher than other terrain, there was water, and many dead cows and other animals were on top of trees, along with the boughs and much debris."

As the train neared Ennis Annie recalled seeing cotton fields for the first time. She thought at first that they were fields of little trees. Annie Nagy (Mrs. Mike) Czákó lived in Ellis County until she died in 1963.[23]

• ⎯⎯⎯⎯⎯⎯⎯⎯⎯⎯ •

Elizabeth Nagy's Rétes

In 1951, at the age of 71, Elizabeth Szénásy (Mrs. Joe) Nagy revealed her recipe for making *rétes*, a Hungarian pastry, to a newspaper in Alice, Texas. Proud to say that she had "never bought a loaf of bread in her life," Mrs. Nagy, who was born in Hungary in 1885, added that "I made all my lard and noodles." Similar to German strudel, the Hungarian *rétes* were made by stretching the dough instead of rolling it out. Consisting of flour, leaf lard, and salt mixed with cold water, the dough had to be worked thoroughly and then stretched, without breaks, until it was paper thin, or large enough to cover a dining table. Filling made of just about anything, except runny jelly, could be used. Mrs. Nagy's favorite was a mixture of ground pecans, sugar, and fine breadcrumbs, but peaches, apricots, or apples could be added. Then, with the tablecloth beneath used for shaping, the thin dough was rolled into sausage shapes which were immediately browned in the oven. The crust was flaky, and the *rétes* could be kept for days without becoming tough.

Mrs. Nagy also raised her own poppies and ground the seeds in a coffee grinder. She mixed poppy seeds with sugar, pecans, and raisins for her *rétes*.[24]

• ⎯⎯⎯⎯⎯⎯⎯⎯⎯⎯ •

A grandson of Joe Nagy, also named Joe, became president of the 48,000-member State Bar of Texas in 1987. A native of Pearsall, he grew up in Hebbronville and then earned a degree at Texas A&M University. After working in the soil conservation service in Carrizo Springs and in a livestock auction ring in his hometown, he did military service in Korea, where he was wounded in 1952. Thereafter Nagy sold insurance in San Antonio and Alice, and worked with his father, also named Joe Nagy, in a clothing store in Pearsall before taking his LL.M.

at the University of Texas School of Law. He practiced civil law in Lubbock for 38 years before becoming president of the State Bar and was also an adjunct professor of law at Texas Tech University.[25]

Individual Hungarians found opportunity in Texas in the late 19th century, but perhaps none had a more exceptional career than Ignatius G. Gaál, who was involved in a famous gun battle at his home in Ysleta (also known as the Ysleta Riot) in 1890. Although his political enemies sought to kill him, Gaál, whose motto was "Do Right and Fear No Man," survived the incident. Who was this controversial figure, and how did the shootout come about? Why did the El Paso *Times* call him "a Hungarian of the school of anarchy"?

Ignatius George Gaál was born in Szomolnok, Szepes County, Hungary, in 1843 and studied medicine under Dr. Jacob Heidel in Vienna before emigrating to the United States in 1865. For the next 15 years he followed a variety of careers which took him as far as California. After a short time in New York, he worked for a furniture factory in Cleveland, Ohio, peddled through northern Ohio in a wagon, and opened a wholesale liquor store in Cleveland called Gaál & Company. By 1869 he was farming on the Kansas prairie; two years later he moved to St. Louis, Missouri. Thereafter he followed the railroad west to Sacramento, California, where he worked for the Central Pacific Railroad, invested in real estate, and married Francisca Rademacher. In 1880 he moved to El Paso, Texas.[26]

Once in El Paso, Gaál bought 6,000 acres of Rio Grande Valley land. During the next few years he was in charge of setting up the shops of the Southern Pacific Railroad, which reached El Paso (then known as Franklin) in 1881, and he also worked for a furniture company. Then, in 1883, he moved his family to the old county seat of Ysleta, where he opened a general mercantile store and continued to do contracting for Southern Pacific, supplying wood and construction work on the roadbed along the river.[27]

Gaál soon began a lifelong involvement with the Republican Party and led the opposition when the county seat was moved from Ysleta to El Paso in 1885. When he arrived in Ysleta there was only one other Republican, Pablo Romera, who feared for his life because of his political affiliation. Gaál soon recruited a group called "young Republicans," who supported his unsuccessful race in 1886 for county commissioners' court. In 1888 he was elected mayor of Ysleta by a six-to-one majority. He was reelected mayor in 1890 and in 1894. He also

Ignatius G. Gaál

served as deputy collector of customs at Ysleta 1891-1895 and was president of the Ysleta school board for seven years.[28]

Always active in business as well as in public life, Gaál was president of the Rio Grande Nursery at Ysleta and of the Rio Grande Irrigation Company in 1888. But it was in the field of politics and civic improvement that Gaál became involved in the "Old West" controversy which resulted in the troubles at Ysleta during the summer of 1890.[29]

Ignatius Gaál's problems began early in 1890. The El Paso *Herald* reported on February 20, 1890, that Mayor Gaál of Ysleta was having troubles, in part because of the El Paso Irrigation Company's ditch being constructed through the town and blocking the flow of water in the old Ysleta ditch. In February his political opponents sought to oust him from the El Paso County Commissioners' Court. In a disputed election in April, Ysleta ended up with two mayors. In May the Ysleta city government obtained an injunction against Gaál for the return of "certain books belonging to that corporation." He was held in contempt of court. Then the *Herald* asked on June 9, "What does the attempt on the life of Mayor Gaál of Ysleta mean?" In unrelated incidents on June 10, the respected Civil War veteran Colonel John

R. Baylor struck him on the side of the head with a quirt, and two men, Santiago Casper and Saturnino Carbajal (Saturiano Carbojal), were charged with assault with intent to murder Gaál. Finally, late in June, the Supreme Court of Texas ruled that he could occupy the seat of county commissioner while serving as mayor of Ysleta, although the local commissioners refused to allow him this honor.[30]

During the summer of 1890 the Ysleta municipal authorities needed to clean out the *acequia* (irrigation ditch) which brought water to the town, but the conflict between the rival mayors caused problems. Gaál's men, headed by his marshal, Milton Gonzales, began working in the ditch on July 9. Gaál visited the work site the next day, only to find rival Mayor Benigno Alderete's men at work there. Trouble loomed. The El Paso *Times* reported on July 12 that "a bloody battle is raging in Ysleta between the factions of I.G. Gaál and Mayor Benigno Alderete." The ditch cleaning resulted in the death of one man. The new mayor had challenged the old mayor, who successfully retained his civic office.[31]

Gaál attended the El Paso County Commissioners' Court meeting for the first time since the Supreme Court ruling that he could hold two public offices simultaneously. His men continued to clean the ditch on July 10. Gaál returned the next day to learn that his life had been threatened in a letter. Meanwhile, Alderete's men under his own marshal, Saturnino Carbajal, armed themselves to take over the ditch work. Tensions built for a showdown. Armed men collected around Gaál's house and corral, where some of his supporters had gathered. Gonzales, Gaál's marshal, and other of his men returned from ditch cleaning late in the afternoon of July 11 and attempted to reach Gaál's house. They were intercepted by Alderete's marshal. Although Carbajal agreed to take Gonzales, unarmed, to Gaál's house, he then tried to arrest him. Shots were fired around the corral at Gaál's house. Other shots came from nearby sites. Gonzales and Gaál's men began firing on this second group. The gunfight continued for the next three hours until dark closed in.

Meanwhile, the El Paso County sheriff was alerted by the Ysleta telegraph operator, whose eyewitness account of the battle ended only when bullets crashed through the window of the depot. With the arrival of the sheriff, the Gaál-Gonzales party was arrested and jailed on the charge of murder. They were released on bail on the 16th and were never indicted by the grand jury, which met in October 1890.

The local Democratic Party paper, the *Times*, blamed the fight on Gaál, who had sent his men to work on the *acequia* where his opponent's men were already working. According to the paper, Alderete attempted to have Gaál arrested and put under a peace bond to prevent further interference, but Gaál resisted and the fight ensued. His chief opponent and rival mayor bitterly accused Gaál of attempting to rule Ysleta illegally. As soon as he was out of jail, Gaál retaliated by having 56 of his opponents, including Alderete, arrested. El Paso's Democratic Party leaders stood bail for them. Although the opposing parties continued to be watchful for further violence, and "it was not unusual to hear a hundred shots fired in the streets of Ysleta on a single night," things gradually quieted along the Rio Grande.[32]

Although Ignatius Gaál's election for the mayoral post at Ysleta in the fall of 1890 was disputed, he continued his leadership in local politics, heading the Republicans who termed themselves the Independents. He was again elected mayor in 1894, but local taxpayers led a successful campaign to abolish the town corporation the next year. In 1899 Gaál was elected superintendent of the County Farm (also called the El Paso City-County Hospital), an office which he held for the remainder of his career. In addition, he continued his farming and business activities at Ysleta. He died at the age of 90 on May 27, 1933, heralded by the local newspapers, Democratic and Republican alike, as an El Paso pioneer.[33]

Another Magyar immigrant founded San Antonio's first museum. On July 13, 1908, the San Antonio *Daily Light* announced that a "Famous Old Man Goes to His Reward: Prof. Jermy Dies after Brilliant Career in His Early Days." In recounting his accomplishments, the obituary stated of Gustav Jermy that he was "one of the most distinguished scientists, botanists, and mineralogists who performed valuable services for the United States government in the way of geological and mineral surveys" and that he was the founder of the first museum in San Antonio, located at San Pedro Springs Park. At the time of his death, Jermy had been a resident of San Antonio for a quarter of a century.[34]

Gustav (Gusztáv) Jermy, born in Hungary in 1832, began his scientific career in Europe and "for many years held responsible positions in several universities." He reportedly spoke eight languages. Jermy came to America in 1883 and worked at the Smithsonian Institution in Washington, D.C., before coming to Texas.

Caged-animal exhibit in San Pedro Springs Park, where Gustav Jermy established his zoological museum

After working for the state government in Austin for a short time, Jermy moved to San Antonio in 1894 and became a botanist at San Pedro Springs Park, the second-oldest public park in the United States. There he founded the first museum of natural history (also known as the San Pedro Springs Zoological Museum) to supplement the caged animal exhibit. It occupied a frame building in the park, and Jermy became its first superintendent, collecting specimens of insects, birds, reptiles, and plants, as well as tending the caged animals. It was described as "the old and much-admired museum, with its collection of typical Texas animals, and including a costly and rare mineral collection of curios." In addition, the "once famed Zoological Garden" contained a "more or less typical Texas and Mexican collection of wild animals." Professor Jermy's skill as a taxidermist provided the museum with mounted specimens for display, particularly of Texas animals, birds, and reptiles, including prairie hawks, owls, armadillos, quail, rabbits, mockingbirds, buzzards, and other such.[35]

Professor Gustav Jermy's last noteworthy assignment came when the Texas State Geologist appointed him to investigate the mineral and agricultural resources in South Texas. Working with T.E. Dumble during the administration of Governor Lawrence Sullivan Ross, he conducted the Third Texas Geological Survey in 1887-1891. Jermy had personal supervision over the geological and mineral survey made in Gillespie County, 1888-1891, which was said to have been "the most complete ever made in Texas." Advanced age and ill health forced him to retire after these projects, and he lived with a son until his death on July 12, 1908.[36]

Railroad companies were not the only recruiters of recently arrived Hungarian workers prior to the First World War. Agents of large lumber companies operating in the pine forests of East Texas and Louisiana recruited Europeans, including Hungarians, on East Coast docks. As a result, foreign-born lumber workers formed a tiny minority of the total manpower employed in these forests and sawmills. Forty-one Hungarians were reported working in Grimes County in 1910, and 75 Austrians were employed in Newton County.[37]

A report on the history of Pineland, Texas, and its lumber and farming industry recalled the settlement of a colony of Bohemians and Magyars around Pineland in Sabine County in 1914. The Hungarians were thrifty, hard-working people who "had some odd ways, such as putting the chickens to roost on the front porch," but they found wages low and the land poor for farming and drifted away to other towns in search of work.[38]

Among the Hungarian families in Pineland was that of Alexander Balla (1886-1950) and his wife, Julie Molnár (1886-1962), who came from their native Budapest to Rochester, New York, in 1902. Their daughter, Ima Balla Creech of Orange, reported that she came to Texas in 1915 at age four and a half, when her father was recruited to work for a lumber company in Pineland. With him came about 25 other Hungarian families. However, the land was too poor for crops in the pine forest. The Balla family, with eight children, moved away and took jobs in industries in Jefferson and surrounding counties.[39]

Northern Harris County also attracted Hungarian truck farmers. Fifteen to 20 families were reported to have farmed around the Cypress and Westfield communities and supplied produce for the Houston market. Six families were also reported to have arrived about 1910 and settled along Kuykendall Road on Green's Bayou, but they left in the 1920's, perhaps for better land upon which to grow potatoes in Fort Bend County.[40]

Hungarian Germans also joined the great economic migration to the United States. Largely urban and composing about 10.4 percent of Hungary's population, they represented 11.5 percent of those who had migrated to America by 1914. Said to have been the "wealthiest of Hungary's nationalities" and holding extensive political influence in their homeland, they settled mainly in Texas' towns and cities, where they maintained their middle-class ethic and supplemented the growing commercial and professional fields. But not all became city dwellers. The lure of ranching in Texas attracted the four Goebel brothers.[41]

According to a descendant's story, three figures were seen one day in 1870 walking down a dusty country road between Shovel Mountain and Cypress Mill in northern Blanco County. At 50-yard intervals Alois (born 1846), Moritz (born 1853), and John (born 1860) Goebel appeared, each carrying their belongings in sacks—thus arrived the orphaned German-Hungarian Goebel brothers from Budapest, who landed at New Orleans on December 1, 1869, and set out to become ranchers in the sheep-growing area of the Texas Hill Country. With the exception of Anton, the fourth brother, who came over later, then returned to Hungary in 1883, the Goebel brothers became part of the Cypress Mill community, and all married daughters of local German sheep raisers.[42]

Lawlessness persisted in the Hill Country during the 1880's, where Anton and Moritz herded sheep for brother Alois and for other ranchers. Minna Fuchs, Moritz's future wife, later recalled an incident when Moritz and Anton herded their sheep near the Fritz Fuchs ranch close to the Pedernales River. One day Moritz was hunting for his horse when he saw thieves breaking into his shack to steal groceries. With the help of the deputy sheriff, he followed the tracks of the thieves to a cave hideout. The men of the neighborhood then gathered and waited for the thieves to return one night. As the thieves approached, the posse shouted "Hands Up!" and shooting began. Unfortunately the thieves got away, although one was wounded. Their horses were captured but later disappeared. Afterwards, when Anton and Moritz went to spend Christmas with Alois, the thieves returned and burned their shack.[43]

Alois married Marie Matern (1854-1917) during the mid-1870's and fathered three daughters and a son. He later moved his family to San Antonio, and he and his daughters formed a string quartet with a piano accompanist, which performed at San Antonio's historic Menger

Minna Fuchs Goebel
and Moritz Goebel, c. 1890

Ida Manna Fuchs Goebel
and John Goebel

The Goebel string quartet at the Menger Hotel, c. 1890 — from left,
unidentified accompanist, Antonia, Marianna, Alois, and Virginia

Hotel on Alamo Plaza. Eventually he moved to Marble Falls, where he had a music store and gave music lessons until his death in 1917.[44]

Moritz Martin Goebel was a sheepherder in Blanco County by 1880. He married Minna Fuchs on June 17, 1891, and rented ranch land from her father at Cypress Mill. According to Minna's memoirs, her father later gave them a ranch on the Pedernales River, to which they moved in 1898 as soon as a house was built. They became the parents of six children.[45]

• ———————————— •

Setting Up Housekeeping on a Hill Country Sheep Ranch

Minna Fuchs Goebel wrote of her marriage in 1891:

> We went to Austin and bought us a bedstead, dresser table, and some chairs. Grandpa [Moritz] had only $90, but Father had given us the money to buy the furniture. On my 21st birthday, Father had given me a pair of shoes, and inside was a $10 gold piece. With that we bought ourselves 6 knives, 6 forks, 6 tablespoons and 6 teaspoons. It was guaranteed for 20 years. For wedding presents Uncle George had made us a table, a bench, and gave us a tablecloth. Theodore Fuchs gave us a churn; Tante [Aunt] Louise gave us 3 jars of pickles, 3 jelly glasses which were half full of sugar. Uncle John Goebel had made a tool box with a saw, square, hatchet, hammer and so on. Aunt Bettie gave us a set of dishes; still have 2 plates and a pitcher left . . . also have 2 bread pans that came with the stove.
>
> We were married at the house, where some of our friends were present. Then we went to Cypress Mill to celebrate with dancing and so on.[46]

• ———————————— •

The two brothers who continued to ranch, Moritz and John, and their families took an active part in the social events of the Cypress Mill community at the Hall built on a hill near the falls of the Pedernales River. "Meeting Days" were held one Sunday a month, and the ranchers and farmers came by horseback or wagon for a day of enjoyment. "The men had their beer, the women talked, and the young folks played games, danced, and so on." With a relative, Eddie Goeth, at the piano (using some of his own compositions), the Goebel brothers played their violins for some "pretty dance music." Those who remembered going to the Hall recalled the spirited Hungarian Gypsy style played by the Goebels, who also played for weddings and song festivals. Many plays, some written and produced by a local rancher, August Schroeter, were performed at the Hall. Nearby was the community one-room schoolhouse, where the ranch children learned arithmetic, history, and geography as well as Latin, Spanish, German, and English.

The Cypress Mill Rifle Club, organized in 1886, held target-shooting competitions with clubs from nearby communities and sponsored other activities at the community hall. In such cases, participants picnicked through the afternoon. The dancing began at dark and lasted until midnight. During the dances John and Moritz Goebel played their violins, Eddie Goeth, the piano, and Paul Pellar accompanied them on a cornet or saxophone. Following the grand march in which everyone participated came a variety of dances, including polkas, waltzes, schottisches, two-steps, and one-steps.[47]

Minna recalled in later years, "To think what little we had to live on. . . . If I had a Sunday dress, I wore it for years, until the people made fun of me." In 1911 the Goebels moved to a farm near Abernathy in the Texas Panhandle. Many children and grandchildren of Blanco and Burnet County pioneers also bought Panhandle farmland, remigrating from the Hill Country, where arable land was very limited. There Moritz died in 1928, and Minna lived until 1955.[48]

Dry Years in the Texas Hill Country

Minna Goebel recalled hard times in Blanco County:

We had some dry years, and . . . we didn't have enough feed for the cattle. In wintertime we would burn cactus or prickly pears. Down there they grew 2 or 3 feet high. We cut them down, then we had sticks sharpened on one end; we would take as many leaves on the stick as it could hold and hold them over a fire to burn off the stickers and thorns. Then the cattle would eat them. They were crazy about them, and as soon as they would smell the cactus burning, they would come a-bawling.

Sometimes an old cow would start eating the cactus with stickers and all, and her mouth would be so full of thorns that she couldn't eat any more. That year we burned so many cactus. We went out in any kind of weather. . . . Sometimes, when people didn't have enough feed [in dry years], they would cut down live oak trees for the cows and sheep to eat.[49]

John, the youngest of the Goebel brothers, was nine years old when he arrived in America in 1869 with his brothers. By 1880 he was herding sheep for Carl Goeth, a rancher at Cypress Mill. His family later recalled that he learned English (his first language was German) by studying a German-English dictionary while herding. In 1887 he married Ida Manna Fuchs, and they had nine children. They settled on a home site in Cypress Mill, and there they remained, ranching and farming. In addition, John carried the mail on the Cypress Mill-Marble Falls route for many years, at first in a gig and later in a Model T Ford. He was also the secretary-treasurer for the Cypress Mill Hall and president of the Rifle Club. John died on April 4, 1931.[50]

Life in Hungary after World War I

In a rare series of letters, Anton Goebel in Budapest reported to his Texas relatives on conditions in post-World War I Hungary, where he was a civil servant until his retirement. He wrote in February 1922, "on my return from Texas in 1883, I changed my dollars and also those that you had sent me at the rate of two and one half guilders or five crowns for one dollar. Now one dollar is worth 530 crowns."

In another letter he wrote:

"We are experiencing bad times over here. Our money has [no] value. Therefore, such items as imported products and food are enormously expensive, also clothing and shoes. Also domestic products such as milk, meat, and grain; in short, everything has experienced a tremendous increase in price. Real estate, houses and land, are no exception.

"For the money I bought 6 percent Hungarian war bonds. Everybody considered these bonds to be safe since the whole country guaranteed them. However, since the Wallachians [Rumanians], Serbians, and Bohemians [Czechs] took away almost all of our land, with the consent of the Great Entente, and left us only a few counties, so that we lost our forests, mines, factories, etc., besides making us pay war reparations and damages, the war bonds have no value . . . and nobody wants to buy them."

And in December 1922 he wrote:

"The conditions over here show no improvement, the high cost of living is getting worse every day, and soon our money will probably be completely worthless, especially if the Entente demands heavy war reparations from us. This would be very unjust, because they have taken away the largest part [of the country] already. Not only the defeated countries but also the victorious nations suffer from the effects of the unfortunate world war. However, the victors will recover more easily and in a shorter . . . time. For us, the prewar times and conditions will never return." [51]

• ———————————— •

Croats, another of Hungary's minorities, also joined the migration to America in search of jobs. They came mainly from the associated state of Croatia, which maintained its own internal government, customs, and institutions under the Hungarian Crown. Along with the other South Slavs, the Serbians and the Slovenians, they lived in the southern part of the Magyar kingdom (as well as in the Austrian portion of the empire), and Croatia bordered on the Adriatic Sea, Hungary's access to maritime commerce. Croats also lived in southern Austria. Further, they were the most tenacious of Hungary's minority nationalities in maintaining their national consciousness and resisting magyarization policies coming from Budapest. [52]

Perhaps recruited from the northeast coal fields or off East Coast docks, Croats, as well as other minority nationals from Hungary, found jobs on Galveston's wharves by the turn of the century. By 1910 Hungarian Magyars, Czechs, Bulgarians, Rumanians, Slovaks, and Germans were working as longshoremen, dock laborers, and warehouse watchmen, but the Croats formed the largest group from Hungary. Others found related employment as merchants, tailors, shoemakers, brewery workers, streetcar men, railroad workers, porters, machinists, cabinetmakers, and hotel proprietors. Other Croats found jobs across the state in El Paso, Harris, Johnson, Tarrant, and Travis counties as railroad workers and meat packers. [53]

Texas' largest concentration of Hungarian-born Croats, before World War I, found employment in the coal mines at Thurber, Texas' most important mine site. Although numbering only 41 in 1910, a small minority among the total number of 1,498 foreign-born miners at the Texas and Pacific Coal Company at Thurber, their numbers were supplemented by another 143 Austrian-born Croats and Italians. By comparison, Italians and Russian, Austrian, and German Poles composed the largest immigrant groups at Thurber, and much has been written about their social life in the company town.

199

Thurber's mixture of ethnic groups made the town unique. The miners and their families represented more than 20 nationalities, mainly European, and gave the company town a "rich variety of their customs, languages, and talents." Of the small minority of Hungarian-born Croats in Thurber, including men, women, and children, only eight families were identified in 1910. The remainder were single men, mainly in their twenties. The largest number of the miners reported that they had arrived in the United States between 1905 and 1907, and most lived as boarders with Croatian families.[54]

Thurber, now a ghost town, was for nearly 50 years (1888-1937) completely owned by the Texas and Pacific Coal Company, including the coal mines, houses, business district, and a brick factory. Everyone lived in a company house, attended a company church, shopped in the company store, danced at the Opera House, and went to a company school. Completely unionized, the miners and their families numbered about 10,000 in 1910, and Thurber was the largest town between Fort Worth and El Paso. When the mines were closed in 1921 following a strike, the population moved away to find jobs in the mines and factories in the Northeast.[55]

A Soldier of Fortune

Italians formed one of Hungary's smallest minorities and came mainly from the Dalmatian Coast, which provided that nation's outlet to world maritime commerce from its port of Fiume. Austria's centuries-old domination of northern Italy brought Italians into imperial service throughout the empire, including Hungary. One Hungarian immigrant of Italian heritage found his way to Texas by a circuitous route.

A variety of Europeans came to Texas by way of the Emperor Maximilian's army in Mexico during the 1860's. One was George Ritter von Tomasini, who was born on April 23, 1818, in Pest to a family of highly placed Austrian officials. According to family memories, Tomasini was a lieutenant in the Austrian force which supported Maximilian's government in Mexico in 1862. Previously Tomasini had been decorated for meritorious military service by the Austrian emperor and the Russian czar.[56]

After Maximilian's fall from power and execution by Mexican patriots, Tomasini landed in New Orleans December 21,

1865. With his Prussian-born wife, Eva Elinor Weiland (1841-1912), he traveled to San Antonio, Texas, where he became a stock raiser and farmer on Salado Creek in the Coker Community. He died at the age of 94 on December 5, 1912.[57]

*Eva Weiland Tomasini
and George Tomasini*

An accurate count of still another Hungarian minority, Jewish Magyars, cannot be made since most identified themselves simply as Magyars to the Texas census takers. Having assimilated in their homeland, they spoke Hungarian and considered themselves culturally Hungarian. Jews were present in Hungary from ancient times, yet they remained a small percentage of the population until the last half of the 19th century. In 1781 a Patent of Toleration granted freedom of religion for Hungary's non-Catholic people, and the Jews, "although not receiving full civil rights, were granted freedom of religion and made subject to the ordinary laws." By 1880 Hungary's Jewish minority concentrated in Budapest and other cities and represented 4.6 percent of the population. That figure approached 5 percent at the turn of the century.

Magyarization, the adoption of the Hungarian language and culture, attracted many among Hungary's Jewish minority, although their religious affiliation was often maintained. They formed an urban middle class of capitalists who predominated in banking and finance. They also were heavily concentrated in the fields of law, medicine, the sciences and arts, journalism, secular education, and Hungarian intellectual life in general. While Jews were facing harsh persecution in Poland and Russia, discrimination against them was more subtle in the Magyar state.[58]

In coming to the United States, and to Texas, many Hungarian Jews shared the common goal of economic opportunity as well as personal freedom which prompted the large-scale emigration from Czarist Russia and other Eastern European states. Most settled in Texas' cities prior to the First World War, but individual families of Hungarian-Jewish merchants were found in small county seats throughout the state. Opportunity was limitless in the growing economy of turn-of-the-century Texas. Those whose fathers were simple tailors or tobacco merchants became economically successful in commerce, banking, real estate, and investments. But not all chose the commercial life. Rabbis and doctors contributed not only to the development of Jewish community life but also to the general welfare of all citizens. Philanthropic interests by more successful individuals and families in many ways benefited not only local and international Jewry, but also their local and general communities. Houston attracted the greatest concentration of Hungarian Jewish immigrants prior to 1914. Occupations identified in 1910 included tailor, tinner, grocer, insurance agent, salesman, peddler, baker, confectioner, watchmaker, and bookkeeper as well as owners of rooming houses and liquor, cigar, shoe, and dry goods stores. One man was cantor of a Jewish congregation, another lived on his investments, and a few worked in cotton gins.[59]

The Taub family from Nagykároly, Hungary, was one which gave back, through philanthropy, to their fellow citizens of Houston much of America's bounty, which they had acquired in just two generations. Jacob Nathan Taub (1849-1931) preceded his family to America during the late 1880's. From New York he went to Galveston and Houston, where he first peddled knickknacks and tobacco from a pushcart. In 1890 he opened a small retail and wholesale cigar store on

Houston's Congress Avenue, and his wife, Johanna, and six children joined him. By the time he died in 1931, Taub and three of his sons had amassed a fortune from his business and real estate dealings.[60]

With the Taub family fortune firmly rooted, Ben, the youngest son, assumed control of the family business and investments. A veteran and hero of World War I and a lifelong bachelor, Taub began a half century of philanthropy. Until his death in 1982 at the age of 93, the Taub name was synonymous with charity and medicine; the Ben Taub Hospital, Harris County's public hospital and outstanding trauma center at the Texas Medical Center, bears his name.[61]

Through his long lifetime of public service, Ben Taub served as an officer and member of 23 boards, including the city-county Jefferson Davis (until 1963) and Ben Taub charity hospitals, two banks, an insurance company, an investment company, a road-building company, and four universities. Always concerned for the less fortunate, he began his longest association in 1927, with the DePelchin Faith Home for unwanted children. In addition to the Taub Foundation, Ben Taub served on the boards of the Wolff Foundation, dedicated to supporting a hospital for indigent children, the Marie Boswell Flake Home, the Texas Institute for Rehabilitation and Research, and the Mading Foundation. He also served on the boards of the Texas Medical Center and the Baylor University Medical College Foundation, which conferred upon him an honorary doctorate of humanities in medicine in 1981.

In addition to giving land for the University of Houston's University Park campus, Taub was instrumental in the moving of Baylor University Medical College to Houston in 1943, where it used the Jefferson Davis Hospital for training. He also gave scholarships to nursing students, headed the United Fund, and expanded hospital care and welfare services to Blacks in Houston. For more than 30 years he made Sunday-morning visits to the hospital wards, where he gave money to the charity patients. His generosity to the indigent touched thousands of his fellow citizens. The plaque under his portrait at the Ben Taub Hospital reads: "His unselfish and untiring work in behalf of the indigent in this community was an inspiration to all who were privileged to serve with him." He remarked, "I've gotten more out of it [all the humanitarian service] than I've ever given."[62]

In 1966 Ben Taub suffered a severe heart attack and spent the remainder of his long life in seclusion at Houston's Methodist Hospital.

After his death in 1982 his youngest nephew, Henry J. N. Taub, became director of the Taub Foundation.

Hungarian-born rabbis served the religious and humanitarian needs of Texas' Jewish communities as well as the general population in their cities. Together two such rabbis, Maurice Faber and Samuel Rosinger, led their congregations for almost a century. In the process they both faced unusual odds, including political as well as social controversies. Little did Rabbi Maurice Faber of Tyler know, when he accepted appointment to the Board of Regents of the University of Texas on February 3, 1915, that he would have a major confrontation with Governor James E. Ferguson. Although meek by nature, Rabbi Faber demonstrated a strength of will equal to that of the highest elected official of the state. He did not back down or resign from the board, but defied the governor who had appointed him.[63]

During Governor James E. Ferguson's attempted takeover of internal operations of the university, he wrote to Rabbi Faber on September 11, 1916:

> It appears from recent developments that certain members of the Board of Regents are conspiring with certain members of the faculty, including the President of the University, to perpetuate certain members of the faculty who are, in my opinion, contrary to every principle of right and decency.
>
> It is quite apparent that the issue is going to be decidedly drawn. I am, therefore, writing you to say that unless I may be assured of your full cooperation I will much appreciate your sending to me at once your resignation as a member of the Board of Regents under my appointment.

In his reply to the governor, the Tyler rabbi stated that, in accepting his high appointment, he had taken an oath to serve the State "to the best of my abilities and according to the dictates of my own conscience." He added, "I never dreamed that such an appointment had any political significance; nor that the appointee is expected to be a mere marionette to move and act as and when the Chief Executive pushes the button or pulls the strings."[64]

Rabbi Faber held that the selection of men who would render good service "to our Commonwealth" without fear of influence from any source and without any hope of remuneration other than that stemming from "service faithfully performed for the common welfare" had prompted him to become a regent. He went on to deny that the regents and faculty were conspiring and upheld them as men of integrity.

Rabbi Maurice Faber

Therefore he denied the governor's request for "full and complete cooperation" without proof of the justice of the governor's demands. Faber refused to concede the governor's right to interfere in the internal affairs of the university, which action he held to be the sole authority of the Board of Regents. Thus Faber cast his lot with the regents in their fight with the governor. Then, having made his stand, the rabbi tendered his resignation as a regent on November 20, 1916, stating "the condition which compelled me to defy the Governor's expressed wish no longer exists. . . . I tendered my resignation.[65]

In August 1917 Faber was summoned by the House of Representatives of Texas to testify as a witness at the impeachment proceedings against Governor Ferguson and to bring all correspondence between himself and the governor relating to the rabbi's service as a regent of the University of Texas. Ferguson was impeached and became the first

Texas governor to be removed from office, although not solely because of Faber's testimony.[66]

University of Texas President Robert E. Vinson wrote to Rabbi Faber in February 1918:

> The faculty of the University of Texas wishes to express to you . . . its sincere appreciation for the unselfish devotion with which you labored during the past summer to preserve the constitutional control of the University and the other state educational institutions from autocratic domination. Your work has had a significance far beyond the limits of Texas. Friends of education throughout the United States anxiously awaited the outcome of your efforts and were encouraged by your success. For ourselves, as citizens of Texas, we feel that you have set an example of patriotic public service the influence of which cannot be measured.[67]

Who was this courageous rabbi? Maurice Faber was born December 30, 1854, in Szinna, Hungary, received his education in secular and religious schools, and was ordained in 1873. After immigrating to the United States in 1879, he lived for a time in New York and Wilmington, Delaware, before working for ten years in Titusville, Pennsylvania, where he taught German literature and history in the local high school. In 1884 he became a citizen of the United States. He moved to Keokuk, Iowa, in May 1898 and then, on September 15, 1900, to Tyler, Texas. He became Temple Beth-El's first rabbi and worked there for the next 34 years. Rabbi Faber died September 16, 1934 — he had been a rabbi for a total of 62 years. A member of the Central Conference of American Rabbis since 1890, he also served as vice-president of the Texas Kallah Association of Rabbis.[68]

Rabbi Faber was a man of profound learning, and "a new spirit of humanism and toleration blew into Tyler with him." Dedicated to Reformed Judaism, he welcomed any "Israelite who is honorable" to the Tyler congregation. Under him the yarmulke was banned, a Sunday School was created, and confirmations rather than bar mitzvahs were held. The women formed an active Sisterhood, and the first parsonage was acquired in 1901. In addition, Rabbi Faber was a "great circuit rider," gathering Jews in surrounding towns into his congregation.[69]

From his early days in Pennsylvania and Iowa as well as in Texas, Rabbi Faber was known for his patriotic speeches on the Constitution, the Fourth of July, and Memorial Day. In Tyler he helped raise funds for charities and educational institutions, the Red Cross, United Charities, a Jewish tuberculosis hospital in Denver, and an orphanage in

New Orleans. He was also a member of the local library board and the Masonic Lodge. Described as a "very meek" man of deep and broad knowledge, Faber also was known as a champion of justice. His death was eulogized by the Central Conference of American Rabbis as well as by the Board of Regents of the University of Texas. Faber Hall at Tyler's Temple Beth-El was named in his memory.[70]

Beaumont's Rabbi Samuel Rosinger served his congregation for 50 years. When Beaumont's Temple Emanuel advertised in 1910 for a rabbi, it specifically asked for a graduate of Hebrew Union College or the Jewish Theological Seminary who was a "good mixer." The Anglo-Jewish press in the United States poked fun at this ad, advising the Beaumont congregation to hire a bartender and not a rabbi. But Samuel Rosinger, a young rabbi in Toledo, Ohio, answered the advertisement and was hired.[71]

Rosinger was born on December 21, 1877, in the small agricultural village of Tibolddarócz in northern Hungary's Carpathian foothills. His father had a small farm and sold the villagers' crops on commission to support his eight children. The family home was a small thatch-roofed cottage with an earthen floor. As a youth Rosinger attended a Jewish school conducted by a government-licensed teacher as well as a yeshiva to learn Hebrew and religion. He then studied at the Rabbinical Seminary in Budapest and later in Bern, Switzerland, and at the Kaiser Friedrich Wilhelm University in Berlin, before emigrating to America in 1904. In New York City he attended lectures at the Jewish Theological Seminary and in 1908 received a master's degree from Columbia University. He accepted his first pulpit in Toledo, Ohio, where he remained for two years.[72]

Through two world wars, the Great Depression in the 1930's, and decades of Ku Klux Klan intimidation, Rabbi Rosinger and his wife faithfully served the Beaumont congregation. Remembered as a man of courage, compassion, dedication to duty, and fierce commitment to his principles, he was also gentle and helpful to his fellow citizens. Rosinger served as the building chairman for the Jefferson County Tuberculosis Hospital, chairman of the Beaumont Municipal Hospital, and president of the Rotary Club and of the Red Cross, and he contributed articles to the *Texas Jewish Herald*.[73]

During his tenure, in 1923, Temple Emanuel was built. Rabbi Rosinger served three generations of the small Beaumont congregation for more than half a century and was named Rabbi Emeritus in 1960.

The temple's Rosinger Center, housing all congregation-sponsored service and social activities, was named in honor of Samuel and Gertrude Rosinger in 1957.[74]

• ———————————— •

Boasting about Texas
by Samuel Rosinger

I would be utterly unworthy of the titles of honor and distinction that go with being called "a Texas Rabbi," had I not caught the contagion of bragging about the glory and grandeur of my great state. Here follows a small and inadequate eulogy that I have penned on this subject:

There is something in the atmosphere of Texas that attracts and holds. Perhaps it is the vastness of the state's area and the variety of its soil and climate that carries a strong appeal. Then, there is the warmth of Texas that manifests itself, not only in the climbing mercury and the semitropical vegetation, but also in the accelerated heartbeat of the Southern people, in the cordiality of their hospitality, the fervor of their friendship, the glow of their faith, and the ardor of their loyalty.

To a man blessed with an independent soul, Texas has an irresistible appeal, by reason of the ruggedness of its people, who still retain distinct traces of their pioneering ancestry, with the quaintness and picturesqueness, and have not yet become obsequious slaves of conventions and standardization. Furthermore, Texas, with its sparse population and undeveloped natural resources, represents the future, and one who does not regard life as fixed and stationary, but as a steady growth, finds great fascination in linking his fate with this youthful state, and sharing the adventures of its romantic unfoldment and the changing fortunes of its colorful development.

The mystic magnetism which Texas exerts upon one by the vast reaches of its prairies, the matchless beauty of its skies, the luxurious growth of its tropical vegetation, and the warm heart of its people, explains the secret of the long tenure of service of the Texas Rabbis, and accounts, very largely, for my lifetime incumbency with my Congregation.[75]

• ———————————— •

*Alice Lang Rottenstein
and Dr. Max Rottenstein
with their children*

Jewish Hungarians also pursued professions such as medicine in Texas. For example, the doctor who installed and operated the first electrocardiograph machine in the Southwest arrived in Laredo, Texas, in 1937 from Mexico. Max Rottenstein was born in 1897 in Kiskún-félegyháza. His medical education in Hungary was interrupted by World War I, during which he rose to the rank of captain in the Austro-Hungarian Army, fought on the Italian and Russian fronts, and was decorated three times for heroism.

In 1922 he received his medical doctorate at the Royal Hungarian Péter Pázmány University of Sciences (previously called the University of Budapest) and served residencies in Prague, Czechoslovakia, and at the Saint Roch Hospital and the Jewish Hospital in Budapest. Rottenstein specialized in electrocardiology and was recognized as an outstanding researcher and diagnostician in heart physiology. Having learned Spanish in Prague from a Jesuit priest, he moved to Mexico in 1925 and practiced medicine in small mining communities, including Aguascalientes, Fresnillo, and Zacatecas.

In Mexico Dr. Rottenstein treated politicians, intellectuals, peasants, miners, and bandits alike — the full spectrum of society. His electrocardiograph machine was at first called a "witch doctor's contraption," but the doctor overcame local medical opposition to new techniques of diagnosis and treatment. He was especially concerned for the well-being of miners and saw to it that their working conditions slowly improved.

He married Alice Lang during a trip to Hungary in 1927, and they had two children while living in Mexico. In 1937 they decided to move to the United States. Reaching the border at Laredo, Dr. Rottenstein thought that his practice would be better suited to that place than to any in the Northeast. In Laredo he served as a diagnostician and heart specialist and became the chief of staff and head of internal medicine at the local Mercy Hospital. He was the first to operate an electrocardiograph machine in the city. When his wife died in 1972, he established the Max and Alice Rottenstein Nursing School Fund. By his death in 1978 he had practiced medicine for a total of 56 years in Mexico and Texas.[76]

Most Hungarian Jews who arrived in Texas prior to 1914 became merchants in the larger cities. One of Dallas's greatest civic leaders was Martin Weiss, born in Eger, Hungary. In 1955, when Martin was 90, he and his wife, Charlotte Szafír Weiss, gave $50,000 to the Dallas Park Board, and the 13-acre Weiss Park was named in their honor.[77]

Martin Weiss came to Texas in the mid-1880's and was a merchant in San Marcos, Gonzales, San Antonio, and Beaumont before settling in Dallas in 1901. There he and his wife owned the Milliners Supply Company and began a long career of civic leadership. He was on the committee that recommended the purchase of Love Field, Dallas's first city-owned airport. He also served on the committee that selected the Methodist Hospital site, was a founder of the Oak Cliff Chamber of Commerce, and played an active role in the Trinity River Improvement Association. Weiss served on the Dallas Park Board, 1935-1937, and helped sponsor the Dallas Museum of Art at Fair Park for the Texas Centennial. His Martin and Charlotte Weiss Foundation benefited the Methodist Hospital in Oak Cliff, where he became a board member in 1927. Weiss was named "Man of the Month" by the Oak Cliff Chamber of Commerce in 1951.

The Weisses generously supported a variety of civic improvements, including viaducts, straightening of the Trinity River, artesian wells, parks, streets and paving, drainage and storm sewers, little theaters, teachers' pensions, zoning, and many other projects in the Oak Cliff neighborhood. The Trinity Improvement Association, which controlled floods by a system of levees, was a favorite project. The title

Martin and Charlotte Szafír Weiss

of his biography, *Hungary Sends a Dallas-Builder*, aptly summed up Martin Weiss' philanthropy and public service to his city.[78]

By the turn of the century, the West Texas city of El Paso offered enterprising businessmen ample opportunity for local and international trade with Mexico. One immigrant, Adolph Schwartz, came to the United States in 1883 at the age of 16 from his native Sztropkó in the vicinity of Eperjes in Hungarian Slovakia and became a leading figure in establishing the Jewish community in El Paso. Once he was settled in business, others of his family followed him to Texas and joined his successful retail business. The Schwartzes and their relations became "the backbone of the El Paso Jewish community."[79]

Adolph Schwartz's rise to prosperity in Texas was typical of many other families across the state. He first worked in New York, Ohio, and California in retail stores before going to Juárez, Mexico, where he and Simon Picard opened a store called the "Tres B" (*Buena*, *Bonita*, *Barata*—Good, Pretty, Cheap) in the Zona Libre, a tariff-free area. In 1900 Schwartz moved to El Paso, Texas, which now had a population of almost 16,000 people. His first store, The Fair, was succeeded by a second, the Popular Dry Goods Company, in 1902. To assist him, Schwartz brought two cousins from Upper Hungary. The penniless immigrant had accumulated a large fortune from merchandising and real estate by his death in 1941. His success was attributed to "astute merchandising, sound finance policies, growing volume, and low labor turnover" as well as to his ability to select associates of high caliber, including his cousins and nephew. The nephew, Maurice Schwartz, succeeded him as president in the family business.

With modern marketing and advertising techniques, including trading stamps, live mannequins, clearance sales, and a mail-order department, the family built the Popular into the store "where the Southwest Shops with Confidence." By the 1980's the Popular was a multimillion-dollar retailer in El Paso, with three locations, including one in a mall. In addition, the Schwartz holdings in local real estate included undeveloped as well as developed land in the border city.[80]

Sixteen-year-old Maurice Schwartz was brought to El Paso by his uncle Adolph in 1899 from his native Jakabvölgye. Growing up in the business, he was responsible for making "a small store into one of the most successful department stores in the Southwest," with his "keen promotional sense" and competitiveness. Both uncle and nephew contributed to clothing for hundreds of students in need. Both were also active in Jewish community life in the B'nai Zion and Temple Mt. Sinai congregations.[81]

The Schwartz family responded to the rise of Nazism in Europe by attempting to bring as many of their relatives as possible from Hungary and Czechoslovakia to the United States. Two nephews were brought to Eagle Pass to live with relatives in 1939. Five other nephews migrated to Mexico in 1940 and settled under family care in Ciudad Juárez until they could be admitted to the United States. In May 1945 five nieces who survived Birkenau concentration camp were brought to America. Others of the family in Europe did not survive the Holocaust.[82]

Like many other immigrants, Jacob Schmidt began as a wagon peddler along farm roads in Central Texas. Born into a Jewish family on January 31, 1889, in Bártfa in Upper Hungary, Jacob was the first of his family to emigrate to the United States. He arrived in New York in 1907. With only a sixth-grade education, he found work in a brewery in Wilkes-Barre, Pennsylvania, and then in a meat-packing house before joining a relative in Seguin, Texas.[83]

Schmidt borrowed enough money to purchase some merchandise and began peddling about 1910. Soon he was able to buy a wagon and mules, with which he could cover a territory of a hundred miles

Jacob Schmidt (right) *and his peddler's wagon. Other man is unidentified.*

Hungarian-Jewish peddlers, Seguin, 1907 — standing, at left, *Jacob Schmidt;* at right, *George Mendlowitz*

213

around Seguin, often with hot bricks under his feet during cold weather. He also learned to trade mules and horses. In 1912 he married Bertha Yahr, and they operated a retail mercantile store in Yorktown. He later had stores in Beeville and San Marcos, but because his children were approaching college age, Schmidt moved his family to Austin to be near the University of Texas. His son and four daughters were educated there during the Great Depression.

The Jacob Schmidt Department Store at Austin's Brazos and East 6th Street dated from 1929. Six years later Schmidt moved to a better location in the 500 block of Congress Avenue, and there he remained until his death in 1964. Meanwhile, he switched from general merchandise to ladies' fashions and began building a chain of retail outlets which would number ten by the 1980's. The firm's name was changed to Yaring's, for Schmidt's wife, Bertha Yahr.

As his son, Leon, recalled, Jacob Schmidt was part of the large Jewish migration from Central and Eastern Europe which sought economic and personal opportunity in America. Rather than accept a ghetto in New York City in place of the ghetto he had fled in the Old Country, he chose the "wild west nature of Texas." His Texas odyssey led him along desolate stretches of Guadalupe, DeWitt, and Gonzales counties selling calico, domestics, socks, shoes, and workpants to his German, Czech, Polish, and Yiddish customers, whose languages he already spoke. He also taught himself to speak, read, and write English and became fluent in Spanish as well.[84]

Some immigrants found success in America's developing technology during the 20th century. One was Eugene (Jenő) Roth, who was born in 1898 in Kisvárda, Hungary. When Roth left his homeland for America at the age of 13, he could not have imagined that one day he and his sons would play a major role in radio and television broadcasting in South Texas. He got his first job selling newspapers for a German printer in New York, while attending night school to learn English. He also worked as a Dow Jones runner for 75 cents a week. With his carefully saved earnings he was able to bring his parents, two brothers, and two sisters to America. The Roth family later moved to Pittsburgh, Pennsylvania, where Eugene had a job at the McMillan Steel Mill, which was making locks for the Panama Canal. After a year or two of the cold northern winters, however, Roth moved to New Orleans and worked for the Southern Pacific Railroad before relocating to San Antonio in 1914.[85]

Gene Roth and staff at KONO, San Antonio

Interested in mechanics, Roth obtained his first job in San Antonio as head machinist at the Southern Pacific Railroad's roundhouse. Just before the First World War he opened his own machine shop and "66 Garage" on Romana Plaza, where he was one of the few early mechanics to hand-grind valves. Shortly thereafter he started the Roth Brothers Garage and also operated a "jitney" taxi service for the doughboys at Camp Bullis during World War I. He began selling radio sets from his garage and machine shop during the early 1920's. Then, because there was nothing to listen to, Roth built a 50-watt transmitter above his garage in 1925 as a hobby and operated it for two years before he received a license. He named his company Paramount Radio Company; its station, KGRC (Come to the Gene Roth Company), was later known as KONO-AM Radio.

Gene Roth soon began commercial radio broadcasting, sending an agent out to sell time to local businesses. During the depression he often took barter for radio time and succeeded in building the first independent music and news station in the nation. By 1950 Roth's AM station broadcast on 250 watts; by 1957 he owned KONO-TV, the third VHF channel available in San Antonio (now KSAT-TV).

Adolph Klein at his Liberty Bell Grocery, 1940

When Gene Roth became ill during the 1960's, his sons, Bob and Jack, ran the family broadcasting business until they sold out in 1968.

As with so many immigrants, Gene Roth came to America as much for economic opportunity as to escape anti-Semitism. Before his death in 1976 he saw his son Jack buy back the radio station and build the business into what was known as Mission Broadcasting Company, which eventually owned six radio stations in four metropolitan markets—Miami, Florida; Charlotte, North Carolina; and Denver, Colorado, in addition to San Antonio. Country music was the format for their KONO-AM and KITY-FM stations in the Alamo City. His other son, Bob, had turned to a career in investments and civic service after the broadcasting company was sold. He was a president of the Chamber of Commerce, a member of the Advertising Club, the San Antonio Executive Association, and the Executive Committee of HemisFair '68, and a fundraiser for the modern Chamber of Commerce building on the San Antonio River.[86]

Gene Roth's emigration to Texas also involved members of his extended family. Al and Lester Klein, cousins of Jack and Bob Roth, turned to careers in law. They graduated from the University of Texas Law School in 1930 and 1941, respectively. Their parents had emigrated from Kisvárda and met and married in America. In 1917 their father,

Adolph Klein, moved his family to San Antonio, where he worked in the livery business with his brother-in-law, Gene Roth. Their Red Star Lines hauled soldiers to and from Camp Bullis. After the war ended Adolph opened his own grocery and meat market. Although Jewish, the Klein and Roth families spoke Hungarian and prepared Hungarian dishes at home.[87]

Governor Dolph Briscoe appointed Al Klein as judge of the 224th District Court of Bexar County on April 1, 1977, capping his 47-year law practice in San Antonio. Born in New York City in 1908 and inspired to a legal career as a boy, Klein later remarked, "I did know at a very, very early age that I would be a lawyer. There had never been anyone in the family who was in the legal profession." He was elected to the 224th District Court in 1978 and served one term before retiring to private practice in 1982. He was the first Hungarian-Jewish Texan to serve on the bench in the Lone Star State.[88]

• —————————————— •

A Hungarian in Western Folklore—
Big-Nosed Kate

The Hungarian heritage of Big-Nosed Kate, an almost legendary "soiled dove" of the Old West, was not known until recently. Variously identified during her long career in dance halls, saloons, and bordellos from Texas to Arizona, she lived with a succession of men, including Doc Holliday. Born Catherine Mary Horony in Pest on November 7, 1850, Kate came to America with her parents, Dr. P. and Catherine Boldizsár Horony, in the 1850's and settled in Davenport, Iowa, in 1858. Tragedy struck in 1865 when her parents both died suddenly. Kate was left to care for six brothers and sisters, all of whom became wards of the city. Kate ran away from home two years later.[89]

Described as a "tall, big-boned, buxom brunette with a nose so determined and handsome that she was known to her cronies as Big-Nosed Kate," she launched her career in the world's oldest profession. In Texas she first lived with John Elder at Fort Griffin, a raw, lawless town in Shackleford County during the 1870's. The military post and town which grew up around it served as an Indian reservation, the center for a flourishing cattle industry, a supply depot for buffalo hunters, the only town on

217

"Big-Nosed Kate" Horony

the famous Western Cattle Trail from South Texas to Kansas City, and a gamblers' paradise and outlaws' rendezvous. Its notorious saloons, gambling halls, and houses of prostitution attracted all elements of society on Texas' frontier.[90]

Kate met Doc Holliday, the "gun-fighting dentist known as the coldest-blooded killer in the West," in Fort Griffin in 1876 or 1877. The Georgia-born Holliday, a tubercular alcoholic who drank two or three quarts of whiskey a day, had killed two men in Georgia, one in Dallas, and a soldier near Fort Richardson, and wounded another man in Denver before coming to Fort Griffin. When accused of killing still another man over a game of cards in 1877, he was arrested and held prisoner in a local hotel. Kate set fire to the rear of the building to distract the townspeople, disarmed the guard, and helped Doc escape to Dodge City, Kansas.[91]

Identified as a "dance-hall girl" when they first met, Kate lived with Doc for the next few years in Kansas and Arizona. In moments of gratitude for saving his life in Texas, Doc referred to her as "Mrs." Holliday, but theirs was a tempestuous relationship.[92] After a brief period in 1879 during which they ran a dental office in Las Vegas, New Mexico, Doc was involved in another shootout, and they moved to Tombstone, Arizona, to join the Earp brothers in 1880. There Kate and Doc came to a final parting of the ways.[93]

Big-Nosed Kate later moved to Globe, Arizona, where she operated a boardinghouse. In 1888 she married a blacksmith in Bisbee but left him to join an innkeeper in Cochise. From 1900 until 1930 she was a housekeeper in Dos Cabezas. Kate finally retired to the Arizona Pioneers' Home in Prescott in 1931. She died on November 2, 1940, at the age of 90. "Viewed in the same light with other pioneer women of her period who had endured similar childhood experiences, had suffered like privations, and had faced the same difficult environmental choices of occupations, Kate, big nose and all, does not suffer by comparison." The Old West was all the more colorful, in folklore as well as in fact, for Big-Nosed Kate's participation.[94]

• ───────────── •

Hungarian Names in the Texas Landscape

Hungarian family and place names were first used to identify a number of streets and sites around the Lone Star State. Streets such as Szabó in Houston, Hamvasy in Tyler, Lorenz and Újházi Road (now Oblate Drive) in San Antonio, and others elsewhere were given names of landowners or honored immigrant citizens. Otherwise, Hungarian names were rare in Texas. There was no Budapest or Pécs or Sopron and certainly no Székesfehérvár or Maramarossziget.

An elusive Hungarian place-name was Kossuth, located on Texas highway and railroad maps in eastern Anderson County near the rural community of Crystal Lake. As late as the mid-1980's, Kossuth was identified as a station on the Texas State Railroad running between Palestine to Rusk (now part of a state historical park). Built between 1896 and 1910, this railroad was state-constructed, -owned, and -operated in order to develop large iron ore deposits in East Texas. Whether Kossuth developed as more than a stop for the train has now faded from memory. There was no surrounding community.

Vidor — for Charles Shelton Vidor, its first large mill operator — is the largest Texas town named for a Hungarian Texan. (See page 139.) Located on the east bank of the Neches River in Orange County in southeast Texas, Vidor originated in 1907 as the headquarters of the woods operation of the Miller-Vidor Lumber Company's Beaumont plant. It also was a station on the Kansas City Southern Railway and on the Galveston, Beaumont, and Northeastern Railroad of the Peach River Lines six miles north of Beaumont. The Vidor logging camp had a daily capacity of 600,000 feet of logs and employed 175 men prior to 1920, when the logging camp was moved to Lakeview.[95]

At first the lumber company provided 30 to 40 houses, a general store, and a blacksmith shop for its workers. Vidor was connected by telephone with the main company office in Beaumont, and a post office was established on February 1, 1909. Practically all of the workmen involved in the logging operations lived in Vidor, where the mules were also kept. The machine shop for the Galveston, Beaumont, and Northeastern Railroad was also maintained there.[96]

Located in a low, marshy area, the town grew slowly, at first depending solely on the lumber industry for jobs. Then the Beaumont Brick Works had a plant in Vidor from 1918 until 1929. Later, with the development of the petrochemical industry on the Gulf Coast, including the North Vidor Oil Field, as well as war plants during World Wars I and II, Vidor experienced sustained growth as part of the Sabine industrial area of the "Golden Triangle." In 1960 it had a population of more than 4,900, and a decade later the population of the town had doubled. Its modern shopping centers, schools, and residential areas provided for the needs of industrial workers throughout the metropolitan area of Beaumont-Port Arthur-Orange.[97]

Milvid, in northeastern Liberty County, was named when the Miller-Vidor Lumber Company established operations in the vicinity. The company town was platted in December 1906, when the sawmill opened. Milvid's first-rate sawmill plant, with a capacity of 100,000 feet daily, drew its supplies of yellow pine from 40,000 acres in Liberty and Hardin counties. The lumber town had graded streets with 125 houses, as well as a post office, commissary, doctor's office, barbershop, meat market, icehouse, drugstore, ice cream parlor, "Union" church, school, hotel, and bathhouses. The railroad shop for the company's Riverside and Gulf Railroad was located there. Milvid had telephone connections to the outside world as well as electric lights.[98]

With connections to the nearby Gulf, Colorado, and Santa Fe Railroad, Milvid also became a lumber shipping station. The company town had a population of more than 1,000 in 1910 and furnished jobs

Miller & Vidor Lumber Mill, Beaumont, 1910

Employees of Miller & Vidor Lumber Company, Milvid, 1910

for 350 men by 1920. Thereafter it declined as the timber land was cut over, and the population dwindled to only 41 persons in 1940.[99]

In addition to place-names, Hungarian saints' names have found a place in Texas. For example, St. Elizabeth of Hungary Catholic Church in Dallas was founded in 1956 and named in honor of a 13th century Hungarian princess. Born in 1207 at Pozsony, she was married at the age of 14 to Duke Louis IV of Thuringia. After the death of her husband during a crusade to the Holy Land, she became a Franciscan tertiary. Elizabeth's charity to the poor and her founding of hospitals were well known. She was canonized in 1235. On the celebration of the Feast Day of St. Elizabeth, November 17 (November 19 in Hungary), Cistercian monks from Our Lady of Dallas Abbey sing the Gregorian Mass in the church. The Mass is followed by a luncheon of Hungarian foods, dances, and the singing of the Hungarian national anthem by members of the Dallas-Fort Worth Hungarian community.[100]

Hungarian Language and Traditions in Texas

Retention of Hungarian language and heritage among the American-born children of the immigrants varied from family to family. For example, Louis Nagy of Boerne, son of Joe Nagy, who spent his Texas career as a cotton farmer in Navarro, Ellis, and La Salle counties, reported that his parents refused to speak Hungarian around their children and observed only American holiday traditions in their home. At Christmas Joe Nagy bought boxes of apples, oranges, and hard candy to be distributed to the children of his farm employees. "That was about the only Christmas that we had," Louis Nagy added. He and his sister, Christine Nagy East, did report, however, that during a weekend dance held on the front porch of their Dilley ranchhouse, their mother danced the csárdás, a very fast Hungarian folk dance. "And could she ever dance! Oh, she was a beautiful dancer. She was a large woman, and I know Mother Szakó [one of Joe's sisters] talked about how popular she was in Europe, because she was such a beautiful dancer. [She] said the boys loved to dance with her."[101]

Other immigrant families encouraged the use of Hungarian in the home. Ann Weigand of San Antonio said that she and her brothers learned Hungarian from their parents. Her father, Norbert Weigand, left his native Váleamáre, Hungary, in 1904 and became a sausage maker in San Antonio. Able to speak German, Hungarian, Polish,

Rumanian, and English, Weigand encouraged his children to speak and read Hungarian. It remained for them to learn English from their playmates before entering school, where, his daughter recalled, she was "ashamed of the Hungarian language." She did not want anyone to "know that we were not just real Americans" and were "talking funny." During his lifetime Weigand subscribed to a Hungarian newspaper published in the North and, until his wife's death in 1929 and occasionally thereafter, spoke Hungarian to his daughter. Typically, the language was forgotten after the deaths of the immigrant parents.

Holidays such as Christmas were celebrated in American fashion in the Weigand home. Ann Weigand remembered: "We had Santa Claus, and I think the first tree I remember was lit with candles. That was just on Christmas Eve that they would light the candles." In speaking of her parents' memories of the Old Country, she continued:

> They would occasionally reminisce and tell about the beauty of their country, and . . . at one time my father was kind of unhappy with the things that were happening here, and said that that would not be allowed in the Old Country. That kind of riled me, and I asked him why he did not go back. He said because there was oppression there. He hadn't a chance to survive there . . . and that is why he came to the United States. He wasn't really unhappy with the United States. He just remembered the good old times.[102]

In a more unusual case, Michael Joseph Balint, the son of Hungarian immigrants to Albany (originally called Árpádhon by its Hungarian founders), Louisiana, and a Texas resident since 1951, said that they spoke Hungarian at home because his deaf mother could only lip-read in that language. Like the Hungarians who worked in the East Texas lumber industry, the Hungarians in Albany had been recruited about 1900 to build a logging railroad for a sawmill. They were paid in part with land after clearing the forests. Because a Magyar community developed, instruction in the public school was held in Hungarian as well as in English. Nothing like that happened where groups of Hungarian-speaking families settled in Texas, although the children of Pakan's Slovak farmers persisted in speaking their native language on an informal basis.[103]

Another aspect of the Hungarian heritage was largely lost during the immigration process. Delicate needlework and colorful folk embroidery traditional in all areas of Hungary were forgotten by most of the immigrants' children. In the case of the Joe Nagy family, fine linen sheets, pillow shams, towels, and scarves woven from flax raised on their Hungarian farm were brought to Texas, but the tradition of weaving and needlework was not retained. The Nagy women did faithfully pluck goose down to make traditional comforters with handmade buttons for each child in Texas. Ann Weigand reported that when her mother came to America, she left a trunk filled with beautiful needlework with a friend, who later refused to send it to her. "That just about broke her heart," the daughter recalled. Her mother did not pass on the needlework tradition to her Texas-born daughter.[104]

Scattered as they were across the width of Texas, the Hungarians of the great economic migration failed to establish ethnically based organizations. Immigrants of various religious affiliations joined local American congregations: Jews joined Conservative or Reformed synagogues, Lutherans and Calvinists attended services with their neighbors, and Catholics joined local parishes. No newspapers, retirement homes, literary and self-culture societies, musical or professional or literary clubs for Hungarians came into being in Texas. And the traditional Hungarian boardinghouse found in the industrial cities of the Northeast existed only for Thurber's coal miners for a short time.

The Economic Immigrants in the Early 20th Century

Personal success stories of many of Hungary's immigrants abound. Whether Magyars or representatives of that nation's many subject nationalities, all shared equally in the economic opportunities available to them in pre-1914 Texas. Hundreds of families immigrated, located new homes, and sought success on farms, in mills and mines, or in towns and cities across Texas. Vastly outnumbering the 48ers and their children, the participants of the great economic migration adapted and assimilated throughout the state. Their talents, skills, labor, and humanism benefited all Texans, no matter what their heritage. And those immigrants who had been members of minority groups in their homeland found personal, social, cultural, and political freedoms which previously had eluded them. As Ed Pakan of Wheeler County said, most found Texas a "real adventure and challenge."

World War I presented a question of loyalty to immigrants, many of whom had not become American citizens. Although no group effort to raise funds for war relief existed, many families undoubtedly helped their relatives in Hungary prior to the entry of the United States in the war in April 1917. When San Antonio's large and prosperous German community staged a giant five-day bazaar and concert series to collect war relief for the widows and orphans in Germany and Austria-Hungary in October 1916, Anglo- and Mexican-Americans participated more enthusiastically than did the Alamo City's few Hungarians. In fact, young Hungarian-Texan men from across the state volunteered and saw action with the American Expeditionary Force in Europe, and their families experienced little harassment at home.[105]

What of immigration between the end of the first and the beginning of the second world conflicts? World War I ended the flood of Eastern European immigration. The United States entered the war in 1917 as an enemy of the German and Austro-Hungarian empires and shared in the celebration of the Allied victory the following year. For Hungary, the Treaty of Trianon formally ended the war in 1920 in a most shattering manner: The peace treaty awarded 72 percent of the old Hungarian kingdom to her four neighboring states, Czecho-slovakia, Rumania, Yugoslavia, and Austria. In all, more than half of her population was lost, including about 3.5 million Magyars living in the awarded territories. Some of these Hungarians emigrated to America along with others from the diminished new Hungarian state during the 1920's and 1930's.

During the surge of nativism which swept the United States after the war, the U.S. Immigration Act of 1921 severely limited the quota for Hungary, allowing only 865 Hungarians, or 3 percent of that national group already living in the United States in 1910, to be ad-mitted each year. In the Immigration Act of 1924, the quota was further limited to 2 percent of those Hungarians living in America in 1890. The Census of 1930 reported that 1,626 immigrants and their Amer-ican-born children were living in Texas. Although slowed by the quota system and the Great Depression, some immigrants, including intel-lectuals, scientists, and Jews fleeing anti-Semitic pressures, sought ad-mission to the United States until the outbreak of World War II in 1939. After Pearl Harbor the United States and Hungary were again on opposite sides in the conflict.[106]

CHAPTER EIGHT

"They cannot go back to Hungary"

Post-World War II Immigrants in Texas

In 1950 Theresa Yanko, a Hungarian displaced person (DP) living in Dallas, said, "There is no life for them here [in Europe]. The American soldiers saved their lives, but now they have no jobs and no homes. They cannot go back to Hungary, to the Russian rule. If they cannot come here, there is nothing." Her simple statement aptly summarized the beginning of the third period of Hungarian immigration, which followed the end of the Second World War. Political refugees who fled before the advancing Soviet army in 1944-1945 and others who crossed through the Iron Curtain within the next few years to escape Communist rule in Hungary flooded displaced persons' camps in Western Europe and waited for admission to new homelands, including the United States. And they soon were followed by thousands of freedom fighters from the abortive Hungarian Revolution of 1956.[1]

Texas' Hungarian minority grew significantly with the arrival of political refugees after 1945. Of the millions of displaced persons in German and Austrian camps, many were ". . . former concentration-camp inmates, persecuted racial and religious minorities, and dissident intellectuals and political leaders who managed to survive the Nazi holocaust and the destructions of the war." Others were members of the defeated Axis armies, "representatives of the upper- and middle-level social and political elites of Germany's former allied and victim states, and hundreds of thousands of others of the lower classes, who were simply driven there by the currents of war." Many others, nationalists and anti-Communists, fled before the advancing Red Army. In all, the refugees included a wide spectrum of Hungary's middle and upper elite from government, military and police, society, and conservative and rightist political parties.[2]

Ed Stern in the Hungarian army, 1939

The Odyssey of a Jewish Tanner

Some of Hungary's Jews fled their homeland in the years immediately preceding World War II. Such was the case of Ed Stern, a native of Budapest, whose family owned a tannery and hide business. Stern graduated from the local Technical University with a doctorate in political economy in 1938, the year of the Nazi Anschluss of Austria, and soon experienced rising anti-Semitism in Hungary.

Stern's family was part of his nation's large Jewish population which had assimilated. "They did not keep the old aspects of the Jewish religion because . . . they thought that they were Hungarians [first] and then Jews." The Sterns had more Gentile friends than Jewish ones, spoke only Hungarian, and learned only Hungarian customs and culture. Ed Stern recalled, "We were more Hungarians than Jews."

Yet subtle discrimination against Jews existed in Hungary and was aggravated by the rise of Nazism during the 1930's. Stern personally experienced it during his university years, in the judiciary, and in the army into which he was inducted in 1939. His decision to leave Hungary was based on that discrimination in Hungary's officer corps.

In spite of his father's protests, Stern fled to France in 1939 on a tourist visa and remained there until the arrival of the German military in 1940. Then, with a purchased transit visa to Haiti, he made his way to Lisbon, Portugal, hoping to obtain entry into an African or South American country. While in Portugal he worked in his father's trade, the hide and skin industry, and married Frieda Mayer, a German-Jewish refugee also seeking escape from Europe.

The odyssey of the Sterns continued. Hoping to join Frieda's brother in South Africa, they obtained transit visas to Portuguese East Africa (Mozambique), where Stern exported hides and leather to Austria and Hungary for a time. But they could not enter South Africa. With increasing Nazi pressure on Portugal, the Sterns then accepted an offer to move to Palestine in 1943. There Ed worked in the diamond industry and became a British subject in 1945.

In 1947 the Sterns decided to rejoin Ed's father, who had survived by hiding in the countryside with friends. For almost a year, in Budapest, Stern imported and exported hides with a government license. But when that was withheld in an attempt to force him to resume Hungarian citizenship, fearing imminent Communist control of the government, he and his wife and small son took the Orient Express to Paris. France became the Sterns' home until 1956.

Ed Stern had first applied for an American visa in 1938. Then, a few months before the October uprising in Budapest in 1956, he received notification that the family would be admitted to the United States on his wife's German quota. They had prospered in France, and Stern asked, "Why, after so many years?" Although almost angry that it had taken so long to gain admission, the Sterns moved to New York, where Ed found immediate employment in the hide business. Their odyssey ended in San Antonio, Texas, where he moved in 1964 to work in a tannery. Ed Stern found that "America is a beautiful refuge for immigrants" seeking religious liberty.[3]

• ———————————— •

With the passage of two Displaced Persons Acts, in 1948 and 1950, tens of thousands of refugees were allowed to enter and settle in the United States. Their number further increased between 1947 and 1949 as postwar Hungarian coalition governments were replaced by one dominated by Communists and their Soviet backers. Centrist and liberal politicians as well as thousands of citizens who could not adjust to a Communist regime fled to the West. By the mid-1950's, 26,532 Hungarian refugees had entered the United States. Included in this wave were members of religious orders, including Cistercian monks, who sought freedom of worship following the confiscation of their schools and properties by the government.[4]

• ———————————— •

The Cistercian Order in Texas

The Cistercian Order first came to Hungary in A.D. 1142 and grew, in spite of setbacks such as the Turkish occupation of 150 years, into a major teaching order with its headquarters at the monastery in Zirc, Hungary. By 1945 the Cistercian educators ran five *gymnasia* (prep schools) in Hungary, but the Red Army occupied the Order's schools and buildings as well as 30,000 acres of farmland, the produce of which contributed to the Order's support. Three years later the Communist government turned the monks out of their schools, and in 1950 the Order was suppressed, and all of its possessions were confiscated. Some monks were imprisoned or deported; the abbot-president was sentenced to 14 years in prison. Others fled to the West.

The first Hungarian Cistercians arrived as refugees in 1946 in the United States and by 1953 in Dallas, where the diocese of that city welcomed them as pastors and educators. With the founding of the University of Dallas at Irving in 1956, they readily formed part of its faculty. Bishop Thomas Gorman of Dallas provided the Cistercians with a residence, which allowed them to again establish their monastic life. The next year the new Cistercian Monastery, Our Lady of Dallas, was begun on the campus of the University of Dallas, where the Fathers worked. In 1962 Texas' first Cistercian Foundation also established a preparatory high school and expanded their facilities to accommodate the students. By 1964 the Fathers numbered 30, and novices were being accepted. Following the Hungarian Revolution of 1956, other Cistercian refugees were welcomed by the Fathers at Our Lady of Dallas Monastery.

By 1964 the Cistercian community represented a wide variety of educational backgrounds and experience — all monks were required to hold master's degrees. Fifteen held doctorates, from Budapest, Rome, Paris, Quebec, and New York and other American universities, in various disciplines. In that year fully half of the Fathers were teaching at the University of Dallas and the others in the Cistercian Preparatory School for Boys, one of Texas' most academically rigorous schools. In addition, the monks served in local parishes, as convent chaplains, and in administrative work. And they rapidly learned English and became American citizens.[5]

Uprooted from their homeland by a hostile government which suppressed religious orders, Texas' Cistercians put down roots in a new land and built their Foundation near Texas Stadium in Irving. Our Lady of Dallas Abbey opened its doors to non-Hungarian novices, teaching young Texans a spiritual life devoted to religion as well as to service through teaching. The Abbey is the only transplanted Hungarian institution in Texas. In its chapel Mass is said in Hungarian on the last Sunday of every month for Hungarians in Dallas and Fort Worth.[6]

Texas' First Cistercian Abbot

The Right Reverend Anselm A. Nagy (1915-1988) of Our Lady of Dallas Cistercian Monastery came to the United States in 1946 knowing no English and having very little money. After a year as an assistant pastor in Ohio, he joined other Cistercians

Abbot Anselm Nagy   *Reverend Mark Major*

Our Lady of Dallas Cistercian Abbey, Irving

232

Cistercians of Our Lady of Dallas

Reverend Roch Kereszty of the Cistercian Abbey

at the Monastery of Our Lady of Spring Bank in Wisconsin, where he became the subprior. He was also named vicar and superior of all refugee monks after the imprisonment of the Abbot of Zirc by the Communists in Hungary. In 1955 he came to Texas at the invitation of Bishop Thomas K. Gorman of Dallas and became the prior of the new monastery of Our Lady of Dallas. His fellow monks elected him their abbot in 1963, and on Sunday, January 5, 1964, the Abbatial Blessing was conferred upon Anselm A. Nagy at Dallas's Sacred Heart Cathedral, marking the elevation of the Cistercian Monastery of Our Lady of Dallas to the rank of Abbey, thus ending the "chapter of pioneering" and opening a "new era of mature growth" for this unique institution.

Anselm A. Nagy, O. Cist., was born in Buják, Hungary, on February 2, 1915, and received his education in Cistercian schools in Eger and Zirc. He became a novice in the Order in 1934 and then studied in Rome at the University of Angelicum of the Dominican Fathers. He was ordained into the priesthood on July 13, 1941, received his doctorate in theology, and, upon returning to Hungary, had an administrative role in the Cistercians' estates. In 1945 the Abbot of Zirc commissioned him to explore the possibilities of transferring the Order to the United States following the confiscation of the Cistercian schools and properties in Hungary.[7]

• ──────────── •

The last group of political refugees came over in 1956 after the failure of the October uprising in Budapest against the repressive Communist government and continued military occupation by the Russian army. Mainly young, single persons at the onset of their careers, many members of this group had participated in the fierce and bloody street fighting in Budapest; others took the opportunity to flee Hungary while the Iron Curtain was temporarily open. Of a different generation and tradition from the earlier waves of displaced persons, the 56ers were professionals whose futures lay in industry and education in America. They assimilated rapidly into the society of their new homeland. In all, 47,643 refugees of the Hungarian Revolution of 1956 came to the United States.[8]

From the American receiving point at Camp Kilmer, New Jersey, these 56ers were resettled across America, including in many Texas cities. There other postwar émigrés joined with earlier arrivals and a variety of agencies to assist the new émigrés in learning English, finding homes and jobs, and fitting into a new society. This was particularly true in Dallas, Houston, and San Antonio, where individuals, churches, and other organizations sponsored the newcomers. In most cases, the 56ers welcomed the assistance of the earlier arrivals to alleviate loneliness and accelerate assimilation in their new homes.

Most postwar refugees arrived in Texas by train or airplane. Those who came before 1956 were usually transported on old troop carriers directly from European displaced persons' camps to Atlantic or Gulf Coast ports and then by train to their Texas destinations. The 56ers were airlifted from Germany to Camp Kilmer, New Jersey, and sent on by train or airplane to their resettlement communities in Texas. One respondent reported a colorful, perhaps apocryphal, tale which was probably enhanced by the telling and retelling:

> The journey from Camp Kilmer to San Antonio was not without incident for some of the refugees, most of whom knew of Texas only from Western movies, although a few did have relatives living here. A poignant story about a young couple on a San Antonio-bound train is worth sharing —
>
> They had enjoyed the trip South thus far and were engrossed in viewing the passing panorama when the conductor, knowing their eagerness to arrive in Texas, land of "kovboys and indianer," approached their coach seat to advise them that they would shortly be crossing the magic border.
>
> As fate would have it, about the time they crossed the state line, several torpedoes (used in those days by repair crews to signal the engineers of oncoming trains that repairs were being made on the tracks ahead) went off with loud bangs. Fearing for their lives and thinking that the train was being attacked by marauding Indians, the two frightened refugees screamed and prostrated themselves, clinging to each other desperately, on the aisle floor.
>
> The petrified couple could not be coaxed up until they were assured by the conductor and reassured repeatedly by their fellow passengers that the loud reports were not gunshots but indeed only warning signals.
>
> It was reported that they spent the remainder of the trip in guarded anticipation of further thrilling events. Upon their arrival at the Missouri-Pacific Depot (in San Antonio), they were welcomed by a jubilant crowd of Hungarian-Americans, some recent émigrés, and other well-wishers.[9]

What the postwar immigrants anticipated finding in Texas varied according to their previous education and experience. Some had preconceived ideas from movies and literature which reflected Old West icons such as cowboys, Indians, and the American frontier. For example, Dr. George Fodor, a San Antonio research chemist, recalled watching old Lone Ranger movies in Hungary before the Communist takeover in 1949, but the Texas summer heat and lack of cultural events in Corpus Christi struck him as the most notable features of the area after his arrival in 1956. Dr. Stephen Juhasz fled Hungary after World War II and only knew that Texas was "the place where the cowboys are," but, arriving in 1953, he quickly realized that "this was not the end of the world." Although he found San Antonio's opera season limited to three days, commerce boomed in the central business district. On the other hand, Dr. Victor Szebehely, an internationally famed celestial mechanical engineer, found Austin a cosmopolitan, cultured city upon his arrival at the University of Texas in 1969.[10]

The postwar period marked the establishment of the first viable Hungarian-centered organizations in the state. Prior to the arrival in those years of hundreds of war-related émigrés, Texas' Magyars had established no mutual benefit societies, cultural clubs, or religious congregations with their fellow countrymen. In part, this may have been due to the lack of ethnic neighborhoods in Texas' larger cities as well as to their small numbers in its general population. Then, with the infusion of new Hungarian immigrants into the Texan metropolitan centers during the 1950's, cohesive ethnic community action was possible for the first time. In fact, the motivation and organizational skills often came from the new arrivals themselves. A summary of Hungarian-centered clubs and religious foundations which took root in Texas after 1945 illustrates this point.

Organizational Efforts in San Antonio

The San Antonio Hungarian Association, founded in 1956, was the first modern organization devoted to the preservation of the Magyar heritage of its members in Texas. Composed of about 30 families of first- and second-generation Hungarian Americans as well as displaced persons who arrived after World War II, SAHA's first goal was to assist refugees of the abortive Hungarian Revolution of 1956 who were spon-

Steve and Rose Safran singing with Steve Juhasz (Johasz) on guitar, San Antonio Hungarian Association picnic, Bandera, 1957

sored by San Antonio agencies such as the Central and Southside Christian Churches and the Council of Catholic Men.[11]

The Austro-Hungarian Society of San Antonio

The earliest-known Texas organization which welcomed Hungarians was the Oesterreichisch-Ungarischer Verein von San Antonio, Texas und Umgegend (Austro-Hungarian Society of San Antonio and Vicinity). Founded November 12, 1916, it received its Texas charter the following March. Still active in the 1980's, it had as its purpose the promotion of closer and friendlier relations among its members, provision of death benefits, and arrangement of social opportunities, including a bowling club. Its membership reflected the multinational composition of the Austro-Hungarian Empire (which was broken up in 1918), and, by the 1980's, its members were mainly descendants of German and Austrian immigrants. The society held quarterly meetings and continued its original purpose as a social club and mutual aid insurance society. As in the beginning, German was the language of its charter, meetings, and publications. Few Hungarian Texans ever became members.[12]

The San Antonio Hungarian Association's founders—Dr. Paul Seabase (Czibész), professor of physics at Trinity University; Professor Alex Nagy, director of research for the Lone Star Brewing Company; and Michael Balint, a graduate student at Trinity University—recognized the need for assisting the freedom fighters and refugees arriving from Camp Kilmer, New Jersey, the Hungarian relocation center in the United States, during the winter of 1956-1957. During the next few years SAHA assisted 38 refugee families and single men who arrived in San Antonio. As Seabase observed in 1957:

> America is truly the promised land for refugees from embattled Hungary. But it isn't easy to adjust from life in an atmosphere of constant fear to enjoyment of the wide degree of freedom the U.S. offers.
>
> Recently arrived refugees are scared of everybody and everything. We have to teach them not to be afraid of the police and other officials and to feel free to express their opinions openly. Such ordinary activities as shopping and getting around town pose major problems for the newcomers faced with living in a community where the language and ways of doing things are vastly different from those to which they are accustomed.[13]

The Story of Paul Seabase

Paul Seabase (Czibész), a postwar political refugee, was born in 1906 in Fiume (Rijeka, now in Croatia) on the Adriatic Sea. He was educated as a mechanical engineer and then worked for a steel company in Hungary. Interested in airplanes and flying, he joined the Aerodynamic Institute in Hungary in 1937 as an aircraft designer but spent World War II in the Hungarian air force, where he rose to the rank of captain. Following the Nazi takeover of Hungary in 1944, he was assigned to repair planes throughout Hungary. Seabase and his family fled westward with other Hungarian military personnel to escape the advancing Soviet army late in 1944. After two weeks, during which Allied planes strafed the Hungarian military convoy, they arrived in southern Germany.

Seabase and his family spent the next few years in displaced persons' camps—Pocking, Funkkaserne, and Dachau—in Germany and later with German Hungarians (called Schwabs)

From left, *Paul and Irene Seabase, Michael Balint, and Rose and Steve Safran, San Antonio, 1957*

at Rastadt in the French military zone in the Black Forest. Seabase soon learned French, worked for the French authorities, and moved his family to a picturesque village. The Seabases were admitted to the United States in 1949. As his wife later recalled:

> After close to five years [as displaced persons], finally we could see the rainbow, for our future. But it . . . turned out to be a nightmare. At the beginning a sponsor with a job was waiting for us in Louisiana. [But] nobody had prepared us to be a slave-worker for a rich rice farmer all day with bleeding hands, for a salary of $17.50 a week. Other compensation [included] a two-room makeshift wooden shack, out of [in the middle of] nowhere with no plumbing. We had two beds, a table, two chairs. The rest of us had to sit on wooden boxes. We had not received any welfare assistance. [My son] Pete was six and a half years old, Tom was four, and I was pregnant. This was the deepest [lowest] point in our life ever . . . in the hot, moist subtropical wind which was blowing from the Gulf over the bare swampland.

Help soon arrived, however, as a priest and nuns from the nearby town of Gueydan took pity on the immigrant family and moved them to a house in town. With his knowledge of French, Paul could communicate with the local Cajuns and so quickly learned English, which enabled him to get a repairman's job with a Western Auto store. Without money or health insurance, Mrs. Seabase, who could not speak English, bore her third son, Johnny, a ten-pound American citizen, with the assistance of a French midwife.

To the Seabases, America was the land of opportunity. Another refugee family, the Alex Nagys in San Antonio, found Seabase a job as an instructor for a French Cadet Program at a military base. Seabase took a bus to San Antonio and soon was assigned to teach aerodynamics to American cadets as well.

He was on his way. He later worked for the Southwest Research Institute and then became a professor of physics at Trinity University, at that time a Presbyterian-affiliated school. When the Soviet Union launched Sputnik, he organized his physics students into Operation Moonwatch, a nonmilitary, non-governmental group which monitored the satellite. To accomplish this, he and his students, because of the lack of university funds, soldered beer cans into an effective antenna and mounted it on the roof of Trinity's science building. Seabase was a cofounder of the San Antonio Hungarian Association, which aided political refugees seeking new homes in the Alamo City. He left Texas the next year to accept a new civil service assignment in St. Louis and was later employed by the U.S. Army in Michigan, where he died.[14]

•———————•

At first SAHA held weekly and monthly meetings, fundraisers (picnics, bridge and card games, and covered-dish suppers), cultural programs, and language classes to help the newcomers. As Seabase observed, "We carry out a rehabilitation program with every newcomer, teaching him American customs, law, and order, and how to use his new-found freedom properly." Then, as its primary goal was achieved, SAHA exhibited Hungarian ethnic pride to the wider San Antonio community, which was noted for its broad range of ethnic diversity. In 1957 the SAHA float won second prize in the Fiesta San Jacinto Battle of Flowers Parade, one of Texas' largest celebrations. The organization also participated in San Antonio's Carnival of Nations in 1959.

As the 1956 Hungarian freedom fighters assimilated into American life (and many moved away), however, SAHA declined and became inactive for 17 years.[15]

Dr. Stephen Juhasz, editor of *Applied Mechanics Review* at the Southwest Research Institute, Alex Nagy, and Michael Balint, both active in the first club, led the revival and rechartering of the San Antonio Hungarian Association in 1977. The original aim of the group had been fulfilled, so new goals were set by the remaining members of the original organization. SAHA's new objectives were civic and cultural: to provide a forum for fellowship by Hungarians in the San Antonio vicinity and throughout the state; to provide information about Hungarian culture; to maintain language skills and instruction; to inform American-born children of their cultural heritage; to assist newly arriving Hungarians; to exchange literature, music, and art among the membership; and to publicize Hungarian culture and achievements.[16]

• ——————— •

From Janitor to Research Professor — Alexander G. Nagy

Alex Nagy, like many other refugees, came to America after World War II and worked his way up from the lowly position of janitor and groundskeeper to adjunct professor at San Antonio's St. Mary's University. Born in Komárom in 1913, he graduated from the Royal Hungarian Ludovica Academy and entered the Hungarian navy, where, during World War II, he was a captain in the Hungarian Danube River Combat Forces. With the approach of the invading Soviet army in 1944, he was ordered to evacuate Hungarian military equipment and naval families to western Hungary and Austria on river barges. As Maria Nagy later recalled, the naval officers' families went aboard the barges early in January 1945, and the Hungarian forces headed westward to Melk, and later Grubweg, Austria, to await the arrival of American forces. "Sometimes the Russians were behind us, like 15 or 20 kilometers, and the Germans would not give us fuel." But Nagy resourcefully traded tobacco for German fuel supplies, and the Hungarian navy surrendered to American forces in May.

Maria and Alexander G. Nagy, with Mary, Alexander Jr., and Thomas

For the next four years Nagy and his family were displaced persons in Austria and Germany. For the first year Alex worked for the Allied Occupation Forces clearing the Danube of destroyed bridges, which German forces had blown up during the last days of the conflict. Later Nagy moved his family to Niederleistein in the French Occupation Zone, where he and some countrymen ran a quartermaster supply system for Hungarian refugees in the Allied Zones. During that time the Nagys applied for admission to Argentina, Venezuela, and even Madagascar, although their real hope was to come to the United States. Two of Nagy's brothers were members of the Catholic order of the Society of Mary. With their assistance and that of the Father General of the order, the Nagy family was sponsored by the president of St. Mary's University in San Antonio in 1949. With more than 1,300 Polish and Estonian refugees, the Nagys landed at New Orleans on the *General Howze*, a converted troop ship, in September and proceeded to San Antonio by train. Maria Nagy later recalled her arrival: "I am in another world; everything was just wonderful, every article, even shoes, there were so many kinds and so many colors!" On the way from the railroad station, she pointed to a tricycle and told her five-year-old son, "There is your tricycle." She was astonished by people's clothing and the plentitude of food, and she remarked that she "could have been in a never-never land." Only San Antonio's terrific heat, 103 degrees the day she arrived, made her ill for a short time.

Maria Nagy, who had learned of Texas from books, found her new home "interesting and absolutely different." As she and her family became accustomed to the climate, she observed that "every day was a surprise." She found people friendly and open, and recalled that "we didn't even have to close the door." At first the Nagys lived in a converted, unair-conditioned classroom at old St. Mary's Law School on the San Antonio River. In the evening they took their children to the courtyard of the building, where they read them Hungarian stories. They wanted the children to learn English rapidly and so enrolled them in the nearby St. Mary's School. Maria learned English by listening to the radio while doing the family's ironing. Although she was initially afraid that someone would break into the family quarters, years later she remarked that she was "just delighted" and "perfectly at home" in Texas. "I never regretted that we came here."

Nagy worked at first as a janitor in St. Mary's University Law School and improved his English. He earned his B.A. and M.A. degrees in economics at night school and became a market analyst for San Antonio's Lone Star Brewery. There he later became director of statistics, planning, and development, and finally, of marketing research. In addition, he spent more than ten years teaching graduate economics at St. Mary's University, which honored him with an International Relations Award Citation in 1976. Thereafter Nagy was instrumental in reestablishing the San Antonio Hungarian Association in 1977 but died within a few months.

Of the Nagy's three Hungarian-born and two American-born children, all earned university degrees, and three received their doctorates and became professors. In addition, two entered Catholic religious orders.[17]

• ———————— •

The rejuvenated Hungarian club began a series of cultural programs, social events, and community participation during the next decade. Its early newsletter, *A Jó Szó* (The Good Word), announced coming events, sometimes in Hungarian and English, as well as social nights and picnics at nearby parks. In 1980 SAHA held a public *Magyar Vasárnap* (Hungarian Sunday) at the University of Texas Institute of Texan Cultures at San Antonio. A giant banner, *Magyar Szüreti Ünnep* (Hungarian Feast of the Harvest of Grapes) greeted visitors, who were treated to a sampling of Hungarian food, music, dance, and history.

In April 1981 SAHA also sponsored "Bartók, A Salute," a public program to mark the centennial of the birth of Béla Bartók (1881-1945), one of Hungary's premier composers and musical folklorists. Other participants were the University of Texas at San Antonio's Division of Music and the Texas Bach Choir. The musical program included Bartok's *Sonata for Two Pianos and Percussion*, *Five Village Scenes*, and four Slovak and three Hungarian folk songs from the *Mikrokosmos*.

The wide separation between San Antonio and the major centers of Hungarian-American life in the Northeast was bridged by the publication of national news in SAHA's newsletter. Yet its main focus of interest and activity was San Antonio and Texas. By 1978 SAHA was a participant in the Texas Folklife Festival, marking the first presentation of the Hungarian ethnic club in its colorful costumes and with its distinctive foods, customs, crafts, and dances for a multi-ethnic audience of more than 100,000 visitors.[18]

American and Hungarian holidays and national observances have been saluted by SAHA in a variety of ways, including the 1981 observance of the 750th anniversary of the death of St. Elizabeth of Hungary at the International Week celebration at Our Lady of the Lake University by the Intercultural Studies and Research Institute. Annual programs on or near March 15 have marked the Hungarian War of Independence, 1848-1849, and in October the anniversary of the Revolution of 1956 is still remembered.

In the mid-1980's SAHA started publishing an expanded, bilingual newsletter, *Paprika*, and at that time membership stood at 50 local and area families. Programs dealing with Hungarian heritage, literature, and music have been interspersed with presentations of leading Hungarian-American scientists and scholars from nearby universities and research institutions. Picnics, dinners, and other social gatherings bring SAHA members together. In addition, the small club gives annual student scholarships to its youth. The civic, cultural, and ethnic impact of the San Antonio Hungarian Association far exceeds its actual size,

Csárdás Dancers at the 1983 Texas Folklife Festival, Institute of Texan Cultures, San Antonio

and its goals have been achieved and implanted in future generations of Hungarian Texans.

SAHA members Adam Bence (age 5), Agnes Rozsa, Zoltan and Margit Balogh, and Monica Nagy were chosen to represent Catholic Hungarians at a huge Papal Mass celebrated on September 13, 1987, during Pope John Paul II's visit to Texas. Dressed in folk costumes, the Magyars represented one of 26 Texas ethnic groups at the event.

The San Antonio Hungarian Association is still active as of this printing in early 1993.

Another organization, the Franz Liszt Foundation of the Americas, moved its charter from Denver to San Antonio during the 1980's. Its focus is to perpetuate Hungarian customs and music and to provide scholarships for serious music students.[19]

Houston's Hungarian American Cultural Association

Hungarian immigrants were attracted to the growing city of Houston. A handful of immigrants were listed in the 1860 census, including Alexander Szabó, who arrived in 1853, J. Veith, a wealthy Hungarian-born grocery merchant, and Maximilian F. de Bajligethy, who, during the 1880's, served as the deputy city assessor and collector.

*Margit and Zoltan Balogh
at the Papal Mass,
San Antonio, 1987*

Recorded as a 34-year-old clerk in 1860, de Bajligethy and his wife, Charlötte, had a large family, including five daughters, who worked during the 1880's as salesladies or milliners. De Bajligethy's sons (Cassimir N.A., Bonaparte N.C., and Attila L.A.) worked in Southern Pacific Railroad shops, the Houston Water Works, and as car inspector and foreman for the Houston and Texas Central Railroad in Houston, respectively. Throughout the remainder of the 19th century, other Hungarians arrived, especially during the large emigration from Hungary in the three decades prior to World War I.[20]

At the turn of the century, 21 heads of households or their wives reported their Hungarian nativity. Almost all had arrived since 1879. Although the immigrants' Hungarian ethnic minority was not given during the 1900 census, their occupations centered mainly on small merchandising and craft shops.[21]

A decade later 121 Hungarian-born and 32 American-born Hungarians lived in Houston and greater Harris County and formed the second-largest concentration, after Galveston County (171 Hungarian-born and 25 children of Hungarian parents). In addition to Magyars, these immigrants formed a representative sampling of ethnic minorities calling themselves Hungarian, including Germans, Jews, Bulgars, Bohemians (Czechs), Serbs, Poles, Slovaks, and Rumanians.

Most worked in blue collar service — industrial, transportation, merchandising, and craft occupations.

The large majority of Hungarian-Jewish immigrants in Houston identified themselves in 1910 as "Hungarian Magyars," indicating their previous assimilation in Hungary. Louis Schwarz, Morris Siegel, and Morris Mauskopf were the exceptions, listing "Hungarian Hebrew" or "Hungarian Yiddish" as their heritage. The majority were small merchants and retailers. Samuel Goldapper was a cantor for the Jewish congregation in Houston.[22]

As the first-generation Hungarian Texans assimilated and advanced economically, fewer Hungarians were arriving in Houston because of the restrictive U.S. immigration laws of the early 1920's and the worldwide depression of the 1930's. Then, following World War II, displaced persons rapidly expanded the numbers of Hungarians in the city. After the Revolution of 1956 still another group of political refugees sought new futures in the Bayou City.

Houston's first Hungarian society was formed in 1957. Dr. Ferenc Györkey, a physician and professor of pathology at the Baylor University School of Medicine; Louis Nagy, a successful shipbuilder and contractor; and Dr. Frank Pető, a professor of French and German at Texas Southern University, organized the Hungarian American Cultural Association of Houston, which was chartered the following year. HACA's immediate objectives were to aid the 60 to 80 incoming 1956 refugees in finding jobs and housing, and in assimilating into American life. Further, HACA sought to enhance Hungarian heritage in America, to supply news and information about events in Hungary, and to provide a social forum for Houston's Hungarians. English-language classes were sponsored for the newly arrived refugees.[23]

· ——————————— ·

Houston's 56ers

The first refugees of the Revolution of 1956 arrived at Houston's Union Depot on the Missouri Pacific Eagle December 20, 1956. One of the first seven men was Miklós (Mike) Oláh, a former chauffeur in a steel factory in Ózd, Hungary, who decided to leave his homeland when he anticipated the failure of the revolution. Hitching a truck ride from Budapest to a spot near the Austrian border, he walked the remaining 50 kilometers, past border guards firing into the air, to safety.

Oláh was among the first refugees airlifted to the United States and was sponsored by a Houstonian who found him a factory job. "Adjusting to life in the United States was difficult at first," he reported, because he did not know English, and the customs were unfamiliar. He said, "I missed the Hungarian music, the folk dances, the weddings, the food and wine . . . and I still do." But within two years he learned English, and "it was easier." Oláh established himself as an auto mechanic and was the first of the 56ers in Houston to become a citizen. In 1975 Oláh commented, "I am here because of the freedom. Free enterprise makes the world go around."

Another of the approximately 50 56ers who came to Houston was Zoltán Gaják, a former Hungarian soldier. When the revolution turned against the Hungarian freedom fighters, his commander advised him to leave the country. With three others he walked five days to the Austrian border, where they used their watches to bribe their way past a Soviet soldier. Gaják, later an engineer for a large construction firm in Houston, recalled that his main adjustment problems were learning English and American customs. Like Oláh, he preferred life in the United States, where there was a higher standard of living as well as political freedom.

Designer Elemér Lengyel, who unsuccessfully tried to leave Hungary in 1948, escaped in November 1956 by hiring a guide and slipping into Austria. After living in England and Canada, he moved to Houston in the mid-1960's to work for a construction firm. He and other 1956 refugees told similar stories of dissatisfaction with conditions in Hungary, escape to the West, and eventual resettlement in Houston, where Lengyel became a leader in the Hungarian American Cultural Association.

Another émigré, René Horváth, recalled joining student demonstrators in front of the Parliament Building in Budapest and being fired upon by Soviet troops. Although wounded, he managed to escape by hiding beneath a railroad car en route to the Austrian border and walking the final 17 miles to freedom. With a slight knowledge of English, Horváth adjusted quickly and soon cut his ties with other Hungarians because he "needed to learn American ways and customs. . . . I was determined to look ahead." He established his own business, married an American, and recalled, "I never could have achieved 25 percent of the things I've done here if I'd stayed in Hungary. . . . Let's face it — I tried to make it better [there], and they shot me for it. So what is there to go back to?"[24]

• ——————————— •

With its first goal accomplished, and in spite of the socials, dances, picnics, and intellectual and cultural activities which sought to help keep the immigrants together, HACA slowly declined during the late 1960's and early '70's. But it revived during the oil boom days of the late '70's and early '80's, attended mainly by post-World War II political refugees and their Texas-born children. HACA sent representatives to the All-Texas Hungarian Picnics held during the late '70's. Dances and picnics at nearby Galveston beaches have always been popular with the members. St. Stephen's Day Mass is celebrated by a Hungarian priest from the Cistercian Abbey, and the anniversary of the October 25, 1956, uprising in Budapest is observed annually with a patriotic program and banquet. HACA's *Bulletin: A Houstoni Magyarok Tájékoztatója* (Bulletin: The Houston Hungarians' Newsletter), begun in 1983, was the second bilingual, Hungarian-language club newsletter published in Texas.[25]

By the 1980's the Houston club was sponsoring a political lobby in Congress, urging the American government to support the human rights of the Hungarian minority living in Transylvania. (Another group supporting this same cause, the American Hungarian Association of the State of Texas, was established in 1992.)[26]

Only a small number of the 3,182 Hungarian-born residents and people of Hungarian heritage (1980) in the widespread Houston-Galveston area belonged to the club, but a 1982 oral history survey of 22 members revealed them to be diverse and well assimilated. The researcher found, however, that because of the "independent nature" of the immigrants consulted, Houston's Hungarians were not very cohesive. They lived in widely separated areas across the sprawling city and held jobs in a variety of fields: entrepreneurship, medicine, business, banking, education, and auto mechanics. Most members of the older generation were multilingual and "displayed an acute historical awareness and strong anti-Communist bent." Loyal and patriotic to the United States, they expressed their gratitude for "the freedom and opportunities available in this country." At the same time, they were proud of their Hungarian heritage.[27]

The study observed that Houston's Hungarians had such traits and values as "strong family awareness, a work ethic, individuality, achievement-mindedness, pride, argumentativeness, and a sense of elitism." Younger members of HACA who wanted more casual social events expressed dissatisfaction with so many intellectual programs. But all recognized that HACA fulfilled a need to host émigré writers and visitors and to observe national holidays. The study concluded that the better-educated members were better assimilated and more cosmopolitan in their world view. HACA's members felt that their position as immigrants gave them a "special vantage point for observing and contributing to American society."[28]

Hungarian Activities in the Dallas-Fort Worth Metroplex

Most Hungarians in the Dallas-Fort Worth area arrived after World War II, and the Revolution of 1956 contributed substantially to the total. In 1980, 2,579 persons reported Hungarian birth or heritage, making this area the second-largest center, after Houston and Galveston, for Hungarians in Texas. But their immigration began more than a century and a quarter ago. Although the 1860 census recorded 32-year-old J.M. Bartay, it was not until the last two decades of the 19th century that significant numbers of Hungarians joined the economically motivated exodus to America. By 1910, 19 heads of household were reported in Dallas County and 18 in Tarrant County.

As in the case of Hungarian immigrants before 1914 in other Texas cities, Dallas's and Fort Worth's communities represented not only Magyars, but also Germans, Slovaks, Czechs, Croats, Rumanians, and Jews from that multi-ethnic Central European kingdom. Their occupations were similar to those of the people who settled in Houston, San Antonio, and elsewhere: crafts, small business, factory work, domestic labor, farming, and railroad work.[29]

Typical of so many others who settled here during this period was A.E. Illés, who lived in Dallas. Illés was born in Balassagyarmat, Nógrád County, on May 29, 1880, and received a degree at the

University of Budapest in pharmaceutical chemistry. He was also on the Austro-Hungarian Olympic track and field team in 1900. Illés then followed a sister and two brothers to the United States about 1904. After living in New York, where he learned English at City University of New York and was on its debating team, he worked for Norwich Chemical Company in Brockton, Massachusetts, as a chemist in the manufacture of extracts. Later he worked in New Jersey, Ohio, and Missouri. In St. Louis, 1910-1912, he was a chemist for the Sanitol Company, the first to put toothpaste and shaving cream into tubes. Illés won a Gold Medal in 1915 at the Panama-Pacific Exposition in San Francisco for his work in the field of dentistry.[30]

During the First World War A.E. Illés was a commodity merchant in Ohio; later he joined the rush to the oil boom town of Burkburnet, Texas, in 1918, where he soon went broke. The next year he moved to Dallas and worked for a supply firm until he set up the A.E. Illés Company in 1929 to produce cosmetics and extracts. Jergens Lotion was one of his formulas. Illés, a Rotarian, operated his company until his death in January 1969.[31]

Hungarians continued to move to the Dallas-Fort Worth area during the first half of the 20th century. Then, after World War II, a new wave of immigration took place. One Dallasite was described as a "one-woman International Refugee Organization." Hungarian-born Theresa Yankó, and her baker husband, Emory, sponsored more than 60 Hungarian refugees. The Yankós found jobs and housing for them and inspired others, including businesses, to do the same, emphasizing that the refugee Hungarians were left with no country, no jobs, and no homes. She pointed out that the refugees were willing to take the most menial jobs in order to begin a new life in America. Often families separated by their flight to the West or by the Iron Curtain were reunited. Some knew English, and others were fast learners. All were faced with establishing new lives.[32]

• ——————— •

Refugee Children Learn English

Refugee children often helped teach their parents to speak English. Such was the case with the Imre Kocsis family, which arrived in Dallas in 1956 from Camp Kilmer, New Jersey. Sons Imre and Gene repeated their own English lessons to their parents, Imre and Maria, after school in order to help their father obtain a new job. Formerly the owner of a clothing and department store in his native Győr, the elder Kocsis and his family were sponsored by the Dallas Junior Chamber of Commerce. Kocsis became a salesman at Neiman-Marcus, and his wife worked as a seamstress and housekeeper to supplement family income.

Gene and Imre Kocsis and Joe and Priscilla Móri, all recently arrived Hungarian children, spent the summer of 1957 in American homes in the northwest Texas counties of Haskell and Knox to increase their command of English. Father Michael Fargó, a Cistercian refugee and parish priest in Rhineland, Texas, conceived the idea to help the children adjust to American society. All had fled Hungary with their parents late in 1956 and eventually enrolled in Dallas public or parochial schools, where they received individual English instruction from PTA volunteers.

According to Father Fargó, the refugee children rapidly adjusted to their new way of life, although they missed their homeland. "One of their happiest discoveries in Texas is a dish of hamburger, sauerkraut, and cabbage leaf called 'Pig in a Blanket,'" which he compared to an old Hungarian dish.[33]

• ———————————————— •

Refugees were also helped by relatives already in Dallas. Attila Telkes and a teenage schoolmate, Imre Lengváry, were sponsored after the Revolution of 1956 by Attila's great-aunt, Dr. Magda Telkes Myers. Dr. Myers was born in Budapest and graduated from the University of Paris, France, in July 1914. She was a Dallas physician for 42 years until her death in 1966. Another family, named Héjjas, was sponsored by a relative and former refugee, Father (later, Abbot) Anselm Nagy of Irving's Cistercian Abbey. He and other Cistercians served as interpreters for the freedom fighters arriving in Dallas.[34]

Father Joseph Nagy, priest and World War II refugee, served parishes in Fort Worth and Dallas during the 1950's and '60's. A native of Mihályfa, Hungary, he was educated at St. Michael's Seminary in Veszprém before being ordained in 1935. Until his flight from Hungary in 1948, Father Nagy served several parishes. In 1952 he emigrated to the United States and became pastor at St. Patrick's C.O. Cathedral in Fort Worth, 1954-1960. Thereafter he served Dallas's St. Monica's and St. Joseph's parishes. He received a citation for meritorious service in the Hungarian Relief Program in Fort Worth from an American Legion Post in that city. Father Nagy also was spiritual director for the Hungarians' Cardinal Mindszenty Movement and took part in the 1961 Mass for the cardinal at St. Joseph's Church in Dallas. He died in February 1964.[35]

The new wave of refugees from the uprising of 1956 needed help. Beginning in December 1956, just two months after battling Soviet tanks in the streets of Budapest, hundreds of Hungarians began arriving at Dallas's Love Field for resettlement. Many were sponsored by the Dallas International Rescue Committee, the National Catholic Welfare Conference, the Jewish Family Service, the Dallas Jewish Welfare Federation, and the Dallas Hungarian Freedom Committee. Others were helped by Fort Worth's Hungarian Relief Program. Dallas Mayor R.L. Thornton, bands, flag wavers, and Hungarian Cistercian monks from the nearby abbey greeted the new arrivals. Hungarian House, Dallas's refugee resettlement center on Lemmon Avenue in 1957 assisted the recently arrived to find employment and housing.[36]

Over the years the anniversary of the 1956 uprising has been remembered annually by Hungarian Catholics with a special Mass. In 1966 Dallas Bishop Thomas K. Gorman celebrated the Mass at St. Joseph's Church. In addition, a Hungarian art exhibit depicting the revolution was held at the studio of local artist André E. Szűcs. It included works by Szűcs, Dr. Julius Zsohár, and Andrew P. Darvas. Other national Hungarian holidays were observed by the Catholic community as well. The Feast Day of St. Elizabeth of Hungary was observed by Mass in that Dallas parish, and monks from the Cistercian Abbey sang a Gregorian Mass (plain chant), which was followed by a covered-dish supper, dances, and the playing of the Hungarian national anthem.

Dallas's Hungarian Catholics also marked the fifth anniversary of the liberation of Cardinal Mindszenty in Budapest during the 1956 revolution with a Mass at St. Joseph's Church in 1961. Mass still is said in Hungarian once a month at Our Lady of Dallas Cistercian Abbey on the campus of the University of Dallas in Irving, where there has been a Hungarian Youth Association for some years.

A Hungarian social club was organized in 1990 in the Dallas-Ft. Worth area—the Metroplex Magyar Cultural Circle—which is active at the time of this printing in early 1993.[37]

Statewide Organization

Ethnic unity among Texas' Hungarians was limited. As earlier, immigrants after World War II scattered to sprawling suburbs, and no ethnic neighborhoods or churches developed.

During the late 1970's three statewide meetings of Hungarian clubs and communities were held. Representatives from Texas' three largest metropolitan areas met at Bastrop State Park in 1977 seeking to create an umbrella organization for all Hungarians living in the state. Thereafter two gatherings were held: at Lake Somerville in 1978 and at Marble Falls in 1979. At the latter meeting Hungarians from Fort Worth were represented for the first time. "Chieftains" from each community met at the *tábortűz*, a traditional bonfire where Hungary's ancient chieftains met to discuss tribal affairs. No subsequent meetings were called, however.

An outgrowth of the statewide gatherings was Hungarians of Texas (HOT), which was chartered by the Texas secretary of state in 1980 as a tax-free, nonprofit organization. Its goal was to bring all persons of Hungarian descent together for preservation and promulgation of Hungarian heritage, but this failed to develop, and HOT was superseded by the Hungarian Foundation of Texas. With the chartering of the new nonprofit foundation, a second effort was made to create an organization for all Hungarians in Texas. A monthly magazine, *The Hungarian Texan*, is in the planning stage; it will, in bilingual format, furnish abundant information on Hungarian culture. A nonreligious, nonpolitical philosophy has been adopted.[38]

In Conclusion

Hungarians have been coming to Texas for more than a century and a half. Their story fell into three broad areas, each with its own motivations. The few who came prior to 1848 were joined by émigrés driven from their homeland by the failure of the Revolution of 1848-1849. They and their children, including the first Hungarian women in Texas, participated in taming Texas' frontier and in the Civil War. With the rapid economic expansion and population growth in the state toward the end of the 19th century, others, the economic migrants, multiplied not only in numbers but also in ethnic diversity. Hungarian minorities, who became known as Czechoslovaks, Yugoslavs, or others in Texas, took part in that large immigration. They were in turn supplemented by hundreds of post-World War II political refugees. Although still few in numbers by the 1980's, Texas' Hungarians formed part of that state's cultural plurality and played contributory roles in building its modern social, economic, and political base.

Hermann Seele's poem to the 48ers who passed New Braunfels in 1853 romantically idealized a popular view of immigrants and their future in the West. "Freedom, home, happiness, and peace," however, were not realized by all. Many found happiness and prospered in new homes. Others found political and personal freedom previously denied them. And still others lived bleak lives or repatriated. In the stories of individuals and their activities through 150 years, Hungarians in Texas experienced both success and failure. Yet, as did those of many other ethnic backgrounds, they played a distinctive part in the history of the state.

ACKNOWLEDGMENTS

The San Antonio Hungarian Association contributed the largest part of the funding for this book, and special appreciation goes to Past Presidents Michael J. Balint, Rose Kovary Safran, the late Mariette Gruber, Milton Caroline, and Stephen Johannes, as well as to all members of the Board of Directors [in the mid and late eighties] and the general membership.

In addition, members of the San Antonio Hungarian Association gave freely of their time to translate materials from Hungarian to English. A special tribute goes to Rose Kovary Safran; Dr. Stephan Juhasz; Maria Nagy Peterson; Dr. Margit Nagy, CDP; Toni Juhasz; Stephen Johannes; Zoltan Balogh; Dr. Leslie André, and others who volunteered their time and loaned books and maps for this project.

Dr. Bela Vassady of Elizabethtown College, Elizabethtown, Pennsylvania, added his expertise in translating as well as sage advice, and Dr. Eniko Molnar Basa of Silver Spring, Maryland, also contributed translations and information. Dr. Steven Bela Vardy of Duquesne University, Pittsburgh, Pennsylvania, was a tremendous help as reader for historical detail as well as provider of diacritics on Hungarian names and words.

A huge debt of gratitude goes to Dr. John J. Alpar of Amarillo, Texas, who voluntarily translated Péter Bogáti's two books, *Édes Pólim!*

and *Flamingók Új-Budán*, and related documents dealing with the Újházi family, with the kind permission of the author.

Péter Bogáti of Budapest, Hungary, followed this work with great interest and contributed copies of rare documents and photographs of László Újházi and his family, the originals of which are in the Újházi Papers in the National Archives in Budapest.

Our appreciation is also extended to Sharon J. Hill and Diane Johnston of Dr. Alpar's staff, who typed — and retyped — translations from Bogáti's books.

Dr. Robert S. Hosh and Dr. August Molnar of the American Hungarian Foundation, New Brunswick, New Jersey, supplied rare books and information from their research library. Dr. Bela Vassady, Dr. Steven Bela Vardy, and Dr. Leslie Konnyu of St. Louis, Missouri, shared their findings on Hungarian Americana freely. Dr. Alfred E. Lemmon of the Historic New Orleans Collection supplied much-needed information as did Dr. Imrich Immer of Houston. Dr. Edward C. Breitenkamp of Bryan, Texas, kindly allowed us to quote from his manuscript translations of Hermann Seele's poetry.

Special thanks go to Helga Maxwell of Universal City, a member of the Institute's volunteer Alliance, who spent many hours translating German manuscripts, as did Irma Goeth Guenther of Austin.

Sarah Smith and Sue McDonald, also Alliance members, became my research assistants, spending uncounted hours reading microfilm, making calls, and searching public records in the San Antonio City Hall and the Bexar County Courthouse. Their interest, humor, and encouragement in following dim trails of the pioneers made this work possible. To them goes my deep appreciation as well as to Elaine Mitrovich of La Marque and Galveston, who worked in the Galveston County Courthouse and braved the local cemetery; to Ann Seaman of Los Angeles, California, who investigated the King Vidor Papers at the University of Southern California; and to Mary Philmon of Lufkin, an Institute Ambassador in her city, who searched fruitlessly for Kossuth, Texas.

The staffs of the repositories of Texas' heritage patiently and expertly helped in locating information. My thanks go to those at the Daughters of the Republic of Texas Library at the Alamo, the San Antonio Public Library, the Dallas Public Library, the Houston Public Library, the El Paso Public Library, the Southwest Collection at Texas

Tech University in Lubbock, the Special Collections Library at Stephen F. Austin State University in Nacogdoches, the Eugene C. Barker Texas History Center at The University of Texas at Austin, the Texas State Library and Archives, the Austin History Center, the Rosenberg Library in Galveston, the Archives of Performing Arts at the University of Southern California in Los Angeles, the Texana Collection at Baylor University in Waco, and many others.

Dr. Frank Pető and Elemer Lengyel of Houston and Imre Kocsis and the Reverend Abbot Anselm Nagy of Dallas gave extra attention to our requests for information on the Hungarian communities in those two metroplexes.

Hundreds of people across the state and nation have answered my pleas for family data and old photographs. Thanks go to David Vidor Adams, Jeffrey W. Alford, Mary Avant, Nell Baldwin, Gabe Balla, Stanley Banks, Dr. Thomas Baron, Gary K. Bartay, Dunya Bean, Ruth Benke, Laszlo Beres, Desi K. Bognar, Henry E. Bowling, A.T. Brainerd, Frank Brenner, Lucille Brown, Sister Julie Budai, Jim Calhoun, Oscar and Ernest Carvajal, Bernice Casey, Ned Comstock, Roger N. Conger, I. Wayne Cox, Ima Creech, Lucy Justine Davis, Esther de Vecsey, Bill Duncan, Christine Nagy East, Josie R. Finger, George Fodor, Norma Friday, Andrew S. Garay, Julia Gardner, Butch Gerfers, Dr. Ted Gish, Rodney Goebel, Dr. William E. Green, Precious and Bill Gregg, Sue Ann Greives, Joe Gross, Dr. George J. Gruber, Irma and Ernest A. Guenther, and Jacqueline Guthrie.

Others are Andrew Haraszti, Loula Újffy Harris, Sallie B. Harris, Mrs. Faulkner Heard, Jean Heard, Marian Hill, Ernest Horvath, Susan Hovorka, Theo Houston, Mrs. John Hrnciar, Robert E. Illes, Royce Jones, Louise Karkalits, Kent Keeth, Dr. Stephen C. King, Vivian King, Judge Al Klein, Lester Klein, Dr. Robert Knutson, Dr. John J. Koldus III, Dr. Frank Korompai, Dr. Z.T. Kosztolnyik, William Krusoe, Lisa Shippee Lambert, Ann Langer, Carol Elizabeth Lee, Doris M. Levy, Billie Lindley, Eugene Lipstate, Lajos Markos, Dr. Denes Monostory, Louis and Edith Nagy, Thomas Barton Nash, Linda Cheves Nicklas, Martin O. Noonan, Marie D. Nordyke, Pamela Lynn Palmer, Richard Parker, Robert J. Parker Jr., Dr. Dan C. Peavy, Mary Ellen Perry, Paul K. Pesthy, Ben Petmecky, Emma Petmecky, and Fred Petmecky.

Thanks also go to Paul Pulitzer of the *Hungarian Heritage Review*, Bill Rakocy, Elma Wadgymar Smith Reeder, Nan L. Reeves,

Phil Rosenthal, Ernest, Eugene J., Bob A., and Jack Roth, Agnes and Klara Rozsa, Annabelle Rylander, Mary A. Sarber, Dr. Zoltan Schelly, Leon and Robert Schmidt, Stephanie N. Schneidler, the late Mrs. C.M. Scholes, Dorothy Schwartz, Edward Stern, Daisy Weirich Strickland, Endre Szabo, Dr. Victor Szebehely, Lela Bell Szenasy, Mitchell Tomasini, Mr. and Mrs. Robert L. Tomasini, Curtis Tunnell, Dr. Tamas Ungar, Dr. Wes Valek, Mr. and Mrs. Milton Varga, Frank Wagner, Lorraine and Frank Watkins, Dr. Bobbie Weaver, Janice Weber, Ann C. Weigand, Selma L. Weiner, Janet Wheeler, Claudia White, Judge John Wildenthal, Alix B. Williamson, Peggy Wingate-Ramage, Dorothea Yorker, Emilie Zinsmeister, and Dr. Julius Zsohár.

The preparation of this Hungarian-Texan study was made possible by [then] Executive Director of the Institute of Texan Cultures Lt. Gen. (U.S. Army, ret.) John R. McGiffert, the Director of Research and Collections Dr. James C. McNutt, and many of my colleagues. Their support, encouragement, and advice have been invaluable. I am grateful.

James Patrick McGuire
San Antonio, 1988

Editor's Note: Patrick McGuire died in January 1992 after a long illness, while this book was in the early stages of production. He is sorely missed by his colleagues and friends at the Institute of Texan Cultures and around the state.

NOTES

Many letters, clippings, articles, and interviews are contained in the Hungarian Files at the Institute of Texan Cultures, cited as HF-ITC.

Please note: When Ibid. follows a note with multiple references, it refers to the *last* listing in that preceding note.

CHAPTER ONE   Hungary and Texas

[1] Hermann Seele, *Verses and Songs of Texas*, trans. and trans. Edward C. Breitenkamp, p. 87.

[2] Steven Bela Vardy, *The Hungarian-Americans*, p. 1; Stephen Sisa, *The Spirit of Hungary: A Panorama of Hungarian History and Culture*, pp. 227-28.

[3] Vardy, *Hungarian-Americans*, pp. 1-3; C.A. Macartney, *Hungary: A Short History*, pp. 1-7. The author wishes to thank *Eastern Europe*, Library of Nations, Time-Life Books, 1986, for permission to use its chronology of Hungarian history as a guide.

[4] Vardy, *Hungarian-Americans*, pp. 2-3; Macartney, *Hungary*, pp. 8-11.

[5] Ibid., pp. 10-14.

[6] Vardy, *Hungarian-Americans*, pp. 2-3.

[7] Macartney, *Hungary*, pp. 33-38; Vardy, *Hungarian-Americans*, pp. 3-4.

[8] Ibid., pp. 4-5.

[9] "Hungary," *Encyclopaedia Britannica*; Istvan Deak, *The Lawful Revolution: Louis Kossuth and the Hungarians, 1848-1849*, p. xiii.

[10] *Encyclopaedia Britannica.*

[11] Ibid., pp. 856-66.

[12] Leslie Konnyu, *Hungarians in the U.S.A.: An Immigration Study*, p. 5.

[13] *Encyclopaedia Britannica.*

CHAPTER TWO   Early Hungarians in Texas

[1] Péter Bogáti, *Édes Pólim!*, p. 337; Vardy, *Hungarian-Americans*, pp. 9-11.

[2] Ibid., pp. 11-12.

[3] Mary Fisher Parmenter, Walter Russell Fisher, and Lawrence Edward Mallette, *The Life of George Fisher (1795-1873) and the History of the Fisher Family of Mississippi*, p. 2; Walter Prescott Webb and H. Bailey Carroll, eds., *The Handbook of Texas* 1:600-601 (hereafter, *Handbook of Texas*).

[4] Parmenter et al., *George Fisher*, p. 2.

[5] *Handbook of Texas* 1:600-601.

[6] Ibid.; Donald W. Whisenhunt, ed., *Texas: A Sesquicentennial Celebration*, p. 55.

[7] *Handbook of Texas* 1:600-601.

[8] Ibid., 2:704-705.

[9] Parmenter et al., *George Fisher*, pp. 133-35; *Handbook of Texas* 1:600-601.

[10] Parmenter et al., *George Fisher*, p. 85.

[11] *Handbook of Texas* 1:600-601.

[12] Houston *Telegraph and Texas Register*, April 9 and 16, 1845.

[13] Ibid., April 16, 1845. Not a few cultured and sophisticated Hungarians assumed ennoblement and titles upon reaching the shores of the New World. So-called counts, princes, and barons competed for the hospitality of gullible frontiersmen, who readily accorded them their new status. Other Hungarians more modestly added only prefixes such as *de* and *von*, disclaiming titles while pointing to noble lineage. The name Zondogi is unknown among the Hungarian nobility, and the nonnoble ending of *i* rather than the noble *y* indicates that the so-called count was unfamiliar with the customary spelling, which should have been Zondogy. There were, of course, valid exceptions to the rule, such as Count Teleki and László Újházi.

[14] New Orleans *Picayune*, April 26, 1845, as quoted in William Ransom Hogan, *The Texas Republic*, pp. 55-56.

[15] Herbert Gambrell, *Anson Jones: The Last President of Texas*, pp. 395-96.

[16] *Handbook of Texas* 1:51-52.

[17] Gambrell, *Anson Jones*, pp. 395-96; Hogan, *Texas Republic*, p. 55; Nancy Nichols Barker, *The French Legation in Texas* 1:660. For a detailed account, see Fayette Copeland, *Kendall of the* Picayune, pp. 121-39.

[18] Houston *Telegraph and Texas Register*, May 28, 1845; *Handbook of Texas* 2:791.

[19] Ibid., 1:128.

[20] Ibid.; Charles Merritt Barnes, *Combats and Conquests of Immortal Heroes*, p. 211.

[21] Daughters of the Republic of Texas, *Founders and Patriots of the Republic of Texas*, p. 487; Thomas Lloyd Miller, *Bounty and Donation Land Grants of Texas, 1835-1888*, pp. 422-23; San Antonio *Express*, November 21, 1932; Mooney and Morrison, comps., *General Directory of the City of San Antonio, 1877-78*.

[22] Frederick Chabot, *With the Makers of San Antonio*, pp. 132-33.

[23] Ibid.; San Antonio *Express*, November 21, 1932; Emily Edwards, *F. Giraud and San Antonio*, pp. 22-23. According to the San Antonio *Express* of March 15, 1890, Lochmar's "boarding house" was called the Navarro House and was located on Acequia Street.

[24] Solms-Braunfels Archives 1:259; *Handbook of Texas* 1:7-8.

[25] Solms-Braunfels Archives 1:258, 259; 30:224-26; 41:34; 61:33-35, 54.

[26] Ibid., 61:82-92, 185-86.

[27] Ibid. Information from another source reported that a Paul Szirmay was a former member of the Hungarian Diet and a member of the Opposition in Sáros County, Újházi's home county. See Ferenc Pulszky, *Életem és korom* [My Life and Times], 2 vols. (Budapest: Szépirodalmi Könyvkiadó, 1958), 1:435, as reported by Steven Bela Vardy to James Patrick McGuire, Pittsburgh, Pennsylvania, March 23, 1988, HF-ITC.

[28] Solms-Braunfels Archives 31:173; 38:162, 180; 39:161, 345.

[29] Ibid., 61:192-201.

[30] Géza Kende, *Magyarok Amerikában* 1:146, 148-49, 193, 273. See also, Péter Bogáti, *Flamingók Új-Budán*, pp. 117-24, for an account of Szirmay at New Buda, Iowa.

[31] Gillespie County Historical Society, *Pioneers in God's Hills: A History of Fredericksburg and Gillespie County, People and Events* 2:109; Jeanette Hastedt Flachmeier, *Pioneer Austin Notables*, p. 82. Flachmeier reported that the king of Hungary granted the family noble status for their fight against the Turks. One source reported that the first Petmecky coming to Germany from Hungary had fought under Prince Eugen against the Turks. See Luise Schulte to Dear Frances, December 29, 1974, HF-ITC.

[32] Ibid.

[33] Flachmeier, *Pioneer Austin Notables*, p. 82. Another source, Gillespie County's *Pioneers in God's Hills* 2:109, reported that she died on March 19, 1849, during the cholera epidemic which struck New Braunfels and other towns.

[34] Gillespie County, *Pioneers in God's Hills* 2:109. Another source, Theodore John Albrecht, "German Singing Societies in Texas" (dissertation), p. 35, reported that Gottfried moved to Austin rather than to San Antonio. From Austin he was made an honorary member of the New Braunfels Germania in November 1853 after the first Texas Sängerfest, held in October 1853 in New Braunfels.

[35] Flachmeier, *Pioneer Austin Notables*, pp. 82-83.

[36] Ibid.; *Handbook of Texas* 2:352, 506.

[37] Flachmeier, *Pioneer Austin Notables*, pp. 82-83; "Joseph Petmecky," Military Service Branch, National Archives and Records Service, Washington, D.C.; *Handbook of Texas* 1:621.

[38] "Frank W. Petmecky," Military Service Branch, National Archives and Records Service, Washington, D.C.; Martin Hardwick Hall and Sam Long, *The Confederate Army of New Mexico*, p. 316.

[39] Flachmeier, *Pioneer Austin Notables*, pp. 84-86.

[40] Gillespie County, *Pioneers in God's Hills* 2:108-10.

[41] *Handbook of Texas* 1:308-309. See also, Bobby D. Weaver, *Castro's Colony: Empresario Development in Texas, 1842-1865* for a more detailed discussion.

[42] A.J. Sowell, *Early Settlers and Indian Fighters of Southwest Texas*, p. 347, 349. The correct spelling of Schorobiny's name is unknown. Sowell spelled it "Charobiny." Declaration of Intent to Become a Citizen, Commissioners' Court Minutes, Medina County, Texas, vol. 1, p. 31; "Rudolph Schorobiny — Sketch of the Old Mexican War Veteran Who Came to Texas in 1845 and Died April 25, 1908," ms., p. 1.

[43] Ibid.; Rudolph Schorobiny to Lorenzo Castro, Quihi, Texas, September 1, 1879, as printed in the San Antonio *Texas Sun*, March 1880.

[44] Schorobiny to Castro, September 1, 1879, HF-ITC.

[45] Ibid.; *Handbook of Texas* 1:141; Sowell, *Early Settlers*, p. 348.

[46] Ibid., pp. 348-49; Schorobiny to Castro, September 1, 1879, HF-ITC.

[47] Ibid.

[48] Ibid.

[49] "Rudolph Schorobiny," ms., p. 1.

[50] Ibid.; Castro Colonies Heritage Association, *The History of Medina County, Texas*, p. 491.

CHAPTER THREE   László Újházi, the Great Exile

[1] L. Éva Gál, *Egy 48-as forradalmás Újházi László*, p. 439; John J. Alpar to James Patrick McGuire, Amarillo, September 4, 1987, HF-ITC.

[2] Gál, *Egy 48-as forradalmás*, p. 439; *Révai Nagy Lexikona* 18:603; J. Siebmacher, *Die Wappen des Adels in Ungarn* 33:689; Chart of Újházy Family from Rozsnyóbánya and Budamér, HF-ITC, with appreciation to Péter Bogáti of Budapest.

[3] Deak, *Lawful Revolution*, pp. 4, 5.

[4] Kende, *Magyarok Amerikában* 1:23-25; Emil Lengyel, *Americans from Hungary*, pp. 29-30; Chart of Újházy Family, HF-ITC. See Lengyel and Kende for additional information on the Benyovszkys in America, including one who supposedly came to Texas, married, and was killed in 1809 on the Rio Grande, leaving three sons, one of whom lived until 1843.

[5] Gál, *Egy 48-as forradalmás*, p. 440.

[6] Ibid.; Bogáti, *Flamingók Új-Budán*, p. 17; Szillányi, *Komorn im Jahre 1849*, p. 113.

[7] Bogáti, *Flamingók Új-Budán*, pp. 17, 22, 46; Gál, *Egy 48-as forradalmás*, pp. 440-41; *Révai Nagy Lexikona* 18:603; Deak, *Lawful Revolution*, p. 136.

[8] Bogáti, *Édes Pólim!*, pp. 17-18; idem, *Flamingók Új-Budán*, pp. 17-18; Gál, *Egy 48-as forradalmás*, p. 441; Deak, *Lawful Revolution*, p. 193.

[9] Bogáti, *Édes Pólim!*, pp. 17, 20-22; Gál, *Egy 48-as forradalmás*, p. 441.

[10] W. Steinert, "W. Steinert's View of Texas in 1849," trans. and ed. Gilbert J. Jordan, p. 408; Francis J. Brown and Joseph Slabey Roucek, eds., *One America*, p. 213.

[11] Carl Wittke, *Refugees of Revolution: The German Forty-Eighters in America*, p. 83; Lengyel, *Americans from Hungary*, p. 48.

[12] Ibid., pp. 48, 50; Brown and Roucek, *One America*, p. 213; Bela Vassady Jr., "Kossuth and Újházi on Establishing a Colony of Hungarian 48-ers in America, 1849-1852," pp. 25-26. Vassady's is the most thorough study available on the Hungarian colony plans in America.

[13] Lengyel, *Americans from Hungary*, p. 50; Eugene Pivány, *Hungarian-American Historical Connections*, p. 48; Vassady, "Kossuth and Újházi," p. 23: Lillian Mae Wilson, "Some Hungarian Patriots in Iowa," pp. 483-84.

[14] Újházi to Pulszky, New Buda, June 26, September 7, 1850, as quoted and summarized in Steven Gaspar, "Four Nineteenth-Century Hungarian Travelers in America" (dissertation), pp. 320-22, 324; Kende, *Magyarok Amerikában* 1:64-66. Gaspar mistakenly stated that Újházi bought 7,680 acres at New Buda.

[15] Gaspar, "Four Hungarian Travelers" (dissertation), pp. 320, 323, 328; Wittke, *Refugees of Revolution*, p. 83.

[16] Gaspar, "Four Hungarian Travelers" (dissertation), p. 335; Kende, *Magyarok Amerikában*, pp. 145-46; Vassady, "Kossuth and Újházi," p. 27.

[17] Leslie Konnyu, *Acacias: Hungarians in the Mississippi Valley*, p. 22; Edmund Vasváry, "A New Budai gyerekek," ms., Edmund Vasváry Collection photocopy 0002611, American Hungarian Foundation, New Brunswick, N.J.; Wilson, "Hungarian Patriots," pp. 484-88. It is interesting to note that Mrs. Újházi died on October 6, which coincided with the anniversary of the execution of the 13 Hungarian Honved generals at Arad and of the former Hungarian prime minister in Budapest by the Austrians in 1849. This date also coincided with the murder of Austrian Minister Latour in Hungary in 1848.

[18] Edmund Vasváry, "Újházi letter [title illegible]," ms., Edmund Vasváry Collection photocopy 0002066-69, American Hungarian Foundation; Wilson, "Hungarian Patriots," p. 488.

[19] Deak, *Lawful Revolution*, pp. 342-43; Konnyu, *Acacias*, p. 27; Vassady, "Kossuth and Újházi," pp. 28-39.

[20] Bogáti, *Édes Pólim!*, p. 121; Gaspar, "Four Hungarian Travelers" (dissertation), p. 369; Kende, *Magyarok Amerikában* 1:71; Vassady, "Kossuth and Újházi," pp. 34-39.

[21] Bogáti, *Flamingók Új-Budán*, pp. 181-88; Újházi to Kossuth, Austin, April 22, 1852, in Gaspar, "Four Hungarian Travelers" (dissertation), pp. 407-409,

citing Dénes Jánossy, *A Kossuth-emigráció Angliában és Amerikában, 1851-1852* [The Kossuth Emigration to England and America, 1851-1852] 2, part 2, p. 797. Bogáti gives a long description of Újházi's journey to Texas, and Gaspar reports in detail on Kinney and Corpus Christi.

[22] Gaspar, "Four Hungarian Travelers" (dissertation), pp. 410-11.

[23] Ibid., pp. 399-402, 17n; Deed Records, Nueces County Clerk's Office, Corpus Christi, book 19, p. 407, plat roll A, image 48; Joseph Majthényi to his wife, New Buda, August 22, 1852, as cited in Tivadar Ács, *New-Buda*, p. 257; Frank Wagner to James Patrick McGuire, Corpus Christi, August 25, 1987, HF-ITC.

[24] Bogáti, *Flamingók Új-Budán*, pp. 187-88.

[25] L. Éva Gál, *Újházi László, a szabadságharc utolsó kormánybiztosa* [László Újházi, the Last Government Commissioner in the War for Independence], p. 72; Gaspar, "Four Hungarian Travelers" (dissertation), pp. 407, 411-13.

[26] Bogáti, *Édes Pólim!*, pp. 126-27.

[27] Alamo Abstract and Title Guaranty Co., San Antonio, Abstract of Title, 211 Mandalay East, Olmos Park, Texas, A.T. Brainerd; Deed Records, Bexar County Clerk's Office, San Antonio (hereafter, BCCO-SA), vol. K2, pp. 420-21, 425. The parcels included 84 acres (Lot No. 3, Range No. 2, District No. 3) and 55 ½ acres (Lot No. 6, Range No. 2, District No. 3), based on Francis Giraud's survey of the city. See also, Bogáti, *Flamingók Új-Budán*, pp. 189-90, for discussion of Újházi's first purchase of land near San Antonio. Újházi asked his son Sándor in Hungary to send money, which would be added to that of Újházi's late wife's estate, and also borrowed money to purchase the Texas property.

[28] Certificate of Marriage of Vilmos Madarász and Helen Újházy, June 4, 1853, Újházy Family Files from Péter Bogáti, Budapest; Ács, *New-Buda*, p. 264; Kende, *Magyarok Amerikában* 1:151-54.

[29] Bogáti, *Édes Pólim!*, p. 136; Gál, *Újházi László*, p. 72; Gaspar, "Four Hungarian Travelers" (dissertation), p. 416; Kende, *Magyarok Amerikában* 1:151-54.

[30] Bogáti, *Édes Pólim!*, pp. 138, 140.

[31] *Neu-Braunfelser Zeitung*, September 2, 1853; *San Antonio Zeitung*, July 30, September 3, 1853; Bogáti, *Flamingók Új-Budán*, pp. 228-31.

[32] Ibid., pp. 231-33.

[33] Seele, *Verses and Songs of Texas*, pp. 83-87.

[34] Bogáti, *Édes Pólim!*, pp. 145, 330; idem, *Flamingók Új-Budán*, pp. 233-34; Albrecht, "German Singing Societies" (dissertation), p. 63.

[35] Bogáti, *Flamingók Új-Budán*, pp. 236-37.

[36] Deed Records, BCCO-SA, vol. L1, pp. 542, 604; vol. L2, pp. 243, 420-21, 443; map of "Lands of Herff and Dittmar, formerly Count General Farkas Újházy, 1146 ⁹/₁₀ acres, on Olmos Creek, Survey by Chas. P. Smith, July 26, 1876," Dittmar Collection, Daughters of the Republic of Texas Library at the Alamo, San Antonio (hereafter, DRT Library, San Antonio); Abstract of Title, Olmos Park. See also, Gaspar, "Four Hungarian Travelers" (dissertation), pp. 414-19.

The Pedro Camarillo Tract, 596 ½ acres, was purchased to the north of the original Sírmező, 550 acres, in 1875. A modern street map of San Antonio

would define the boundaries of Újházi's property as running along McCullough Avenue from Annie Street northward to Jackson-Keller Road and then
northwest to Blanco Road, northward again, then east on Oblate Drive (once
called Újházi Road, then apparently Lorenz and Újházi Road) to Jones-
Maltsberger Road. The boundary then went southward, becoming Devine
Road to its southern boundary, which follows the present southern boundary
of the City of Olmos Park. Included in this area are the present City of Olmos
Park, the Olmos Flood Basin, Olmos Park (picnic area and sporting fields),
Olmos Golf Course, and the residential additions of Shearer Hills. See "Lands
of Herff and Dittmar," Dittmar Collection, DRT Library. Újházi paid off
the liens on the original purchase of 550 acres in June 1864. See Deed
Records, BCCO-SA, vol. T1, p. 136; vol. 3, p. 320.

[37] Bogáti, *Flamingók Új-Budán*, pp. 235-38, 267.

[38] Brand Books, BCCO-SA, book A, p. 275.

[39] Bogáti, *Flamingók Új-Budán*, pp. 339-48. Bogáti gives a long account of Újházi's problems in obtaining ownership of the site of his house and of the
hillside located on Sírmező.

[40] Frederick Law Olmsted, *A Journey through Texas, or, A Saddle-Trip on the
Southwestern Frontier*, pp. 356-57. Olmsted, as did other of Újházi's contemporaries in America, afforded the respected exile the honorary title of "governor," possibly because of his prior service in his home county of Sáros as
well as because of his role at the fortress of Komárom during the revolution.
Újházi was also variously called "general" and "count." Such titles in relation
to Újházi appear nowhere in Hungarian literature, but abound in American
sources concerning him.

[41] Bogáti, *Flamingók Új-Budán*, pp. 348-49.

[42] Ibid., p. 237; idem, *Édes Pólim!*, pp. 145-46.

[43] Ibid., pp. 146-53.

[44] Ibid., p. 148; idem, *Flamingók Új-Budán*, pp. 269-70.

[45] Bogáti, *Édes Pólim!*, pp. 178-79. See also, idem, *Flamingók Új-Budán*, pp.
280-81, for Újházi's division of his Hungarian properties. He divided his
estates and legal rights in Hungary equally between his eight children, in
return for $6,000 and the money to pay for his land in Texas, which was
under litigation. The children were to share the expenses of his trip to
Switzerland. In addition, Helen and her four siblings then living in Hungary
were to be paid their maternal inheritance, which Újházi had been holding
for them. Finally, his eight children were to pay all his debts in Hungary.
He retained only Sírmező, his American farm, which was eventually reserved
for Helen, Farkas, and László Jr., who shared his Texas home at the end
of his life.

[46] Bogáti, *Édes Pólim!*, pp. 153, 212-21; Marriage Records, BCCO-SA, book D1,
p. 5, no. 1164.

[47] Bogáti, *Flamingók Új-Budán*, pp. 277-78.

[48] Bogáti, *Édes Pólim!*, pp. 190, 226.

[49] Bogáti, *Flamingók Új-Budán*, pp. 276-77.

[50] 4th Civil Court Minutes, Naturalization Records, Bexar County District Clerk's
Office, book B, nos. 431, 432, and 433; Bogáti, *Édes Pólim!*, pp. 227-28;

Chart of Újházy Family, HF-ITC. Their naturalization papers gave their names as Ladislaus (László), Theodore (Tivadar), and Wolfgang (Farkas).

[51] Bogáti, *Édes Pólim!*, p. 228.

[52] Ibid., pp. 246-47, 250; Gaspar, "Four Hungarian Travelers" (dissertation), p. 441.

[53] Bogáti, *Édes Pólim!*, pp. 252-85. (The information in the next eight paragraphs is taken from this source.)

[54] Ibid., pp. 266, 285; Ács, *New-Buda*, p. 88; John J. Alpar to James Patrick McGuire, Amarillo, August 28, 1987, HF-ITC.

[55] San Antonio *Daily Herald*, October 28, 1858.

[56] Bogáti, *Édes Pólim!*, pp. 288-91.

[57] Ibid., pp. 292-97; *The Madarasz Book*, p. 3.

[58] Bogáti, *Édes Pólim!*, pp. 299-304.

[59] Ibid., pp. 306-307.

[60] Gaspar, "Four Hungarian Travelers" (dissertation), pp. 426-31.

[61] Ibid., p. 443.

[62] Bogáti, *Édes Pólim!*, pp. 308-46. (The next eleven paragraphs are taken from this source.)

[63] Ladislaus Újházi to William H. Seward, Sírmező, April 6, 1861, Record Group 59, Applications and Recommendations for Public Office, 1861-69, Diplomatic Papers, letter box 107, National Archives, Washington, D.C.

[64] Bogáti, *Flamingók Új-Budán*, p. 311; Ács, *New-Buda*, p. 89.

[65] Deed Records, BCCO-SA, vol. S3, pp. 247-48; San Antonio *Tri-Weekly Alamo Express*, March 25, 1861; Gaspar, "Four Hungarian Travelers" (dissertation), p. 450.

[66] Ibid., pp. 456-64.

[67] Ibid., pp. 464-65; Bogáti, *Édes Pólim!*, p. 352; Gál, *Újházi László*, pp. 79-80.

[68] Bogáti, *Édes Pólim!*, pp. 355-63. (The next six paragraphs are from this source.)

[69] Bogáti, *Flamingók Új-Budán*, pp. 341-42; Kende, *Magyarok Amerikában* 1:172-76.

[70] Bogáti, *Flamingók Új-Budán*, pp. 341-44; Sam Woolford, ed., *San Antonio . . . A History for Tomorrow*, p. 88.

[71] Bogáti, *Flamingók Új-Budán*, p. 344.

[72] Deed Records, BCCO-SA, vol. U, p. 117; vol. 2, p. 258. In 1873 Klára Kellerschön was living at Schönbornslust near Koblenz, Germany, and certified to American consular agent George Holscher that the agreement was valid.

[73] Gaspar, "Four Hungarian Travelers" (dissertation), p. 472; San Antonio *Daily Herald*, December 25, 1865. "Ladislaus Ujhazy, Jr., Ladislaus Ujhazy, Sr., and Faker [*sic*] Ujhazy" were all listed as registered voters in Bexar County in February 1868. See San Antonio *Express*, February 13, 1868; see also, January 20, 24, and 28, February 5, 1868.

[74] Kende, *Magyarok Amerikában* 1:172-76; Frederick Chabot Papers, Eugene C.

Barker Texas History Center, University of Texas at Austin; Gál, *Újházi László*, p. 83; Gaspar, "Four Hungarian Travelers" (dissertation), pp. 484-85. The majority of Hungarians supported the efforts of Deák and other statesmen and welcomed the Compromise of 1867, viewing it as a partial reassertion of Hungary's autonomy. Until World War I, Hungary experienced almost five decades of progress. Újházi's views reflected, therefore, those of a bitter exile unwilling to face reality as far as political progress in Hungary was concerned. See Steven Bela Vardy to James Patrick McGuire, "Comments on *The Hungarian Texans*," HF-ITC.

[75] Record Group 59, Applications and Recommendations for Public Office, 1861-1869, Diplomatic Branch, National Archives, Washington, D.C.; Elisha Marshall Pease Papers, Austin History Center, Austin, Texas; Gaspar, "Four Hungarian Travelers" (dissertation), pp. 477-80.

[76] Ács, *New-Buda*, pp. 316-22; Gaspar, "Four Hungarian Travelers" (dissertation), pp. 473-77.

[77] Ibid.

[78] Ibid.

[79] San Antonio *Express*, September 11, 1867.

[80] Bogáti, *Flamingók Új-Budán*, pp. 353-63. The San Antonio *Express* of June 6, 1869, reported that "Laszlo Ujhazy [*sic*]" offered to rent "the storehouse on Main Street, now occupied by Moke & Bro."

[81] Deed Records, BCCO-SA, vol. V2, p. 501; Bogáti, *Édes Pólim!*, pp. 368-71. Reported to have been a lonely old lady living in Germany in the 1880's and 1890's, Klára wrote in her diary that, in Texas, she, who hadn't married until age 34, had been "a hopeless spinster, a jack of all trades of the family, who is different from a hired hand only that she can sleep with the family and they cannot be rude to her, is now richer and more stable than her other bloods [relatives] in Texas and in the County Sáros, put together." Although her family patronized Joseph Kellerschön for being a German and of the working, or peasant, class, Klára reported also that her brother Farkas had made peace with Joseph as they worked in the fields of Sírmező, watching for rain. Although Joseph's handiwork was everywhere evident at Sírmező, it was always known as the Újházi settlement and his name never mentioned.

[82] Bogáti, *Édes Pólim!*, pp. 371-75. Bogáti, in *Flamingók Új-Budán*, pp. 363-73, presents a long discussion of Újházi's natural death versus his suicide, weighing all sides of the question. Further, Bogáti details the final return of Újházi's and his wife's remains for reburial on October 16, 1879, in the ancient family crypt in the Lutheran Church at Budamér in Sáros County.

[83] Ibid.; San Antonio *Daily Express*, March 9 and 10, 1870; *Flake's Daily Bulletin* (Galveston), March 12, 1870; San Antonio *Freie Presse für Texas*, March 8, 1870; Gaspar, "Four Hungarian Travelers" (dissertation), pp. 486-87. The newspapers lamented Újházi's death by suicide, reporting that he was suffering from despondency and melancholy caused by old age and infirmity. The report also said that he aimed his gun through his mouth and fired it with the help of a string bound to the trigger. It ended, "Peace to his soul." A lively debate subsequently developed among historians and biographers over László Újházi's reported suicide. Those denying it based their reasoning upon Farkas's letter to his relatives; those accepting it quoted the newspaper reports.

[84] Bogáti, *Flamingók Új-Budán*, p. 367.

[85] Bogáti, *Édes Pólim!*, pp. 377, 380, 389.

[86] Ferdinand Peter Herff, *The Doctors Herff: A Three-Generation Memoir*, ed. Laura L. Barber, vol. 1, pp. 69-70.

The Pedro Camarillo Tract, 596½ acres, was purchased to the north of the original Sírmező, 550 acres, in 1875. A modern street map of San Antonio would define the boundaries of Újházi's property as running along McCullough Avenue from Annie Street northward to Jackson-Keller Road and then northwest to Blanco Road, northward again, then east on Oblate Drive (once called Lorenz and Újházi Road) to Jones-Maltsberger Road. The boundary then went southward, becoming Devine Road to its southern boundary, which follows the present southern boundary of the City of Olmos Park. Included in this area are the present City of Olmos Park, the Olmos Flood Basin, Olmos Park (picnic area and sporting fields), Olmos Golf Course, and the residential additions of Shearer Hills. See "Lands of Herff and Dittmar," Dittmar Collection, DRT Library. Újházi paid off the liens on the original purchase of 550 acres in June 1864. See Deed Records, BCCO-SA, vol. T1, p. 136; vol. 3, p. 320.

CHAPTER FOUR   Újházi's Family in Texas after 1870

[1] Bogáti, *Édes Pólim!*, pp. 18, 34-49.

[2] Ibid., pp. 60-90.

[3] Ibid., pp. 96-136.

[4] Ibid., pp. 153-65.

[5] Ibid., pp. 166-202, 221-23, 228-45.

[6] Ibid., pp. 262-77.

[7] Ibid., pp. 280-97.

[8] Ibid., pp. 301-13, 320.

[9] Ibid., pp. 314-16; Deed Records, BCCO-SA, vol. R, p. 612; vol. V2, p. 277.

[10] Bogáti, *Édes Pólim!*, pp. 324-30.

[11] Ibid., pp. 328-44.

[12] Bexar County, Texas, U.S. Bureau of Census, Census of Population, 1860; Civil Court Cases, District Clerk's Office, Bexar County, vol. F, pp. 304-305, 590.

[13] Ibid., vol. F, pp. 304-305; *Madarasz Book*, p. 3.

[14] Bogáti, *Édes Pólim!*, pp. 331-39.

[15] Ibid., pp. 352-53; Ács, *New-Buda*, pp. 307-308.

[16] Bogáti, *Édes Pólim!*, pp. 358, 361-63.

[17] Ibid., pp. 364-67, 484; San Antonio *Express*, August 28, 1867.

[18] Deed Records, BCCO-SA, vol. V2, pp. 35, 119, 277; vol. V3, p. 353; Gaspar, "Four Hungarian Travelers" (dissertation), p. 481.

[19] Bogáti, *Édes Pólim!*, pp. 381-82; Gaspar, "Four Hungarian Travelers" (dissertation), p. 489; Chart of Újházy Family, HF-ITC.

[20] Bogáti, *Édes Pólim!*, pp. 382-85.

[21] Ibid.; U.S. Ninth Census (1870), Schedule IV: Agricultural, Bexar County.

[22] Bogáti, *Édes Pólim!*, p. 386; St. Mary's College Record Books, 1858-69, St. Mary's University Special Collections Library, San Antonio.

[23] Deed Records, BCCO-SA, vol. 13, pp. 85, 87. László Jr.'s power of attorney was witnessed by Samuel Baloghy and Joseph Kossuth. The document moved through official channels from the District Judge of Gömör County to the Royal Court of Justice at Rimaszombat to the Ministry of Justice. Translated into German and then into English, it was signed by the U.S. consular agent in Pest before being sent to Texas and recorded in the Deed Records at the Bexar County Courthouse.

[24] Ibid., BCCO-SA, vol. 3, p. 320.

[25] Gaspar, "Four Hungarian Travelers" (dissertation), pp. 489-91; San Antonio *Freie Presse für Texas*, January 11, 1870, December 4, 1873; San Antonio *Express*, January 11, 1870.

[26] H. v. Liffreing to J.P. Newcomb, San Antonio, May 28, 1870, James P. Newcomb Papers, San Antonio Public Library; San Antonio *Daily Express*, October 14, 1875. The 1876 survey map of Sírmező included the location of the cotton gin just to the north of the house and outbuildings. See "Lands of Herff and Dittmar," Dittmar Collection, DRT Library, San Antonio.

[27] Deed Records, BCCO-SA, vol. 3, pp. 64, 268, 320, 615; vol. X2, pp. 23, 376; vol. 7, pp. 163-64. See also, Gaspar, "Four Hungarian Travelers" (dissertation), pp. 493-98.

[28] "Trustee's Sale," handbill, James Collection, DRT Library, San Antonio; San Antonio *Daily Express*, December 22, 1877; San Antonio *Weekly Express*, April 25, 1878. The last citation stated that Farkas Újházy's property was also listed under Notice of Tax Sales in 1877.

[29] *North San Antonio Times*, December 23, 1976, November 26, 1987.

[30] Deed Records, BCCO-SA, vol. 7, p. 333.

[31] Marriage Records, BCCO-SA; Gaspar, "Four Hungarian Travelers" (dissertation), p. 496; Chart of Újházy Family, HF-ITC; Klára Kellerschön to her niece Ilona, daughter of Pauline Nagy, Schönbornslust, Germany, February 2, 1881, HF-ITC. Klára reported that the bankrupt Farkas had returned from America with his wife and small daughter in April 1879, visited her at Schönbornslust, and then gone on to Hungary, where he sought employment.

[32] Bogáti, *Édes Pólim!*, pp. 380-84.

[33] Ibid., p. 379.

[34] Deed Records, BCCO-SA, vol. T3, pp. 582, 597; vol. V3, p. 494.

[35] Ibid., vol. V1, p. 269; vol. V2, p. 277; vol. X2, pp. 267-69, 322, 410; vol. 3, pp. 72, 108, 397.

[36] Bexar County, Census of Population, 1870; Mooney and Morrison, *Directory of San Antonio, 1877-78, 1879-80, 1881-82, 1883-84*.

[37] Bexar County, Census of Population, 1880; Mooney and Morrison, *Directory of San Antonio, 1883-84*; *Madarasz Book*, pp. 3-4. The time of Louis Madarász's departure from San Antonio is uncertain. *The Madarasz Book*, p. 7,

reproduces a letter from L. Madarász to J.D. Day, New York, December 20, 1877, indicating that he had moved to the Northeast, c. 1876-77. Another source gave more personal information on him, stating that he was a "peculiar man" with a basically good nature, but that he did not make friends easily. It was said that he had a "special talent" in all games of gambling, especially cards. He was also an excellent billiards player and had learned to play chess from his mother. While summering in Ogunquit, Maine, he posted signs at the local post office, challenging people to different games. See Edmund Vasváry, "A Madarász," ms., photocopy #0000468-0000476, Vasváry Collection, American Hungarian Foundation.

[38] *Madarasz Book*, pp. 3-5.

[39] San Antonio *Daily Express*, July 16, 1879, May 1, 1899; San Antonio *Freie Presse für Texas*, September 20, 1877; Donald E. Everett, *San Antonio: The Flavor of Its Past, 1845-1898*, p. 69.

[40] San Antonio *Express*, November 28, 1879, as quoted in Everett, *Flavor of Its Past*, p. 69.

[41] San Antonio *Freie Presse für Texas*, October 15, November 12, 1880, November 2, 1881; San Antonio *Daily Express*, October 30, 1881.

[42] Deed Records, BCCO-SA, vol. 25, p. 612; vol. 26, p. 484.

[43] San Antonio *Freie Presse für Texas*, August 7, 1882, July 25, 1884; San Antonio *Light*, March 6, 1883, August 5, 1884; San Antonio *Evening Light*, March 6, 1883; Stephen Gould, *The Alamo City Guide*, pp. 100-101.

[44] San Antonio *Freie Presse für Texas*, June 5, September 19 and 30, December 10, 1885; Mooney and Morrison, *Directory of San Antonio, 1883-84, 1885-86, 1887-88, 1889-90*; Johnson and Chapman, *General Directory of the City of San Antonio, 1891*; Jules A. Appler, *General Directory of the City of San Antonio 1892-93, 1895-96, 1897-98, 1899-1900*; Barnes, *Combats and Conquests*, p. 99.

[45] San Antonio *Freie Presse für Texas*, May 10, 1886; San Antonio *Daily Express*, August 21, 1886; San Antonio *Light*, July 9, 1886.

[46] San Antonio *Daily Express*, February 10, 1887; Elton R. Cude, *The Wild and Free Dukedom of Bexar*, pp. 134-36; Everett, *Flavor of Its Past*, pp. 80-81. Cude's description of McCoy's trial included the following poem, reportedly sent to the sheriff by the jury before it returned from its deliberations:
> We the jury in the McCoy case,
> Have found his actions very base,
> We think that this is only just
> When to us is given trust
> No reason why we should abuse
> Our bodies further with misuse.
> To waste our time in vain endeavor
> The Judge would say 'twas very clever
> But no, their guns went together — Bang-Bang
> Then why in hell should he not hang.
> " 'Twill be a lesson in after time
> To warn men from crime
> So should our lives be pure and sue
> For life or property or divorce

For law will surely have its force
As it did in this case."

[47] San Antonio *Daily Light*, September 3, 1888, March 9, 1889; San Antonio *Daily Express*, February 4, 1891.

[48] Marilyn McAdams Sibley, *George W. Brackenridge: Maverick Philanthropist*, p. 135; Samuel Nugent Townshend, *Our Indian Summer in the Far West*, p. 112.

[49] Klára Kellerschön to relatives, Schönbornslust, Germany, February 9, 1885, February 14, April 28, May 12, August 8, September 27, 1889, HF-ITC.

[50] Everett, *Flavor of Its Past*, pp. 63-64; Vinton Lee James, *Frontier and Pioneer Recollections of Early Days in San Antonio and West Texas*, p. 115.

[51] Klára Kellerschön to relatives, Schönbornslust, Germany, September 17, 1890, March 6, June 1, 1891, HF-ITC.

[52] Ibid., December 19, 1891.

[53] Ibid., August 12, 1893.

[54] Ibid.; Marriage Records, El Paso County Clerk's Office, El Paso; Appler, *Directory of City of San Antonio, 1892-93, 1895-96*; Újházi Biography File, Eugene C. Barker Texas History Center, University of Texas at Austin.

[55] Klára Kellerschön to relatives, Schönbornslust, Germany, December 21, 1893, HF-ITC.

[56] Ibid., April 24, May 6, 1894.

[57] San Antonio *Daily Express*, May 2, 1895.

[58] Ibid., October 9, 1904; Appler, *Directory of City of San Antonio, 1897-98, 1899-1900*; Újházi Biography File, Eugene C. Barker Texas History Center, University of Texas at Austin.

[59] San Antonio *Express*, May 1, 1899.

[60] Ibid., June 20, 1899.

[61] San Antonio *Daily Express*, June 16, 1901; Rudolph Menger, *Texas Nature Observations and Reminiscences*, p. 314.

CHAPTER FIVE   Hungarian 48ers in Bexar County, Texas

[1] Vardy, *Hungarian-Americans*, p. 14.

[2] Vassady, "Kossuth and Újházi," pp. 22-28. This article contains a clear, concise explanation of Kossuth's and Újházi's ideas concerning an American colony for the exiles.

[3] Ibid., pp. 26-27; Bogáti, *Édes Pólim!*, pp. 36-38, 47; Lengyel, *Americans from Hungary*, p. 52.

[4] Gaspar, "Four Hungarian Travelers" (dissertation), p. 4. Excellent biographies on Xantus have been published in recent years. See Henry Miller Madden, *Xantus: Hungarian Naturalist in the Pioneer West*; Leslie Konnyu, *John Xantus, Hungarian Geographer in America (1851-1864)*; John Xantus, *Letters from North America*, trans. and ed. Theodore Schoenman and Helen Benedek Schoenman.

[5] Madden, *Xantus*, pp. 17-19.

[6] Konnyu, *John Xantus*, pp. 6-13.

[7] Ibid., pp. 13-16; Xantus, *Letters*, pp. 54-55; Kende, *Magyarok Amerikában* 1:207-26.

[8] Konnyu, *John Xantus*, pp. 16-37. Konnyu gives an excellent summary of the kinds of information and samples exchanged, including skulls of American Indians for those of different Hungarian tribes, including Kún, Székely, and Jász.

[9] Ibid., pp. 37-40.

[10] Bogáti, *Flamingók Új-Budán*, pp. 26, 71, 93-94; Edmund Vasváry, *Lincoln's Hungarian Heroes: The Participation of Hungarians in the Civil War, 1861-1865*, p. 73. Bogáti related that Pomutz was a major at Komárom and had been a lawyer before becoming a police commissioner in the military group of government commissioner Gáspár Noszlopi, military commander of Somogy. Thereafter he met Újházi and was the chief of police at Komárom.

[11] Bogáti, *Édes Pólim!*, pp. 21, 45, 48-49.

[12] Vasváry, *Lincoln's Hungarian Heroes*, p. 74; Wilson, "Hungarian Patriots," pp. 479, 502-504. Wilson reported that Pomutz stayed with Újházi for a year or so before he returned to Iowa. She also said that he appeared at public functions in St. Petersburg, Russia, in the full regimentals of an American brigadier general.

[13] "Kerényi Frigyes," *Révai Nagy Lexikona* 11:495-96. Another source reports that Kerényi was born in Bártfa, Sáros County. See Kende, *Magyarok Amerikában* 1:190-94. See also, Leslie Konnyu, *A History of American Hungarian Literature*, pp. 12-13, and Ács, *New-Buda*, p. 86.

[14] "Kerényi," *Révai Nagy Lexikona* 11:495-96.

[15] Kende, *Magyarok Amerikában* 1:190-94; Edmund Vasváry, "The First Letter of Frigyes Kerényi from America" (1961); "Where Is the Grave of Frigyes Kerényi?" (1966); "Once More about Frigyes Kerényi" (1969); "The Rank of Frigyes Kerényi as a Poet" (1971), ms. photocopies, Edmund Vasváry Collection Index and Photocopies, American Hungarian Foundation; Gaspar, "Four Hungarian Travelers" (dissertation), pp. 232-36. Kerényi is remembered in his homeland with a marble tablet on a wall at the college in Eperjes. His poems were published in Hungary in 1844, 1846, and 1879. See *Révai Nagy Lexikona* 11:495-96.

Tivadar Ács, in *New-Buda*, p. 86, gave another account of Kerényi's death: Having reached San Antonio, Kerényi began walking to Újházi's farm but collapsed on the road. A nearby coal-burning furnace attracted his attention, and he sought its heat, fell in, and burned to death. In his pockets were found his poems, "which is how Újházi learned of his fate." If true, then Kerényi died in present Brackenridge Park, San Antonio, where there once was a stone quarry with limekilns. In February 1854 Justice of the Peace H. Matson of Bexar County presented his bill to the Bexar County Commissioners' Court for three inquests. One may have been for Kerényi. See Commissioners' Court Minutes, 1837-1855, BCCO-SA, p. 303. See also, Bogáti, *Flamingók Új-Budán*, pp. 117-24, for a discussion of Kerényi's arrival at New Buda, Iowa.

[16] Joseph Széplaki, *The Hungarians in America, 1583-1974*, p. 11; Vardy, *Hungarian-Americans*, p. 14; Rezsoe Gracza and Margaret Gracza, *The Hungarians in America*, pp. 23-24; Wilson, "Hungarian Patriots," pp. 513-14.

[17] Ibid.; Gracza and Gracza, *Hungarians*, pp. 23-24; Széplaki, *Hungarians in America, 1583-1974*, p. 11.

[18] Ibid.

[19] Ödön [Edmund] Vasváry, "Könyv Újházy Lászlóról" [A Book about László Újházy], ms., Edmund Vasváry Collection, American Hungarian Foundation; Deed Records, BCCO-SA, vol. N2, p. 40. The Kosztas gave a promissory note for the property to the seller, C.C. Cove, to be paid in three yearly installments at 12 percent annual interest. See also, Bogáti, *Édes Pólim!*, p. 260, and *Flamingók Új-Budán*, pp. 266-67, for László Újházi's commentary concerning Koszta, his wife, and his Texas farm and slaves. According to Újházi, the slaves were valued at $1,500 of the $9,000 purchase price of the farm.

[20] Deed Records, BCCO-SA, vol. N2, p. 41; vol. O2, p. 345; vol. S2, pp. 66-67.

[21] San Antonio *Herald*, July 17, 1858; Lengyel, *Americans from Hungary*, pp. 59-61; Kende, *Magyarok Amerikában* 1:252-56.

[22] Bogáti, *Flamingók Új-Budán*, pp. 254-57.

[23] Bogáti, *Édes Pólim!*, pp. 30, 71, 74, 92; idem, *Flamingók Új-Budán*, pp. 67, 254-56; Gaspar, "Four Hungarian Travelers" (dissertation), p. 474; Kende, *Magyarok Amerikában* 1:155, 172-76.

[24] Commissioners' Court Minutes, Naturalization Records, book 2A, p. 601, no. 220, and Deed Records, vol. 27, p. 333, BCCO-SA; Bexar County, Census of Population, 1880; Bogáti, *Édes Pólim!*, pp. 280, 295, 302; idem, *Flamingók Új-Budán*, pp. 256-57, 279; Gaspar, "Four Hungarian Travelers" (dissertation), p. 426; San Antonio *Light*, March 19, 1884.

Katona made his declaration of intent to become a citizen in Decatur County, Iowa, on July 29, 1853, and was granted his citizenship in San Antonio on January 10, 1866. His witnesses were Francis Böröndi and Joseph Kellerschön.

Small glimpses of the Katonas' lives in Texas included Teris (Terez, Terus) bringing the first spring flowers to Helen Madarász in January 1859. In 1864 his cattle brand, KG, was recorded in the Bexar County Courthouse. In the Census of 1880 Katona was 63 years of age, and his wife was 57. Teris Katona died in 1883. Her tombstone in Coker Cemetery, San Antonio, bears the inscription "Katona Teris, born 1823, died 1883, 60 years of age." Katona sold the Mud Creek farm and livestock (eight yearlings, seven cows and two calves, four horses, and a yoke of oxen) the same year and married Anna Keresztes on March 19, 1884.

[25] Bogáti, *Flamingók Új-Budán*, pp. 254-57, 279.

[26] Commissioners' Court Minutes, Naturalization Records, BCCO-SA, book 2A, p. 601; San Antonio Genealogical and Historical Society, "1867-1869 Registration of Voters, Bexar County, Texas"; Bogáti, *Flamingók Új-Budán*, pp. 255, 259; Kende, *Magyarok Amerikában* 1:155; Gaspar, "Four Hungarian Travelers" (dissertation), p. 495; Deed Records, BCCO-SA, book S1, p. 287; Benjamin Varga to John Varga, San Antonio, July 8, 1879, HF-ITC; "Trustee's Sale," A. Dittmar, Trustee, November 14, 1877, flyer in James Collection, DRT Library, San Antonio.

27 Gaspar, "Four Hungarian Travelers" (dissertation), p. 474; Deed Records, BCCO-SA, vol. 32, p. 364; Bexar County, Census of Population, 1880. Included in the 1883 sale of the restaurant were tables, tablecloths, castors, knives, forks, dishes, silverware, chairs, lamps, heating stove, kitchen stove, utensils, counters, and "all fixtures of 'my restaurant' in the house situated in the northwest corner of Commerce Street and Navarro Street, known as Boshart's [sic] Saloon, said property and restaurant being in rear of said saloon and known as Globe Restaurant." The total sale amounted to $250 and was dated December 20, 1883, many months after his death. In the Coker Cemetery, San Antonio, Böröndi's tombstone is inscribed "Frank Brandi, died March 1, 1883, aged 52 years." On the iron gate to the fenced plot, a nameplate is spelled "Boerendy." See also, San Antonio *Daily Express*, March 1 and 3, 1883.

28 San Antonio *Light*, February 2, September 15, 1954; San Antonio *Express*, September 15, 1954; *The San Antonian*, September 22, 1954.

29 San Antonio *Light*, February 2, 1954.

30 Gaspar, "Four Hungarian Travelers" (dissertation), p. 433; "Benjamin Varga" obituary, S.W. Pease Collection, Institute of Texan Cultures; Ethel Hander Geue, *New Homes in a New Land: German Immigration to Texas, 1847-1861*, p. 57.

The Institute of Texan Cultures's Varga files contain assorted unidentified documents, copies, and notes furnished by Mr. and Mrs. Milton Varga, San Antonio. Varga family traditions hold that there were seven sons: one remained in Hungary, one went to California, one was in New York, and only four came to Texas. The San Antonio Vargas were not kin to another refugee family, that of Francis Varga, which settled in Iowa, although the legends of both are often borrowed and confused.

Benjamin Varga obtained a baptismal certificate, copied "word for word" and "written and presented to the parents," from John Pápay, preacher of the Calvinist Reformed Church in Patas on November 28, 1854. (Apparently his wife, Magdalene, was still living at that time.) His sons, John, born December 6, 1833, and Alexander, born November 12, 1836, were born in Patas. Attached to this document was a note in Hungarian: "The honorary saddle master, Mr. Benjamin Varga, who lives in Szerdahely, would like to clear and prove all dates of birth and baptism of his sons before he leaves the country to prevent any deriving doubts in the future. He also wants to have his fourth son, Joseph's, name be recorded, just like the rest of his sons, Lajos, John, and Alexander. Joseph was born in Szerdahely and was baptized by the preacher in the Lutheran Church, also in Szerdahely."

Geue's reading of the German immigrant ship lists identified the Varga sons as "A. and J. Borga" and "F. and P. Borga," all of whom arrived at Galveston on the *Weser* from Bremen in 1858.

31 Bexar County, Census of Population, 1860; Gaspar, "Four Hungarian Travelers" (dissertation), pp. 432-34, 496, 499, 501, 505; Deed Records, BCCO-SA, vol. R2, p. 42.

32 Certificate from the Register of Births and Baptisms from the Calvinist Church, Patas, Hungary, November 28, 1854; Emigration Edict, John Varga, Oedenburg (Sopron), July 17, 1858; Austrian Imperial-Royal Passport, John Varga,

Oedenburg (Sopron), July 17, 1858; Declaration of Intent, Bexar County District Clerk's Office, November 8, 1873; "John Varga," Military Service Branch, National Archives and Records Service, Washington, D.C.

[33] Imperial-Royal Siebenbürgischen General-Commando Reisepass, Roselia Deák; Marriage Records, vol. D2, p. 560, and Probate Records, Rose Varga, November 12, 1866, BCCO-SA; San Saba County, Census of Population, 1880; Mooney and Morrison, *Directory of San Antonio, 1883- 84, 1885-86, 1887-88, 1889-90;* Johnson and Chapman, *General Directory of San Antonio, 1891;* Appler, *Directory of City of San Antonio, 1892-93, 1894, 1895-96, 1897, 1897-98, 1898, 1899-1900;* Bexar County, Census of Population, 1900; "John Varga Is Dead," undated, unidentified newspaper obituary, HF-ITC.

[34] "Alexander Varga," Military Service Branch, National Archives and Records Service, Washington, D.C.; 23rd Civil Court Minutes, Naturalization Records, Bexar County District Clerk's Office, vol. H, p. 70; Bexar County, Census of Population, 1870; San Antonio *Daily Herald,* June 5, 1867; Mooney and Morrison, *Directory of San Antonio, 1877-78, 1879-80, 1883-84, 1885-86, 1887-88, 1889-90.* Alexander Varga received his citizenship in San Antonio on October 18, 1872.

[35] Johnson and Chapman, *General Directory of San Antonio, 1891;* Appler, *Directory of City of San Antonio, 1892-93, 1894, 1895-96, 1897, 1897-98, 1898, 1899-1900;* Bexar County, Census of Population, 1900; Andrew Morrison, comp., *San Antonio, Texas,* p. 98.

[36] "Joseph H. Varga," Military Service Branch, National Archives and Records Service, Washington, D.C.; San Antonio *Express,* November 23, 1942; San Antonio *Light,* March 7, 1943; Benjamin Varga to John Varga, San Antonio, July 8, 1879, HF-ITC. In this letter Benjamin Varga said, "Joseph has his shop on Military Plaza after separating from Alex."

[37] Frank W. Johnson, *A History of Texas and Texans* 5:2315-16; San Antonio *Light,* February 2, 1942; *Southwest Texans,* p. 84; Proof of Heirship, Emory L. Varga and Bart J. Varga, San Antonio, HF-ITC; San Antonio *Light,* March 7, 1943.

[38] "Paul Varga," Military Service Branch, National Archives and Records Service, Washington, D.C.; Hall and Long, *Confederate Army of New Mexico,* p. 172.

[39] Baptismal Certificate of Pál Varga, Evangelical Church, Szerdahely, December 21, 1854; Permission to Emigrate, Sopron, July 17, 1858; Austrian Imperial-Royal Passport, Paul Varga, Sopron, July 17, 1858; Marriage Records, BCCO-SA, no. 2720; Bell County, Census of Population, 1870; San Saba County, Census of Population, 1880; Mary Ellen Varga Johnson, "The Varga Story," ms., HF-ITC; Deed Records, BCCO-SA, Benjamin Varga to Paul Varga, July 12, October 12, 1876, vol. F, p. 417. The Bell County Census of 1870 identified Paul's wife as "Nancy." The children of Paul and Blanche Varga were William A., Elvira, and Mary.
See also, "Death of Old Settler, Paul Varga," unidentified newspaper obituary, c. August 15-17, 1912; "Varga Chapel Named for Early Settler Who Gave Land," unidentified newspaper article; "Homecoming at Bowser Recalls Former Glory," Brownwood *Bulletin,* August 28, 1960, HF-ITC.
Born on May 28, 1841, in Bős and baptized in the Reformed Church at Szerdahely, Paul was identified as a "brushmaker" from Győr when he applied

to emigrate in July 1858. The old Varga Chapel at Richland Spring was later demolished, but the cemetery remained in use. One daughter, Mary Ellen, lived on part of the Varga ranch until 1976, a century after her father acquired the property.

[40] Everett, *Flavor of Its Past*, p. 132; Deed Records, BCCO-SA, vol. R2, p. 42; vol. T3, pp. 38, 126; vol. T1, p. 175; vol. U1, pp. 226-28; vol. U2, p. 87; 4th Civil Court Minutes, Naturalization Records, Bexar County District Clerk's Office, vol. F, p. 540; Benjamin Varga to John Varga, San Antonio, March 23, 1878, July 8, 1879, HF-ITC. Varga received his American citizenship on August 3, 1867.

[41] Benjamin Varga to John Varga, San Antonio, July 8, 1879, HF-ITC.

[42] Benjamin Varga to Paul and John Varga, San Antonio, February 14, 1880; Benjamin Varga to John Varga, San Antonio, March 13, 1880; Benjamin Varga to Paul and John Varga, San Antonio, August 1881, HF-ITC.

[43] Benjamin Varga to John Varga, San Antonio, September 27, 1881, HF-ITC; San Antonio *Light*, November 20, 1889; Mooney and Morrison, *Directory of San Antonio, 1883-84, 1889-90.*

[44] Amos Lorenz, Affidavit, September 11, 1926, Deed Records, BCCO-SA, vol. 8, p. 230; vol. 907, p. 450; Bogáti, *Édes Pólim!*, pp. 263, 273, 282-83, 290, 296-97, 302, 320, 324. In a total of seven land transactions between 1874 and 1883, Lorenz acquired additional acreage for his farming and ranching operation. See Index to Deed Records, BCCO-SA. See also, Commissioners' Court Minutes, Naturalization Records, BCCO-SA, book 2A, p. 601, box A, document 173; interview with Robert J. Parker Jr., San Antonio, May 21, 1987, HF-ITC.

[45] Bogáti, *Édes Pólim!*, pp. 263, 273, 287, 290.

[46] Ibid., pp. 296-97, 320, 324.

[47] Bexar County, Census of Population, 1880, 1910; Commissioners' Court Minutes, January 10, 1866, BCCO-SA, book 2A, p. 601; "Anton Lorenz," Military Service Branch, National Archives and Records Service, Washington, D.C.; San Antonio Genealogical and Historical Society, "1867-1869 Registration of Voters, Bexar County, Texas"; Brand Books, book B, p. 506, book C, p. 55, and Marriage Records, vol. D2, p. 314, BCCO-SA.

In the 1900 census Lorenz gave his age as 70 and declared that he had entered the U.S. in 1851. In the same census Julia said that she was 62 and had entered the U.S. in 1860. Further, Anton reported that he was born in September 1829; Julia's birthdate was given as November 1837. In the 1910 census he gave his age as 83 and reported that he had entered the country in 1848, and his wife, in 1860.

There is some evidence that Julia had previously been married. Writing in late 1859, Helen Madarász said, "Julcsa [Julia] left her husband behind [in Hungary] the same way I did mine. . . . The faithless Julcsa left me two weeks ago, or, to be precise, I was forced to fire her." See Bogáti, *Flamingók Új-Budán*, pp. 295.

Anton Lorenz made his declaration of intent to become an American citizen in New York City. He was naturalized by a special term of the Bexar County Commissioners' Court on January 10, 1866, with Francis Böröndi and Gabriel

Katona as witnesses. When registering to vote in 1869, he reported that he had been a resident of San Antonio for 14 years.

[48] *North San Antonio Times*, August 19, 1982; interview with Robert J. Parker Jr., San Antonio, May 21, 1987, HF-ITC.

[49] Ibid. In the Coker Cemetery, San Antonio, an ornate iron fence with a gate plate inscribed "Anton Lorenz" surrounds a seemingly empty plot. This may be the burial place for the children who died of smallpox. In the Lorenz Family Cemetery, San Antonio (a small fenced plot behind the tennis courts at the Chateau Dijon Apartments on Broadway), dates given for Julie Lorant [*sic*] are January 17, 1839, to August 4, 1916 (77 years). The life dates for Anton Lorant [*sic*] are February 20, 1824, to May 22, 1911 (87 years).

[50] For information on Alexander Benke, see Ruth Todd Benke, comp., "Genealogical Information on the Benke Family," ms., San Antonio, 1976, HF-ITC; Gyula Andrássy, count, *Magyarország Címeres Könyve*, pp. 64-65; J. Siebmacher, *Die Wappen des Adels in Ungarn* 33:54-55; Bexar County, Census of Population, 1860, 1900; 4th District Civil Court Minutes, July 15, 1867, Bexar County District Clerk's Office, book F, p. 495.

Benke family stories maintained that Benke was "descended from a royal family," possibly meaning that he was of noble rank. The Benke (originally Benkő) name is recorded among Hungary's noble families. In Texas Benke gradually dropped the *ő* ending of his name, although he maintained it when signing official documents. He reportedly was born in 1823 and entered the U.S. in 1855, giving his nationality as German. For information on John Finto, see Nell Baldwin, comp., "Finto Family Records," ms., HF-ITC; Bexar County, Census of Population, 1880, 1900; Brand Book, BCCO-SA, book E, p. 284; Appler, *Directory of City of San Antonio, 1892- 93, 1895-96, 1897*; Lurinda and Sarah Finto tombstone, Coker Cemetery, San Antonio; John Finto tombstone, Fairview Cemetery, Wilson County, Texas.

[51] Benke, "Benke Family," ms., HF-ITC.

[52] Marian Finto Hill to James Patrick McGuire, Trinidad, Texas, c. November 14, 1988, HF-ITC.

[53] Bexar County, Census of Population, 1860; Ferenc Badalik Journeyman's Travel Pass Book, HF-ITC.

CHAPTER SIX   Other 48ers in Texas

[1] Galveston *News*, September 15, 1904; King Vidor, Beverly Hills, California, to Mrs. Lajosné Csatári, June 12, 1960, in King Vidor Collection, Archives of Performing Arts, University of Southern California Library, Los Angeles, (hereafter, King Vidor Collection, USC); Lengyel, *Americans from Hungary*, p. 275; *Révai Nagy Lexikona* 16:151-52; "Peach River Pine and the Peach River Lines," p. 65. Although no mention of Charles Vidor is made, Géza Kende reported in *Magyarok Amerikában* 1:140, that Ede Reményi, "who became the world-famous violin virtuoso," arrived in America on the steamer *Hermann* in 1851. Could Charles Vidor have accompanied him? In Péter Bogáti's *Flamingók Új-Budán*, p. 88, a Vidor, from Miskolc, was reported working as a "scriber" for a newspaper office in New York City in 1850.

2   Galveston County, Census of Population, 1860; W. and D. Richardson, *Galveston Directory for 1859-1860*, p. 30; Emily Vidor Tombstone, Episcopal Cemetery, Galveston; Marriage Records, Galveston County Clerk's Office, vol. B, p. 369. Yellow fever struck Galveston in 1859 and was followed by typhus in 1860. Emily Vidor died at the age of 20 years, 11 months, and 13 days. Her name and those of her two small children are recorded on a single shaft in Galveston's Episcopal Cemetery.

3   David G. McComb, *Galveston: A History*, pp. 47-49, 55, 61, 66, 67, 172; Charles W. Hayes, *Galveston: History of the Island and the City*, p. 483.

4   "Charles Vidor," Military Service Branch, National Archives and Records Service, Washington, D.C.; Galveston *News*, September 15, 1904; Harold B. Simpson, *Hood's Texas Brigade: A Compendium*, pp. 77-78.

5   Galveston *News*, September 15, 1904; *Flake's Daily Galveston Bulletin*, December 28, 1865; W. Richardson and Co., *Galveston Directory for 1866-67*, p. 27; C.W. Marston, *Galveston City Directory for 1868-1869*, pp. 59, 103-104; Morrison and Fourmy, *General Directory of the City of Galveston, 1886-87*, p. 379; Maggie Abercrombie, *Sketch of Galveston County*, p. 333.

6   Marriage Records, Galveston County Clerk's Office; Vidor Family Genealogy, King Vidor Collection, USC; Register of Deaths, Galveston County Clerk's Office.

7   Dermot H. Hardy and Ingham S. Roberts, eds., *Historical Review of South-East Texas* 2:775-76; Morrison and Fourmy, *Directory of Galveston, 1882-83*, p. 400, *1884-85*, p. 379, *1899-1900, 1901-02*; Galveston County, Census of Population, 1900; "Peach River Pine," p. 66.

8   Hardy and Roberts, *Historical Review* 2:776; Elaine Mitrovich, La Marque, Texas, to James Patrick McGuire, April 30, 1986, HF-ITC.

9   Hardy and Roberts, *Historical Review* 2:950-51; Morrison and Fourmy, *Directory of Galveston, 1903-04*.

10 S.G. Reed, *A History of the Texas Railroads*, pp. 466, 515, 520, 528, 534, 536; "Peach River Pine," pp. 88-89.

11 Ibid., p. 102.

12 Morrison and Fourmy, *Directory of Galveston, 1909-10, 1911-12*; *Directory of Houston, 1913, 1915*.

13 King Vidor Collection, USC. Vidor's business papers provide extensive detail on the operation of the large lumbering and wholesaling empire of Miller-Vidor Lumber Company. A 1910 reprint on the Peach River Company from the *American Lumberman* gives excellent in-depth coverage of this empire, as well as photographs of the mills, railways, lumber towns, and all other aspects of the Miller-Vidor enterprises.

14 Ibid.

15 Ibid.

16 *New York Times*, November 2, 1982; King Vidor Collection, USC.

17 Ibid.; King Vidor, "Southern Storm," pp. 56-57, 128, 131; Kevin Brownlow, *The War, the West, and the Wilderness*, p. 186.

18 *New York Times*, November 2, 1982; Brownlow, *The War, the West*, pp. 186-87.

[19] *New York Times*, November 2, 1982.

[20] Ibid.

[21] Declaration of Intent, Fayette County District Clerk's Office, June 30, 1856, La Grange, Texas; Leonie Rummel Weyand and Houston Wade, *An Early History of Fayette County*, pp. 117, 298. In Weyand and Wade, Újffy was listed as "William F. Újffy."

[22] "John H. Újffy," Military Service Branch, National Archives and Records Service, Washington, D.C.

[23] Lucia L. Williams, "The Yellow Fever Epidemic of La Grange in 1867," in *Fayette County: Past and Present*, ed. Marjorie L. Williams, pp. 40-43.

[24] John H. Heller, *Galveston City Directory, 1878-79*; idem, *Heller's Galveston Directory, 1880-81*; Morrison and Fourmy, *Directory of Galveston, 1881-82, 1882-83, 1884-85, 1886-87, 1899-1900, 1901-02, 1903-04, 1905*.

[25] Loula Újffy Harris of Austin, the daughter of Maurice Újffy, provided family information, scrapbooks, and photographs.

[26] Elise von Johnson to Loula Harris, Munich, Germany, n.d., typescript, HF-ITC.

[27] HF-ITC.

[28] Ibid.

[29] Houston *Chronicle*, August 5, 1905.

[30] Ibid.; Ellis A. Davis and Edwin H. Grobe, comps. and eds., *The New Encyclopedia of Texas*, p. 759; Marriage Records, Harris County Clerk's Office, Houston, vol. 1; Harris County, Census of Population, 1860. In the census he was listed as "Seabo."

Szabó was the father of one daughter, Eloise Eleanora, by his first wife, and a second daughter, Marian, by his second wife, Harriet M. Baker. Her brother, W.R. Baker, was a pioneer merchant and reputedly the wealthiest man in Houston, which city he served as mayor. Marian Szabó married Judge Charles E. Ashe of the 11th District Court in Houston. He was the grandson of the last president of the Republic of Texas, Anson Jones. See Davis and Grobe, *New Encyclopedia*, p. 759; Houston *Chronicle*, August 5, 1905.

[31] Morrison and Fourmy, *Directory of Houston, 1866, 1867-68, 1870-71, 1873, 1877-78, 1880-81, 1882-83, 1884, 1886-87, 1887-88, 1889-90, 1890-91, 1892-93, 1894-95, 1895, 1897-98, 1899, 1900-01, 1903-04, 1905-06*.

[32] Houston *Chronicle*, August 8 [?], 1905.

[33] "János [John] M. Bartay, Founder of the Oldest Hungarian Family in Texas," pp. 8-9; Gary Kent Bartay, "Bartay Family Emigration from Hungary to Texas," ms., HF-ITC; Dallas *Morning Herald*, July 3, 1858.

Bartay was the son of Endre [András] and Katharina Bauer Bartay. His father founded a singing school, or "choir school," in Pest in 1829. In 1843 he leased the National Theater and made it a consciously *Hungarian* theater by performing only Hungarian works. He was said to have devised and promoted a national contest for the best musical score for the Hungarian national anthem in 1844. Endre Bartay also was reportedly the composer of ballets, the Coronation Mass for the Emperor Ferdinand V of Austria, operas, oratories, and piano music.

[34] Ibid.

[35] Vasváry, *Lincoln's Hungarian Heroes*, p. 93; Brownson Malsch, *Indianola: The Mother of Western Texas*, pp. 154-56; "J.R. Holmy," Military Service Branch, National Archives and Records Service, Washington, D.C.

[36] Ibid. It is interesting to note that a commissioned officer's rations for one month included bacon, fresh beef, flour, corn meal, sugar, vinegar, candles, soap, salt, molasses, and meal coffee.

[37] Dewitt Clinton Baker Biographical File, Austin History Center; M.K. Kellogg, *M.K. Kellogg's Texas Journal 1872*, ed. Llerena Friend, pp. 6, 9; Mike Kingston, ed., *1986-1987 Texas Almanac and State Industrial Guide* (Dallas: A.H. Belo Corp., 1985), p. 530.

[38] Ibid.; Anton Roessler to Texas Military Board, State of Texas, April 6, 1863, Texas State Military Board Papers, Texas State Archives, Austin.

[39] *Handbook of Texas* 2:608; Eldon S. Branda, ed., *The Handbook of Texas* 3:809-10; Texas State Military Board Papers, Texas State Archives, Austin.

[40] Ibid.; Frank Wagner, "Wm. DeRyee of Corpus Christi," ms.; Frank Wagner, Corpus Christi, to James Patrick McGuire, July 10, 1987, HF-ITC.

[41] Wagner, "Wm. DeRyee," ms.; James M. Day, comp., *Maps of Texas, 1527-1900*, pp. 74-76.

[42] Wagner, "Wm. DeRyee," ms.; *Handbook of Texas* 3:810.

[43] Day, *Maps of Texas*, pp. 90-93.

[44] Kellogg, *Texas Journal*, pp. 6, 7, 11-13, 60-61, 74; *Handbook of Texas* 3:810.

[45] Austin *Daily Statesman*, June 8, 1873; Bogáti, *Flamingók Új-Budán*, pp. 67, 85-88; Mary J. Hayes and Frances T. McCallum, comps., *A Record of Faith, 1867-1967*; Robert M. Hayes, "Tyler's Spiritual Debt to a Hungarian Refugee," pp. 20-24; Kende, *Magyarok Amerikában* 1:161, 267; Gaspar, "Four Hungarian Travelers" (dissertation), p. 346; Thomas Barton Nash, "Soldier for Christ: Emir Hamvasy in Texas," ms., HF-ITC. The author wishes to express appreciation to Thomas B. Nash of San Antonio and Frank Wagner of Corpus Christi for calling his attention to the Reverend Hamvasy.

[46] Ibid.

[47] Ibid.; Lengyel, *Americans from Hungary*, pp. 48-49.

[48] Ibid.

[49] Ibid.

[50] Ibid.

[51] Hayes and McCallum, *Record of Faith*; Nash, "Soldier for Christ," ms., HF-ITC.

[52] Ibid.

[53] Ibid.

[54] *Flake's Daily Galveston Bulletin*, January 3, 1866; "Major Ruttkay Dead," Galveston *Daily News*, November 13, 1888. Ruttkay's first advertisement in the Galveston paper was placed on October 7 for three months. Initially the firm comprised three partners, Albert Ruttkay, C.B. Zulavsky, and S.A. Masters, but Masters withdrew on January 1, 1866. Ruttkay and Zulavsky continued the business.

[55] Galveston *Daily News*, November 13, 1888; Lengyel, *Americans from Hungary*, p. 46; Ilona Madarász to Pauline Nagy, July 12, 1858, in Bogáti, *Édes Pólim!* Louise Ruttkay remained in New York until 1883 when she moved to Turin, Italy, to care for her brother, Louis Kossuth. After his death in 1894 she returned to Budapest, where she died in 1902.

[56] Frank Preston Stearns, *The Life and Public Works of George Luther Stearns*, pp. 75-76; Lengyel, *Americans from Hungary*, pp. 46, 82.

[57] "Albert Ruttkay," Military Service Branch, National Archives and Records Service, Washington, D.C.; Eugene Pivány, *Hungarians in the American Civil War*, p. 35; Széplaki, *Hungarians in America, 1583-1974*, pp. 10, 16; Kende, *Magyarok Amerikában* 1:366-67; Vasváry, *Lincoln's Hungarian Heroes*, pp. 26, 79, 89; Lengyel, *Americans from Hungary*, p. 82.

[58] Edmund Vasváry Collection Index and Photocopies, American Hungarian Foundation; Robert S. Hosh, New Brunswick, New Jersey, to James Patrick McGuire, January 22, 1987, HF-ITC; "Albert Ruttkay," Military Service Branch, National Archives and Records Service, Washington, D.C.

[59] Morrison and Fourmy, *Directory of Houston, 1882-83, 1884, 1886-87, 1887-88, 1889-90*; Imrich Immer to James Patrick McGuire, Houston, September 29, 1986, and Elaine Mitrovich, Galveston, to James Patrick McGuire, October 17, 1986, HF-ITC; Probate Records, Harris County Clerk's Office, Houston; Houston *Daily News*, November 13, 1888; Jan Kelsey, Rye Historical Society, Rye, New York, to James Patrick McGuire, May 21, 1987, HF-ITC.

[60] Houston *Daily Post*, November 14, 1888; Kende, *Magyarok Amerikában* 1:267.

[61] "Emeric Szabad," Military Service Branch, National Archives and Records Service, Washington, D.C.; Vasváry, *Lincoln's Hungarian Heroes*, p. 83; Pivány, *Hungarians in the Civil War*, pp. 47, 59; Kende, *Magyarok Amerikában* 1:365.

[62] Ibid.; Emeric Szabad File, Boerne (Texas) Area Historical Preservation Society.

[63] Ibid.; "A marker at last for Emeric Szabad," (Boerne) *Hill Country Recorder*, August 12 and 19, 1987; Probate Records, Kendall County Clerk's Office, Boerne.

[64] L.E. Daniell, *Types of Successful Men of Texas*, p. 241 [Editor's Note: All of this information was supplied by Arthur Wadgymár himself, with no secondary confirmation.]; S.W. Geiser, "Men of Science in Texas, 1820-1880," p. 230; idem, "Notes on Some Workers in Texas Entomology, 1839-1880," pp. 593-98.

Efforts by the Wadgymár descendants to trace the name have met with complete failure. Some family members believe that the first names of the parents, Belezar and Bianca, are correct, but that the correct surname of these ancestors and facts of heritage may only be discovered if some record of a duel fought about 1856-1857 in Vienna between a father and son exists and details match family legend closely.

[65] Elma Wadgymar Smith Reeder, Rancho Palos Verdes, California, to John Wildenthal, April 7, 1987; John Wildenthal, Houston, to James Patrick McGuire, August 1, 1986; Joe Gross, San Antonio, to James Patrick McGuire;

"Legends told to Annabelle Rylander by Arthur Wildenthal and Mary Wildenthal," in "Family of Arthur August von Wadgymár, M.D.," ms., HF-ITC.

One family story, reported by Joe Gross, but unconfirmed by any records, was that Wadgymár's father was a general in the Austrian army during the Hungarian Revolution of 1848. Gross also stated that Wadgymár had a silver plate in his skull when he died in 1899 and that he carried a sword cane.

[66] "Family of Wadgymár," "Family Record [Wadgymár Family from old Bible], Births and Deaths," ms., HF-ITC.

[67] "Arthur Wadgymar," Military Service Branch, National Archives and Records Service, Washington, D.C.; Daniell, *Types of Successful Men*, p. 241; "Family Record," HF-ITC.

[68] Geiser, "Men of Science," p. 230; "Family Record," "Family of Wadgymár," HF-ITC.

[69] Ibid.; Wildenthal to McGuire, Houston, August 1, 1986.

[70] Ibid.; Annabelle Rylander, Denton, Texas, to John Wildenthal Jr., n.d., HF-ITC.

[71] Wildenthal to McGuire, Houston, August 1, 1986. Wadgymár's appeal of his conviction of violation of the local option law, with fines of $50 and $100, was made to the Court of Appeals of Texas in June 1886. The conviction was set aside, and the judgments were reversed and causes remanded. See *Southwestern Reporter* 2:768.

[72] Annette Martin Ludeman, *La Salle: La Salle County, South Texas Brush Country, 1856-1975*, pp. 213-14; Geiser, "Men of Science," p. 230; Annabelle Rylander, Denton, to John Wildenthal Jr., n.d.; Wildenthal to McGuire, Houston, August 1, 1986, HF-ITC.

[73] Vassady, "Kossuth and Újházi," p. 40; Vardy, *Hungarian-Americans*, p. 14.

CHAPTER SEVEN   The Great Economic Immigration

[1] Reed, *Texas Railroads*, pp. 179-80.

[2] Vardy, *Hungarian-Americans*, pp. 18-22.

[3] State of Texas, Census of Population, 1910. Of the Hungarians counted, only 56 could not be identified in the 27 most populous counties reporting Hungarians. This was possibly because of illegible handwriting by the census takers, damaged census rolls, or omission or confusion of information given to the census takers. Some minority peoples, such as the Bohemians and the Moravians, called themselves Hungarians but reported that they were born in Austria rather than in Hungary. The Texas counties consulted were Anderson, Angelina, Bell, Bexar, Bosque, Cooke, Dallas, DeWitt, Ellis, El Paso, Erath, Falls, Fayette, Fort Bend, Galveston, Goliad, Harris, Jack, Jefferson, Johnson, Navarro, Smith, Tarrant, Travis, Wharton, and Wheeler. Information in the next three paragraphs is taken from this source.

[4] A.C. Green, Brooklyn, New York, to James J. Hill, February 4, 1910, in "Hungarian Colony Location, File 50755" and "Immigration to Wichita Valley Territory, File 50381," Southwest Collection, Texas Tech University, Lubbock.

[5] Sallie B. Harris, comp., *Hide Town in the Texas Panhandle: 100 Years in Wheeler County and Panhandle of Texas*, pp. 239-43; Wheeler County History Book Committee, *The History of Wheeler County*, pp. 83, 123-25, 187; Vardy, *Hungarian-Americans*, pp. 20-21.

[6] Ed Pakan, "Pakan Community and the Pakan Family," ms., HF-ITC.

[7] Harris, *Hide Town*; Wheeler County Committee, *History*.

[8] Ibid.; *Shamrock Texan*, May 8, 1975.

[9] Pakan, "Pakan Community," ms., p. 5, HF-ITC.

[10] Harris, *Hide Town*; Wheeler County Committee, *History*; Wheeler County, Census of Population, 1910.

[11] Ibid.; Anna P. Dolak, "16-Family Telephone System," "Education Posed a Problem," "Pakan Community Established," "Pioneers in Early-Day Pakan," undated articles from *The Shamrock Texan*, c. 1975.

[12] Pakan, "Pakan Community," ms., p. 4, HF-ITC.

[13] Dolak articles in *Shamrock Texan*.

[14] Pakan, "Pakan Community," ms., pp. 6-7, HF-ITC; Dolak, "16-Family Telephone System," *Shamrock Texan*.

[15] Ellis and Navarro counties, Census of Population, 1910.

[16] Ibid.

[17] Telephone interview with Ernest Horvath, DeSoto, Texas, September 20, 1986, HF-ITC.

[18] Family documents and history were furnished by Mr. and Mrs. Louis Nagy and Mrs. Christine Nagy East, Boerne, Texas.

[19] Ellis County Genealogical Society, ed., *Ellis County, Texas, Naturalization Records*, p. 44.

[20] Interview with Mr. and Mrs. Louis Nagy and Mrs. Christine Nagy East, Boerne, Texas, May 18, 1988, HF-ITC.

[21] Davis and Grobe, *New Encyclopedia*, p. 1046; Ludeman, *La Salle*, p. 192; undated, unidentified obituary, "Joe Nagy Meets Tragic Death," HF-ITC.

[22] Ibid.

[23] Fay Casebolt, "On the Avenue," unidentified newspaper clipping, HF-ITC.

[24] Alice *Daily Echo*, January 28, 1951.

[25] Lubbock *Evening Journal*, August 10, 1987.

[26] B.B. Paddock, *A Twentieth Century History and Biographical Record of North and West Texas* 1:493-95; El Paso *Times*, May 27, 1933; Nancy Hamilton, "The Ysleta Riot of 1890," pp. 101-11.

[27] El Paso *Herald Post*, May 27, 1933; Paddock, *Biographical Record* 1:493-94.

[28] Ibid.

[29] Ibid.

[30] El Paso *Times*, April 7, 1888; El Paso *Herald*, February 1 and 20, May 26, June 4, 5, 9, 10, 17, 18, and 29, 1890.

[31] El Paso *Times*, July 12, 1890; Hamilton, "Ysleta Riot," p. 102. Her account of the bloody incident is the best available.

[32] Ibid., pp. 105-10.

[33] Ibid., pp. 110-11; Paddock, *Biographical Record* 1:494-95; El Paso *Times*, May 27, 1933; El Paso *Herald Post*, May 27, 1933.

[34] San Antonio *Daily Light*, July 13, 1908.

[35] Ibid.; Mooney and Morrison, *Directory of San Antonio, 1883-84, 1885-86*; Menger, *Texas Nature*, pp. 135, 176-77, 249-51; Cornelia E. Crook, *San Pedro Springs Park*, p. 59.

[36] San Antonio *Daily Light*, July 13, 1908; James R. Underwood, "Edwin Theodore Dumble," pp. 53-78.

[37] Ruth A. Allen, *East Texas Lumber Workers: An Economic and Social Picture, 1870-1950*, pp. 52-53.

[38] Charles Forse, "A History of Pineland, Texas, and Its Industries" (research paper), May 18, 1949.

[39] Telephone interview with Mrs. Ima Balla Creech, Orange, Texas, May 29, 1986, HF-ITC.

[40] Imrich Immer, Houston, to James Patrick McGuire, September 29, 1986; telephone interviews with Louis Nagy, Waller, Texas, July 17, 1986; with Louis Pali, Houston, July 17, 1986; with Charles Aranyas, Houston, July 16, 1986, HF-ITC; American Association of University Women, *The Heritage of North Harris County*, p. 53.

[41] Vardy, *Hungarian-Americans*, pp. 20-22.

[42] Norma Goebel Wenmohs to Bernice Casey, October 8, 1968; Bernice Casey, Waco, to James Patrick McGuire, September 7, 1986, HF-ITC; John Stribling Moursund, *Blanco County History*, pp. 500, 519.

[43] Ibid.; Minna Goebel, *A Collection of Memories by Grandmother Minna Goebel*, comp. Hilda Goebel Smith, pp. 5, 6, 8.

[44] Moursund, *Blanco County History*, p. 519; Goebel, *Collection of Memories*, pp. 24, 58-59.

[45] Ibid., pp. 5, 16-18, 51-52.

[46] Ibid., pp. 16, 18.

[47] Ibid., pp. 19, 21; Donald Earl Casey, "John and Ida Manna Fuchs Goebel," ms., HF-ITC.

[48] Ibid., pp. 19, 20, 26, 28.

[49] Ibid., pp. 23-24.

[50] Ibid., pp. 55-57; Moursund, *Blanco County History*, p. 500; Casey, "John and Ida Goebel," ms., HF-ITC.

[51] Anton Goebel, Budapest, to Moritz Goebel, February 20, 1922; Anton Goebel, Budapest, to Moritz and Minna Goebel, December 8, 1922; Anton Goebel, Budapest, to John Goebel, December 29, 1922; Theresia Niederkirchner, Budapest, to John Goebel, n.d., HF-ITC.

[52] Vardy, *Hungarian-Americans*, pp. 19-21.

[53] Galveston County, Census of Population, 1910.

[54] Erath County, Census of Population, 1910.

[55] "Thurber, Texas . . . TP's Birthplace," pp. 4-13. See also, Mary Jane Gentry, "Thurber: The Life and Death of a Texas Town" (thesis).

[56] San Antonio *Light*, December 16, 1912; Tomasini Tombstones, Coker Cemetery, San Antonio, Texas.

[57] Ibid.; Declaration of Intent, July 2, 1887; Brand Book H, BCCO-SA, p. 34; interview with Mitchell Tomasini, San Antonio, July 14, 1987, HF-ITC. George Ritter von Tomasini's brand, SINI, was recorded on March 20, 1880. One family story held that Tomasini returned briefly to Europe after the collapse of the Maximilian regime in order to reunite with his first wife and four children. But his wife had thought that he had died in the fighting in Mexico and had remarried, so Tomasini returned to America, subsequently married again, and raised his second family in Texas.

[58] Macartney, *Hungary*, pp. 31, 118-19, 122-23, 190-93.

[59] Harris County, Census of Population, 1900, 1910.

[60] Ibid.; Houston *Post*, September 21, 1986; Houston *Chronicle*, November 4, 1931. Nathan Taub's obituary in 1931 reported that he came to America in 1889. The Harris County census returns for 1900 and 1910 identify the Taub family as Hungarian Magyars. Further, all of the Taub children were reported as born in Hungary. Nathan Taub was listed as a "grocer" in 1900 and as a "cigar merchant" in 1910. His wife emigrated with the children in 1890 to join her husband. Nathan Taub was a member of Congregation Beth Israel in Houston.

[61] Ibid.; Houston *Chronicle*, July 1 and 3, 1964, June 9, 1981; Houston *Post*, July 3, 1964, June 18, 1979, September 10, 1982.

[62] Ibid.

[63] Rabbi Martin Zielonka, "Eulogy," El Paso, September 1934, HF-ITC.

[64] James E. Ferguson, Austin, to Dr. M. Faber, September 11, 1916, HF-ITC.

[65] [Maurice Faber,] Tyler, to Governor James E. Ferguson, September 20, November 20, 1916, HF-ITC; Dallas *Morning News*, November 25, 1916.

[66] Bob Barker, Chief Clerk, House of Representatives, Austin, to Rabbi M. Faber, August 6, 1917, HF-ITC.

[67] Robert Ernest Vinson, Austin, to Rabbi M. Faber, February 20, 1918, HF-ITC.

[68] Tyler *Journal*, c. September 16-18, 1934; "Rabbi M. Faber of Tyler Dies Today," undated newspaper obituary; Eugene Lipstate, Lafayette, Louisiana, to James Patrick McGuire, September 29, 1986, HF-ITC.

[69] "Temple Beth El, 1887-1987, Centennial Journal (Tyler, Texas)," pp. 23-24.

[70] HF-ITC.

[71] *Temple Emanuel 75th Anniversary*.

[72] Samuel Rosinger, *My Life and My Message*, pp. 1-14.

[73] Ibid.

[74] *Temple Emanuel 75th Anniversary*.

[75] Rosinger, *My Life*, pp. 19-20.

[76] All materials relating to Dr. Max Rottenstein were provided by his granddaughter, Stefanie N. Schneidler of Dallas.

[77] Dallas *Morning News*, November 15, 1955.

[78] Ibid., March 20, 1955; Carolyn Holmes Moses with Myrtle E. Lowe, comps., *Hungary Sends a Dallas-Builder: The Story of Martin Weiss.*

[79] Floyd S. Fierman, *The Schwartz Family of El Paso: The Story of a Pioneer Jewish Family in the Southwest*, pp. 6-7.

[80] Ibid., pp. 8-29.

[81] Ibid., pp. 29-33; El Paso *World News*, March 3, 1935.

[82] Fierman, *Schwartz Family*, pp. 33-45.

[83] Austin *American-Statesman*, March 3, 1985; September 14, 1987; February 28, 1988.

[84] Ibid.

[85] Interview with Bob A. Roth, San Antonio, October 23, 1986; interview with Jack Roth, San Antonio, November 11, 1986, HF-ITC.

[86] Ibid.

[87] Interview with Judge Al Klein, San Antonio, November 3, 1986, HF-ITC.

[88] Ibid.; interview with Lester Klein, San Antonio, November 5, 1986, HF-ITC; San Antonio *News*, April 5, 1977; San Antonio *Light*, March 28, 1977.

[89] Leslie Konnyu, "The Identity Problem of Mrs. Doc Holliday Has Been Solved," pp. 22-23.

[90] Pat Jahns, *The Frontier World of Doc Holliday: Faro Dealer from Dallas to Deadwood*, p. 111; Don H. Biggers, *Shackelford County Sketches*, ed. Joan Farmer, pp. 38-39.

[91] Konnyu, "Identity Problem"; Jahns, *Frontier World*, p. 111; Cy Martin, *Whiskey and Wild Women: An Amusing Account of the Saloons and Bawds of the Old West*, p. 162. See also, Peter Lyon, *The Wild, Wild West.*

[92] Stuart N. Lake, *Wyatt Earp: Frontier Marshal*, pp. 197, 202, 223; Carl W. Greihan, *Great Lawmen of the West*, as quoted in Ramon F. Adams, *More Burs under the Saddle: Books and Histories of the West*, p. 15.

[93] Jahns, *Frontier World*, pp. 112, 136-43, 147-49, 177-78.

[94] Ibid., pp. 178-79; Konnyu, "Identity Problem," pp. 22-23.

[95] State of Texas, *Cities and Towns of Texas*, p. 1; Reed, *Texas Railroads*, pp. 275-77. The author wishes to thank Mrs. Maria Nagy Peterson, San Antonio, for calling his attention to the "Kossuth" spotted on the Texas road map during her vacation trip through East Texas in 1986.

[96] *Handbook of Texas* 2:841, 3:1068; "Peach River Pine," pp. 85-88.

[97] Ibid.

[98] *Handbook of Texas* 2:202; "Peach River Pine," pp. 85-88.

[99] Ibid.

[100] Sisa, *Spirit of Hungary*, p. 31; Dallas *Morning News*, November 21, 1972.

[101] Interview with Louis and Edith Nagy and Christine Nagy East, Boerne, Texas, May 28, 1986, HF-ITC.

[102] Interview with Ann Weigand, San Antonio, July 10, 1988, HF-ITC.

[103] Interview with Michael J. Balint, San Antonio, June 6, 1988, HF-ITC.

[104] Interviews with Louis Nagy and Ann Weigand, HF-ITC.

[105] *Bazar-Zeitung, Herausgegeben für den Deutsch-Texanischen Bazar, Beethoven Halle und Garten, San Antonio, Texas, October, 1916*; interview with Ann Weigand, San Antonio, July 10, 1988, HF-ITC.

[106] Konnyu, *Hungarians in USA*, pp. 54-55.

CHAPTER EIGHT   Post-World War II Immigrants in Texas

[1] Dallas *Times-Herald*, January 8, 1950.

[2] Vardy, *Hungarian-Americans*, pp. 115-16.

[3] Interview with Ed Stern, San Antonio, May 11, 1988, HF-ITC.

[4] Vardy, *Hungarian-Americans*, pp. 116-18.

[5] *Texas Catholic* (Diocese of Dallas-Fort Worth), September 29, 1956, January 15, 1958.

[6] Abbot Anselm Nagy, O. Cist., Irving, Texas, to James Patrick McGuire, November 28, 1987, HF-ITC.

[7] *Texas Catholic*, September 29, 1956, January 15, 1958, January 4, 1964; Galveston *Daily News*, September 6, 1986; Dallas *Morning News*, November 21, 1972.

[8] Vardy, *Hungarian-Americans*, pp. 118-19.

[9] Michael J. Balint to James Patrick McGuire, San Antonio, June 10, 1987, HF-ITC.

[10] Interviews with George Fodor, San Antonio, May 28, 1966; with Stephen Juhasz, San Antonio, June 15, 1988; with Victor Szebehely, Austin, July 20, 1988, HF-ITC.

[11] Special recognition goes to Michael Balint and Rose Safran for their summaries of the history of SAHA, HF-ITC.

[12] *Gedenkschrift zum 50. Stiftungsfest Oesterreichisch-Ungarischer Verein von San Antonio, Texas und Umgegend, 1916-1966* (San Antonio, c. 1966).

[13] Ibid.; Dorothy Adler, "Refugees Helped in S.A.," unidentified newspaper clipping, c. 1957, HF-ITC.

[14] Irene Seabase Tripak, "History of the Seabase (alias Czibész) family," ms., HF-ITC.

[15] Adler, "Refugees Helped," HF-ITC.

[16] HF-ITC.

[17] Interview with Maria Nagy Peterson, San Antonio, May 24, 1988, HF-ITC.

[18] HF-ITC.

[19] Interview with Rose K. Safran, San Antonio, August 5, 1988, HF-ITC; phone conversation between Michael Balint and Sandra Hodsdon Carr (ITC editor), December 1992.

[20] Harris County, Census of Population, 1860, 1910; W.A. Leonard, *Houston City Directory for 1866*; Morrison and Fourmy, *General Directory of the City of Houston, 1882-83, 1887-88, 1889-90, 1900-01*.

21 Harris County, Census of Population, 1900.

22 Harris County, Census of Population, 1910.

23 HF-ITC.

24 Houston *Chronicle*, May 11, 1975, October 25, 1976; interview with Dr. Frank Pető, Houston, November 8, 1986, HF-ITC.

25 Ibid.

26 Ibid.

27 Marie Dobay Nordyke, "Tracing the Assimilation of the Hungarian Immigrants into the Houston Community," 1982, ms., University of St. Thomas, Houston, courtesy of the Houston Metropolitan Research Center. Nordyke received a grant of $100 for the preparation of this report from HACA as well as support from the National Endowment for the Humanities.

28 Dallas County, Census of Population, 1860, 1910, 1980; Tarrant County, Census of Population, 1910, 1980.

29 Dallas *Morning News*, January 14, 1969; telephone interview with Robert E. Illes, Dallas, May 2, 1986, HF-ITC. Much post-World War II information on Dallas's Hungarians comes from newspaper clippings from Dallas newspapers in Imre Kocsis' Scrapbook, copies in HF-ITC, courtesy of Imre Kocsis. Further information was supplied by the "Foreign Born Citizens" File, Dallas Public Library.

30 Ibid. Family stories claim that Illés was a count in the Austro-Hungarian Empire and that his father had earlier freed his serfs, thus becoming unpopular with other noblemen in his immediate neighborhood. Upon becoming an American citizen, Illés renounced his title. There is no secondary confirmation of these stories.

31 Dallas *Daily Times Herald*, November 2, 1949, January 8 and December 24, 1950.

32 Unidentified, undated newspaper clippings, "Hungarian Refugees Like Life in Dallas," "Jaycees Adopt Refugees," "Hungarian Says He'd Face Noose If Returned Home," HF-ITC.

33 Dallas *Morning News*, December 19, 1956, April 5, 1966.

34 "Father Nagy Dies; Rosary Set Sunday," unidentified clipping, February 28, 1964, HF-ITC.

35 Dallas *Times Herald*, March 10, 1957, April 4, 1974; Dallas *Morning News*, December 12, 1956, May 11, 1975.

36 "Hungarians Recall Homeland at Mass," unidentified clipping; "Mass to Mark Hungary Revolt," unidentified clipping, October 20, 1966, HF-ITC.

37 "Fifth Anniversary of the Hungarian Revolution," October 22, 1961, Mass program, St. Joseph's Church, Dallas; invitation to Hungarian Folkdance Exhibition, University of Dallas, October 30, no year, HF-ITC; phone conversation between Imre Kocsis and Sandra Hodsdon Carr (ITC editor), January 29, 1993.

38 HF-ITC; phone conversation between Michael Balint and Sandra Hodsdon Carr (ITC editor), December 1992.

BIBLIOGRAPHY

BOOKS AND ARTICLES

Abercrombie, Maggie. *Sketch of Galveston County*. Galveston, 1881.

Ács, Tivadar. *New-Buda*. Budapest, 1941.

Adams, Ramon F. *More Burs under the Saddle: Books and Histories of the West*. Norman: University of Oklahoma Press, 1979.

Allen, Ruth A. *East Texas Lumber Workers: An Economic and Social Picture, 1870-1950*. Austin: University of Texas Press, 1961.

American Assn. of University Women. *The Heritage of North Harris County*. Houston: North Harris County Branch, AAUW, 1978.

Andrássy, Gyula, Count. *Magyarország Címeres Könyve*. Budapest: Grill Károly Könyvkiadóvállalata, 1913.

Appler, Jules A., comp. *General Directory of the City of San Antonio, 1892-93*. San Antonio: Jules A. Appler, 1892.

———. *General Directory of the City of San Antonio, 1894*. San Antonio: Jules A. Appler, 1894.

———. *General Directory of the City of San Antonio, 1895-96*. San Antonio: Jules A. Appler, 1895.

———. *General Directory of the City of San Antonio, 1897*. San Antonio: Jules A. Appler, 1897.

———. *General Directory of the City of San Antonio, 1897-98*. San Antonio: Jules A. Appler, 1897.

———. *General Directory of the City of San Antonio, 1898*. San Antonio: Jules A. Appler, 1898.

———. *General Directory of the City of San Antonio, 1899-1900*. San Antonio: Jules A. Appler, 1899.

_____. *General Directory of the City of San Antonio, 1901-02*. San Antonio: Jules A. Appler, 1901.

Balassa, Ivan, and Gyula Ortutay. *Hungarian Ethnography and Folklore*. Budapest: Corvina Kiadó, 1974.

Barker, Nancy Nichols. *The French Legation in Texas*. Vol. 1. Austin: Texas State Historical Assn., 1973.

Barnes, Charles Merritt. *Combats and Conquests of Immortal Heroes*. San Antonio: Guessaz and Ferlet, 1910.

Bazar-Zeitung: Herausgegeben für den Deutsch-Texanischen Bazar, Beethoven Halle und Garten, San Antonio, Texas, Oktober, 1916. San Antonio: Wilson-Schwegmann Printing Co.; c. 1916.

Bógati, Péter. *Édes Pólim!* [My dear Polí!]. Budapest: Móra Könyvkiadó, 1979.

_____. *Flamingók Új-Budán* [The Flamingo of New Buda]. Budapest: Kossuth Könyvkiadó, 1979.

Bognár, Desi K. *Hungarians in America*. Philadelphia: Alpha Pub., 1971.

Biggers, Don H. *Shackelford County Sketches*. Ed. Joan Farmer. Albany, Tx.: Clear Fork Press, 1974.

Branda, Eldon S., ed. *The Handbook of Texas*. Vol. 3. Austin: Texas State Historical Assn., 1976.

Brown, Francis J., and Joseph Slabey Roucek. *One America: The History, Contributions, and Present Problems of Our Racial and National Minorities*. New York: Prentice-Hall, 1952.

Brownlow, Kevin. *The War, the West, and the Wilderness*. New York: Alfred A. Knopf, 1979.

Bull, Kristy. "New Times for Modern Pentathletes." *The Olympian* 12, no. 8 (March 1986).

Castro Colonies Heritage Assn. *The History of Medina County, Texas*. Dallas: National ShareGraphics, 1986.

Chabot, Frederick. *With the Makers of San Antonio*. San Antonio: Artes Graficas, 1937.

Copeland, Fayette. *Kendall of the* Picayune. Norman: University of Oklahoma Press, 1943.

Crook, Cornelia E. *San Pedro Springs Park*. San Antonio, 1967.

Cude, Elton R. *The Wild and Free Dukedom of Bexar*. San Antonio: Munguia Printers, 1978.

Daniell, L.E. *Types of Successful Men of Texas*. Austin: Von Boeckmann, 1890.

Daughters of the Republic of Texas. *Founders and Patriots of the Republic of Texas*. n.p; n.d.

Davis, Ellis A., and Edwin H. Grobe, comps. and eds. *The New Encyclopedia of Texas*. Dallas: Texas Development Bureau, [1929].

Day, James M., comp. *Maps of Texas, 1527-1900*. Austin: Pemberton Press, 1964.

Deak, Istvan. *The Lawful Revolution: Louis Kossuth and the Hungarians, 1848-1849*. New York: Columbia University Press, 1979.

Dinnerstein, Leonard, and David M. Reimers. *Ethnic Americans: A History of Immigration and Assimilation*. New York: Harper and Row, 1975.

Doráti, Antal. *Notes of Seven Decades*. Detroit: Wayne State University Press, 1981.

Edwards, Emily. F. *Giraud and San Antonio*. San Antonio, 1979.

Ellis County Genealogical Society, ed. *Ellis County, Texas, Naturalization Records*. Waxahachie: Ellis County Genealogical Society, 1980.

Encyclopaedia Britannica. 15th ed. 1985.

Everett, Donald E. *San Antonio: The Flavor of Its Past, 1845-1898*. San Antonio: Trinity University Press, 1975.
———. *San Antonio Legacy*. San Antonio: Trinity University Press, 1979.
Fekete, Martón. *Prominent Hungarians; Home and Abroad*. London: Fehér Holló Press, 1973.
Fierman, Floyd S. *The Schwartz Family of El Paso: The Story of a Pioneer Jewish Family in the Southwest*. Southwestern Studies Monograph no. 61. El Paso: Texas Western Press, 1980.
Flachmeier, Jeanette Hastedt. *Pioneer Austin Notables*. Austin: Ginny's Copying Service, 1980.
Gál, L. Éva. *Egy 48-as forradalmás Újházi László* [The Revolutionary of 1848 — László Újházi]. Budapest, 1971.
———. *Újházi László, a szabadságharc utolsó kormánybiztosa* [László Újházi, the Last Government Commissioner in the War for Independence]. Budapest: Akadémiai Kiadó, 1971.
Gambrell, Herbert. *Anson Jones: The Last President of Texas*. Austin: University of Texas Press, 1964.
Gedenkschrift zum 50. Stiftungsfest Oesterreichisch-Ungarischer Verein von San Antonio, Texas und Umgegend, 1916-1966. San Antonio, [1966].
Geiser, S.W. "Men of Science in Texas, 1820-1880." *Field and Laboratory* 27, no. 4 (October 1959).
———. "Notes on Some Workers in Texas Entomology, 1839-1880." *Southwestern Historical Quarterly* 49 (1946).
Geue, Ethel Hander. *New Homes in a New Land: German Immigration to Texas, 1847-1861*. Waco: Texian Press, 1970.
Gillespie County Historical Society. *Pioneers in God's Hills: A History of Fredericksburg and Gillespie County, People and Events*. 2 vols. Fredericksburg, Tx.: Gillespie County Historical Society, 1960, 1974.
Goebel, Minna. *A Collection of Memories by Grandmother Minna Goebel*. Comp. Hilda Goebel Smith. Lubbock, 1970.
Goetzmann, William H., and William N. Goetzmann. *The West of the Imagination*. New York: W.W. Norton and Co., 1986.
Gould, Stephen. *The Alamo City Guide*. New York: Macgowan and Slipper, 1882.
Gracza, Rezsoe, and Margaret Gracza. *The Hungarians in America*. Minneapolis: Lerner Publications Co., 1969.
Greihan, Carl W. *Great Lawmen of the West*. London: John Long, 1963.
Hall, Martin Hardwick, and Sam Long. *The Confederate Army of New Mexico*. Austin: Presidial Press, 1978.
Hamilton, Nancy. "The Ysleta Riot of 1890." *Password* 24 (Fall 1979).
Hardy, Dermot H., and Ingham S. Roberts, eds. *Historical Review of South-East Texas*. 2 vols. Chicago: Lewis Publishing Co., 1910.
Harris, Sallie B., comp. *Hide Town in the Texas Panhandle: 100 Years in Wheeler County and Panhandle of Texas*. Hereford, Tx.: Pioneer Book Pub., 1968.
Hayes, Charles W. *Galveston: History of the Island and the City*. Austin: Jenkins Garrett Press, 1974.
Hayes, Mary J., and Frances T. McCallum, comps. *A Record of Faith, 1867-1967: Christ Episcopal Church, Tyler, Texas*. Waco: Texian Press, 1968.
Hayes, Robert M. "Tyler's Spiritual Debt to a Hungarian Refugee." *Chronicles of Smith County, Texas* 5, no. 2 (Fall 1966).
Heller, John H. *Galveston City Directory, 1878-79*. Galveston: Strickland, 1878.
———. *Heller's Galveston Directory, 1880-81*. Galveston: Strickland, 1880.

Herff, Ferdinand Peter. *The Doctors Herff: A Three-Generation Memoir*. Ed. Laura L. Barber. 2 vols. San Antonio: Trinity University Press, 1973.

Hogan, William Ransom. *The Texas Republic*. Austin: University of Texas Press, 1969.

Hungarian Heritage Review. "Dr. Daniel N. Hortobagyi: The Hungarian-American Cancer-Fighter." *Hungarian Heritage Review* 16, no. 9 (September 1987).

Jackson, W.H., and S.A. Long. *The Texas Stock Directory*. San Antonio: Herald Office, 1865.

Jahns, Pat. *The Frontier World of Doc Holliday: Faro Dealer from Dallas to Deadwood*. Lincoln: University of Nebraska Press, 1957.

James, Vinton Lee. *Frontier and Pioneer Recollections of Early Days in San Antonio and West Texas*. San Antonio: Artes Graficas, 1938.

"Janos (John) M. Bartay, Founder of Oldest Hungarian Family in Texas." *The Eighth Tribe* 6, no. 7 (July 1979).

Johnson, Frank W. *A History of Texas and Texans*. 5 vols. Chicago and New York: American Historical Society, 1914.

Johnson and Chapman, comps. *General Directory of the City of San Antonio, 1891*. San Antonio: Johnson and Chapman, 1891.

Katona, Anna. "Hungarian Travelogues on the Pre-Civil-War U.S." *Hungarian Studies in English* 5. Debrecen, Hungary, 1971.

Kellogg, M.K. *M.K. Kellogg's Texas Journal 1872*. Ed. Llerena Friend. Austin: University of Texas Press, 1967.

Kende, Géza. *Magyarok Amerikában* [Hungarians in the United States]. 2 vols. Cleveland: A Szabadság Kiadása, 1927.

"The Kodaly Method in America." *Hungarian Studies Newsletter*, no. 2 (Fall 1973).

Komlos, John H. *Louis Kossuth in America, 1851-1852*. Buffalo, N.Y.: East European Institute, 1973.

Konnyu, Leslie. *Acacias: Hungarians in the Mississippi Valley*. Ligonier, Pa.: Bethlen Press, 1976.

———. *A History of American Hungarian Literature*. St. Louis: Cooperative of American Hungarian Writers, 1962.

———. *Hungarians in the U.S.A.: An Immigration Study*. St. Louis: American Hungarian Review, 1967.

———. "The Identity Problem of Mrs. Doc Holliday Has Been Solved." *Hungarian American Review* 16, no. 11 (November 1987).

———. *John Xantus, Hungarian Geographer in America (1851-1864)*. Köln: American Hungarian Pub., 1965.

Lake, Stuart N. *Wyatt Earp: Frontier Marshal*. Boston: Houghton Mifflin Co., 1955.

Lengyel, Emil. *Americans from Hungary*. Philadelphia: J.B. Lippincott Co., 1948.

Leonard, W.A., comp. *Houston City Directory for 1866*. Houston: Gray, Strickland and Co., 1866.

Linthicum, Leslie. "A&M professor challenges cut-and-dried violin theory." Undated Houston *Post* clipping.

Ludeman, Annette Martin. *La Salle: La Salle County, South Texas Brush Country, 1856-1975*. Burnet, Tx.: Nortex Press, 1975.

Lyon, Peter. *The Wild, Wild West*. New York: Funk and Wagnalls, 1969.

Macartney, C.A. *Hungary: A Short History*. Edinburgh: Edinburgh University Press, 1962.

The Madarasz Book: Containing a Collection of the Work of L. Madarasz. Columbus, Ohio: Zaner and Bloser Co., 1911.

Madden, Henry Miller. *Xantus: Hungarian Naturalists in the Pioneer West*. Palo Alto, Calif.: Books of the West, 1949.

Malsch, Brownson. *Indianola: the Mother of Western Texas*. Austin: Shoal Creek Pub., 1977.

Markos, Lajos. "The Siege of the Alamo;" "Lajos Markos; Romantic Legend of the West." Advertising poster. Houston: Art-Mark, n.d.

Marston, C.W. *Galveston City Directory for 1868-1869*. Galveston: Shaw and Blaylock, 1868.

Martin, Cy. *Whiskey and Wild Women: An Amusing Account of the Saloons and Bawds of the Old West*. New York: Hart Publishing Co., 1974.

McComb, David G. *Galveston: A History*. Austin: University of Texas Press, 1986.

McGuire, James Patrick. "László Újházi: A Most Unusual Hungarian Texan." *Texas Passages* 1, no. 2 (Spring 1986). San Antonio: University of Texas Institute of Texan Cultures at San Antonio.

_____. "László Újházi: A Most Unusual Hungarian Texan." *Hungarian Heritage Review* 15, no. 6 (June 1986).

Menger, Rudolph. *Texas Nature Observations and Reminiscences*. San Antonio: Guessaz and Ferlet Co., 1913.

Men of Texas. Chicago: A.N. Marquis and Co., 1903.

Miller, Thomas Lloyd. *Bounty and Donation Land Grants of Texas, 1835-1888*. Austin; University of Texas Press, 1967.

Modern Pentathlon: San Antonio, Texas. San Antonio: U.S. Modern Pentathlon Assoc., [1986].

Mooney and Morrison, comps. *General Directory of the City of San Antonio, 1877-78*. Galveston: Galveston News, 1877.

_____. *General Directory of the City of San Antonio, 1879-80*. Marshall, Tx.: Jennings Bros., [1879].

_____. *General Directory of the City of San Antonio, 1883-84*. Galveston: Clarke and Courts, 1883.

_____. *General Directory of the City of San Antonio, 1885-86*. Galveston: Clarke and Courts, 1885.

_____. *General Directory of the City of San Antonio, 1887-88*. Galveston: Clarke and Courts, 1886.

_____. *General Directory of the City of San Antonio, 1889-90*. Galveston; Clarke and Courts, 1888.

Morrison, Andrew, comp. *San Antonio, Texas*. St. Louis: Geo. W. Engelhart and Co.; reprint, San Antonio: Norman Brock, 1977.

Morrison [C.D.] and [J.V.] Fourmy. *General Directory of the City of Galveston, 1881-82*. Galveston: Strickland and Co., 1880.

_____. *General Directory of the City of Galveston, 1882-83*. Galveston: Clarke and Courts, 1882.

_____. *General Directory of the City of Galveston, 1884-85*. Galveston: M. Strickland and Co., 1883.

_____. *General Directory of the City of Galveston, 1886-87*. Galveston: Clarke and Courts, 1886.

_____. *General Directory of the City of Galveston, 1899-1900*. Galveston: Clarke and Courts, 1899.

_____. *General Directory of the City of Galveston, 1901-02*. Galveston: Clarke and Courts, 1901.

_____. *General Directory of the City of Galveston, 1903-04*. Galveston: Clarke and Courts, 1903.

_____. *General Directory of the City of Galveston, 1905.* Galveston: Clarke and Courts, 1904.

_____. *General Directory of the City of Galveston, 1909-10.* Galveston: Clarke and Courts, 1909.

_____. *General Directory of the City of Galveston, 1911-12.* Galveston: Clarke and Courts, 1911.

_____. *General Directory of the City of Houston, 1866.* Galveston: Clarke and Courts, 1866.

_____. *General Directory of the City of Houston, 1867-68.* Galveston: Clarke and Courts, 1867.

_____. *General Directory of the City of Houston, 1870-71.* Galveston: Clarke and Courts, 1870.

_____. *General Directory of the City of Houston, 1873.* Galveston: Clarke and Courts, 1872.

_____. *General Directory of the City of Houston, 1877-78.* Galveston: Clarke and Courts, 1877.

_____. *General Directory of the City of Houston, 1880-81.* Galveston: Clarke and Courts, 1880.

_____. *General Directory of the City of Houston, 1882-83.* Galveston: Clarke and Courts, 1882.

_____. *General Directory of the City of Houston, 1884.* Galveston: Clarke and Courts, 1883.

_____. *General Directory of the City of Houston, 1886-87.* Galveston: Clarke and Courts, 1885.

_____. *General Directory of the City of Houston, 1887-88.* Galveston: Clarke and Courts, 1887.

_____. *General Directory of the City of Houston, 1889-90.* Galveston: Clarke and Courts, 1889.

_____. *General Directory of the City of Houston, 1890-91.* Galveston: Clarke and Courts, 1890.

_____. *General Directory of the City of Houston, 1892-93.* Galveston: Clarke and Courts, 1892.

_____. *General Directory of the City of Houston, 1894-95.* Galveston: Clarke and Courts, 1894.

_____. *General Directory of the City of Houston, 1895.* Galveston: Clarke and Courts, 1895.

_____. *General Directory of the City of Houston, 1897-98.* Galveston: Clarke and Courts, 1897.

_____. *General Directory of the City of Houston, 1899.* Galveston: Clarke and Courts, 1899.

_____. *General Directory of the City of Houston, 1900-01.* Galveston: Clarke and Courts, 1900.

_____. *General Directory of the City of Houston, 1903-04.* Galveston: Clarke and Courts, 1903.

_____. *General Directory of the City of Houston, 1905-06.* Galveston: Clarke and Courts, 1905.

_____. *General Directory of the City of Houston, 1907.* Galveston: Clarke and Courts, 1907.

_____. *General Directory of the City of Houston, 1908-09.* Galveston: Clarke and Courts, 1908.

_____. *General Directory of the City of Houston, 1910-11.* Galveston: Clarke and Courts, 1910.

_____. *General Directory of the City of Houston, 1911-12.* Houston: Texas Publishing Co., 1911.

_____. *General Directory of the City of Houston, 1913.* Houston: Texas Publishing Co., 1912.

_____. *General Directory of the City of Houston, 1915.* Houston: Texas Publishing Co., [1914].

Moses, Carolyn Holmes, and Myrtle E. Lowe, comps. *Hungary Sends a Dallas-Builder: The Story of Martin Weiss.* Dallas, 1948.

Moursund, John Stribling. *Blanco County History.* Burnet, Tx.: Nortex Press, 1979.

O'Keeffe, Kevin. "Balla's life lofty as Berlin Wall." San Antonio *Express*, November 1, 1982.

Olmsted, Frederick Law. *A Journey through Texas, or, A Saddle-Trip on the Southwestern Frontier.* New York: Burt Franklin, [reprint] 1969.

Paddock, B.B. *A Twentieth Century History and Biographical Record of North and West Texas.* Chicago: Lewis Publishing Co., 1906.

Parmenter, Mary Fisher, Walter Russell Fisher, and Lawrence Edward Mallette. *The Life of George Fisher (1795-1873) and the History of the Fisher Family of Mississippi.* Jacksonville, Fla.: H. and W.B. Drew Co., 1959.

"Peach River Pine and the Peach River Lines." *American Lumberman*, October 8, 1910.

Piványi, Eugene. *Hungarian-American Historical Connections: From Pre-Columbian Times to the End of the American Civil War.* Budapest: Royal Hungarian University Press, 1927.

_____. *Hungarians in the American Civil War.* Cleveland: n.p., n.d. Reprint from *Dongo*, 1913.

Puskás, J[ulianna]. *Emigration from Hungary to the United States before 1914.* Budapest: Akadémiai Kiadó, 1975.

Reed, S.G. *A History of the Texas Railroads.* Houston: St. Clair Publishing Co., 1941.

Révai Nagy Lexikona [Encyclopaedia, 21 vols.]. Vols. 2, 16, 18. Budapest: Révai Testvérek Irodalmi Intézet Részvénytársaság, 1910-1935.

Richardson, W., and Co. *Galveston Directory for 1866-67.* Galveston: News Book and Job Office, 1866.

Richardson, W., and D. Richardson. *Galveston Directory for 1859-1860.* Galveston: News Book and Job Office, 1859.

Rodgers, John William. "Views and Previews." Dallas *Daily Times Herald*, December 26, 1948.

Rosenfield, John. "Dorati's Direct Appeal." Dallas *Morning News*, February 13, 1955; July 28, 1963.

Rosinger, Samuel. *My Life and My Message*. Beaumont, Tx., 1945.

Roussel, Hubert. *The Houston Symphony Orchestra, 1913-1971*. Austin: University of Texas Press, 1972.

San Antonio Genealogical and Historical Society. "1867-1869 Registration of Voters, Bexar County, Texas." *Our Heritage* 17, no. 1 (October 1975); no. 2 (January 1976).

Seele, Hermann. *Verses and Songs of Texas*. Trans. and trans. Edward C. Breitenkamp. Bryan, Tx., 1984.

Sibley, Marilyn McAdams. *George W. Brackenridge: Maverick Philanthropist*. Austin: University of Texas Press, 1973.

Siebmacher, J. *Die Wappen des Adels in Ungarn*. Vol. 33. Neustadt an der Aisch: Bauer und Raspe, Inhaber Gerhard Gessner, 1982.

Simpson, Harold B. *Hood's Texas Brigade: A Compendium*. Hillsboro, Tx.: Hill Junior College Press, 1977.

Sisa, Stephen. *America's Amazing Hungarians*. Huddleston, Va., 1987.

_____. *The Spirit of Hungary: A Panorama of Hungarian History and Culture*. Toronto, Ont.: A Wintario Project of the Rakoczi Foundation, 1983.

Souders, D.A. *The Magyars in America*. New York: George H. Doran Co., 1922; reprint, San Francisco: R&E Research Assn., 1969.

Southwestern Reporter 2: 768.

Southwest Texans. San Antonio: Southwest Pub., 1952.

Sowell, A.J. *Early Settlers and Indian Fighters of Southwest Texas*. New York: Argosy-Antiquarian, 1964.

Spell, Lota M. *Music in Texas*. Austin, 1936.

Stearns, Frank Preston. *The Life and Public Works of George Luther Stearns*. Philadelphia: J.B. Lippincott Co., 1907; reprint, New York: Arno Press and the New York *Times*, 1969.

Steinert, W. "W. Steinert's View of Texas in 1849." Trans. and ed. Gilbert J. Jordan. *Southwestern Historical Quarterly* 80, no. 4 (April 1977).

Steinfeldt, Cecilia. *San Antonio Was: Seen through a Magic Lantern*. San Antonio: San Antonio Museum Assn., 1978.

Széplaki, Joseph. *The Hungarians in America, 1583-1974: A Chronology and Fact Book*. Ethnic Chronology Series No. 18. Dobbs Ferry, N.Y.: Oceana Pub., 1975.

_____, comp. and ed. *Hungarians in the United States and Canada; A Bibliography*. Minneapolis: Immigration History Research Center, University of Minnesota, 1977.

Szilagyi, Pete. "Scientist is calling the tune." Austin *American-Statesman*, February 16, 1987.

Szillányi, [?]. *Komorn im Jahre 1849; mit besonderem hinblick auf die Operationen der ungarischen Armee an der obern Donau und Waag*. Leipzig: F.W. Grunow und Comp., 1851.

Szy, Tibor. *Hungarians in America*. New York: Hungarian University Assn., 1963.

Tefft, B.F. *Hungary and Kossuth, or, An American Exposition of the Late Hungarian Revolution*. Philadelphia: John Ball, 1852.

"Temple Beth El, 1887-1987, Centennial Journal (Tyler, Texas)." *Chronicles of Smith County, Texas* 26, no. 2 (Winter 1987). Tyler: Smith County Historical Society, 1987.

Temple Emanuel 75th Anniversary. Beaumont, 1975.

Texas, State of. *Cities and Towns of Texas*. [Austin]: State Dept. of Highways and Public Transportation, Transportation Planning Div., and U.S. Dept. of Transportation, Federal Highway Admin., 1985.

Townshend, Samuel Nugent. *Our Indian Summer in the Far West*. London: Charles Whittingham, 1880.

"Thurber, Texas . . . TP's Birthplace." *TP Voice* 2, no. 3 (May-June 1966). Dallas: Texas Pacific Oil Co., 1966.

Underwood, James R. "Edwin Theodore Dumble." *Southwestern Historical Quarterly* 68 (July 1964).

U.S. Dept. of Commerce, Bureau of Census. *General Social and Economic Characteristics, Texas; Census of Population, 1980*. Washington, D.C.: U.S. Dept. of Commerce, 1983.

Vardy, Steven Bela. "Maygars in America." *The World and I*, March 1987.
_____. "The 'Mystery of the Hungarian Talent'." *The World and I*, April 1987.
_____. *The Hungarian-Americans*. Boston: Twayne Pub., 1985.

Vassady, Bela Jr. "Kossuth and Újházi on Establishing a Colony of Hungarian 48-ers in America, 1849-1852." *Canadian-American Review of Hungarian Studies* 6, no. 1 (Spring 1979).

Vasváry, Edmund. *Lincoln's Hungarian Heroes: The Participation of Hungarians in the Civil War, 1861-1865*. Washington, D.C.: Hungarian Reformed Federation of America, 1939.

Vidor, King. *A Tree Is a Tree*. New York: Harcourt, Brace and Co., 1953.
_____. "Southern Storm." *Esquire*, May 1935.

Wagner, Francis S. *Hungarian Contributions to World Civilization*. Center Square, Pa.: Alpha Pub., 1977.

Weaver, Bobby D. *Castro's Colony: Empresario Development in Texas, 1842-1865*. College Station: Texas A&M University Press, 1985.

Webb, Walter Prescott, ed. *The Handbook of Texas*. 2 vols. Austin: Texas State Historical Assn., 1952.

Weyand, Leonie Rummel, and Houston Wade. *An Early History of Fayette County*. La Grange, Tx.: La Grange Journal, 1936.

Wheeler County History Book Committee. *The History of Wheeler County*. Dallas: Taylor Publishing Co., 1985.

Whisenhunt, Donald W., ed. *Texas: A Sesquicentennial Celebration*. Austin: Eakin Press, 1984.

Williams, Lucia L. "The Yellow Fever Epidemic of La Grange in 1867." *Fayette County: Past and Present*. By students of La Grange High School. Ed. Marjorie L. Williams. La Grange, Tx., 1976.

Wilson, Lillian Mae. "Some Hungarian Patriots in Iowa." *Iowa Journal of History and Politics* 11 (October 1913).

Windeler, Diane. "Long-lost secret of Stradivarius near discovery." San Antonio *Light*, June 24, 1984.

Wittke, Carl. *Refugees of Revolution: The German Forty-Eighters in America*. Philadelphia: University of Pennsylvania Press, 1952.

Woolford, Sam, ed. *San Antonio, A History for Tomorrow*. San Antonio: Naylor Co., 1963.

Xantus, John. *Letters from North America*. Trans. and ed. Theodore Schoenman and Helen Benedek Schoenman. Detroit: Wayne State University Press, 1975.

UNPUBLISHED DISSERTATIONS AND MANUSCRIPTS

Albrecht, Theodore John. "German Singing Societies in Texas." Unpublished Ph.D. dissertation. North Texas State University, Denton, 1975.

Forse, Charles. "A History of Pineland, Texas, and Its Industries." Research paper (History 444), May 18, 1949. R.W. Steen Library Special Collections. Stephen F. Austin State University, Nacogdoches, Texas.

Gaspar, Steven. "Four Nineteenth-Century Hungarian Travelers in America." Unpublished Ph.D. dissertation. University of Southern California, Los Angeles, 1967.

Gentry, Mary Jane. "Thurber: The Life and Death of a Texas Town." Unpublished M.A. thesis. University of Texas at Austin, 1946.

Lazaro, Gina Yvette. "Hungarians in Early Texas," ms. 1982. Harlandale High School, San Antonio, Texas.

"Rudolph Schorobiny — Sketch of the Old Mexican War Veteran Who Came to Texas in 1845 and Died April 25, 1908," ms. Special Collections Library, St. Mary's University, San Antonio, Texas.

PRIMARY SOURCES

The Hungarian Files at The University of Texas Institute of Texan Cultures at San Antonio, cited as HF-ITC, contain correspondence, clippings, articles, photographs, interviews, and notes taken during the preparation of this book.

Alamo Abstract & Title Guaranty Co., San Antonio, Texas. Abstract of Title, 211 Mandalay East, Olmos Park, Texas. A.T. Brainerd.

Aranyas, Charles. Telephone interview, July 16, 1986, Houston, Texas. HF-ITC.

Baker, Dewitt Clinton, Biographical File. Austin History Center, Austin, Texas.

Baldwin, Nell Finto, comp. "Finto Family Records," ms. HF-ITC.

Bartay, Gary Kent. "Bartay Family Emigration from Hungary to Texas," ms. HF-ITC.

Bell County, Texas. U.S. Bureau of Census. Census of Population, 1870.

Benke, Ruth Todd, comp. "Genealogical Information on the Benke Family," ms. San Antonio, 1976. HF-ITC.

Bexar County, Texas. Brand Book. Bexar County Clerk's Office, San Antonio, Texas.

———. Civil Court Cases. Bexar County District Clerk's Office, San Antonio, Texas.

———. Commissioners' Court Minutes. Bexar County Clerk's Office, San Antonio, Texas.

———. County Court for the Settlement of Estates. Bexar County Clerk's Office, San Antonio, Texas.

———. Declaration of Intent. Bexar County District Clerk's Office, San Antonio, Texas.

———. Deed Records. Bexar County Clerk's Office, San Antonio, Texas.

———. Marriage Records. Bexar County Clerk's Office, San Antonio, Texas.

———. Naturalization Papers. Bexar County Clerk's Office and Bexar County District Clerk's Office, San Antonio, Texas.

———. Probate Records. Bexar County Clerk's Office, San Antonio, Texas.

———. U.S. Bureau of Census. Census of Population, 1860, 1870, 1880, 1900, 1910.

Casey, Donald Earl. "John and Ida Manna Fuchs Goebel," ms. HF-ITC.

Dallas County, Texas. U.S. Bureau of Census. Census of Population, 1860, 1910, 1980.

Diplomatic Branch. National Archives and Records Service, Washington, D.C.

Diplomatic Papers. Record Group 59, Letterbox 107. National Archives, Washington, D.C.

Dittmar, Emmy, Papers. Daughters of the Republic of Texas Library at the Alamo, San Antonio, Texas.

Dolak, Anna P. "16-Family Telephone System Operated in Early-Day Pakan"; "Education Posed a Problem in Early-Day Pakan Community"; "Pakan Community Established by Hardy Czechs in May 1905"; "Pioneers in Early-Day Pakan Bore Hardships with Courage." Undated newspaper articles from *The Shamrock* [Texas] *Texan*, 1975.

Ellis County, Texas. U.S. Bureau of Census. Census of Population, 1910.

El Paso County, Texas. Marriage Records. El Paso County Clerk's Office, El Paso, Texas.

Erath County, Texas. U.S. Bureau of Census. Census of Population, 1910.

"Family Record (Wadgymár Family from Old Bible), Births and Deaths," ms. HF-ITC.

Fayette County, Texas. Declaration of Intent. Fayette County District Clerk's Office, La Grange, Texas.

Foreign Born Citizens File, Hungarian. Dallas Public Library, Dallas, Texas.

Galveston County, Texas. Marriage Records. Galveston County Clerk's Office, Galveston, Texas.

———. Register of Deaths. Galveston County Clerk's Office, Galveston, Texas.

———. U.S. Bureau of Census. Census of Population, 1860, 1900.

Green, A.C., to James J. Hill. Brooklyn, New York, February 4, 1910. In "Hungarian Colony Location, File 50755" and "Immigration to Wichita Valley Territory, File 50381." Southwest Collection, Texas Tech University, Lubbock, Texas.

Harris County, Texas. Marriage Records. Harris County Clerk's Office, Houston, Texas.

———. Probate Records. Harris County Clerk's Office, Houston, Texas.

———. U.S. Bureau of Census. Census of Population, 1860, 1900, 1910.

Hovorka, Sue, letter to James Patrick McGuire, Austin, Texas, December 26, 1986.

James Collection. Daughters of the Republic of Texas Library at the Alamo, San Antonio, Texas.

Johnson, Mary Ellen Varga. "The Varga Story," ms. HF-ITC.

Kellerschön, Klára Újházy. Typescript of letters, photographs, 1878-1894. Péter Bogáti, Budapest, Hungary. Original letters in Újházi Papers (1539 P. Szekcio, Újházi iratok), Hungarian National Archives, Budapest, Hungary.

Kendall County, Texas. Probate Records. Kendall County Clerk's Office, Boerne, Texas.

Medina County, Texas. Declarations of Intent. Commissioners' Court Minutes. Medina County Clerk's Office, Hondo, Texas.

Military Service Branch. National Archives and Records Service, Washington, D.C.

Monostory, Denes, letter to James Patrick McGuire, Arlington, Texas, October 29, 1986.

Nagy, The Rev. Abbot Anselm, letter to James Patrick McGuire, Dallas, Texas, November 28, 1987.
Nash, Thomas Barton. "Soldier for Christ: Emir Hamvasy in Texas," ms. HF-ITC.
Navarro County, Texas. U.S. Bureau of Census. Census of Population, 1910.
Nordyke, Marie Dobay. "Tracing the Assimilation of the Hungarian Immigrants into the Houston Community," ms. University of St. Thomas, Houston, Texas. Houston Metropolitan Research Center, 1982.
Nueces County, Texas. Deed Records. Nueces County Clerk's Office, Corpus Christi, Texas.
Pease, Elisha Marshall, Papers. Austin History Center, Austin, Texas.
Pease, S.W., Collection. Institute of Texan Cultures, San Antonio, Texas.
St. Mary's College. "Complete Register, 1857-1865," "Record Book, 1857-1891." Microfilm. Special Collections Library, St. Mary's University, San Antonio, Texas.
San Saba County, Texas. U.S. Bureau of Census. Census of Population, 1880.
Schneidler, Stefanie N. "Biographical Sketch of Dr. Max Rottenstein," ms. HF-ITC.
Solms-Braunfels Archives. 70 bound German typescript vols. Eugene C. Barker Texas History Center, University of Texas at Austin.
Szabad, Emeric, File. Boerne Area Historical Preservation Society, Boerne, Texas.
Tarrant County, Texas. U.S. Bureau of Census. Census of Population, 1910, 1980.
Texas State Military Board Papers. Texas State Library and Archives, Austin, Texas.
Tripak, Irene Seabase. "History of the Seabase (alias Czibész) family," ms. HF-ITC.
Újházi Biographical File. Eugene C. Barker Texas History Center, University of Texas at Austin.
Újházi Family Research Files. Péter Bogáti, Budapest, Hungary.
U.S. Bureau of Census. Census of Population. Texas, 1910.
Vásváry, Edmund, Collection. Photocopies and Index. American Hungarian Foundation, New Brunswick, New Jersey.
Vásváry, Ödön [Edmund]. "A Madarász," ms. Photocopied typescript, 1954; "The First Letter of Frigyes Kerényi from America," ms. Photocopied typescript, 1961; "Könyv Újházy Lászlóról," ms. Photocopied typescript, 1972; "Madarász László emlekezete," ms. Photocopied typescript, 1959; "Once More about Frigyes Kerényi," ms. Photocopied typescript, 1971; "The Rank of Frigyes Kerényi as a Poet," ms. Photocopied typescript, 1971; "Where Is the Grave of Frigyes Kerényi?" ms. Photocopied typescript, 1966; Title illegible, ms. Photocopied typescript, pages 0002066-0002069 [Letter; László Újházi to My Highly Respected Father, New Buda, Iowa, October 25, 1851]. Edmund Vásváry Collection. American Hungarian Foundation, New Brunswick, New Jersey.
Vidor, King, Collection. Archives of Performing Arts, University of Southern California Library, Los Angeles, California.
Wagner, Frank. "Wm. DeRyee of Corpus Christi," ms. HF-ITC.
Wheeler County, Texas. U.S. Bureau of Census. Census of Population, 1910.
[Wildenthal, Arthur, and Mary Wildenthal.] "Legends told to Annabelle Rylander, to Arthur Wildenthal and Mary Wildenthal," in "Family of Arthur August von Wadgymár, M.D.," ms. HF-ITC.
Wingate-Ramage, Peggy, letter to James Patrick McGuire, Houston, Texas, August 21, 1987.
Yorker, Dorothea. "The Family of Stephen and Mary Eross," ms. HF-ITC.

PHOTO CREDITS

All prints are from the collections of The University of Texas Institute of Texan Cultures at San Antonio, courtesy of the following lenders. Credits of photographs positioned left to right are separated by semicolons, from top to bottom by dashes.

Page 2   Institute of Texan Cultures.
Page 6   Institute of Texan Cultures.
Page 7   Institute of Texan Cultures.
Page 9   Institute of Texan Cultures.
Page 12   Archives Division, Texas State Library, Austin.
Page 15   Amon Carter Museum, Fort Worth.
Page 25   Louis Nagy, Boerne.
Page 26   Fred Petmecky, Buchanan Dam.
Page 29   A[ndrew].J[ackson]. Sowell, *Early Settlers and Indian Fighters of Southwest Texas* (New York: Argosy-Antiquarian, 1964; reprint of 1900 edition).
Page 30   Josie R. Finger, D'Hanis.
Page 33   Daisy B. Weirich, Hondo.
Page 36   Péter Bogáti, Budapest, Hungary.
Page 37   Istvan Deak, *The Lawful Revolution: Louis Kossuth and the Hungarians, 1848-1849* (New York: Columbia University Press, 1979).
Page 38   Istvan Deak, *The Lawful Revolution: Louis Kossuth and the Hungarians, 1848-1849* (New York: Columbia University Press, 1979).

Page 39 Istvan Deak, *The Lawful Revolution: Louis Kossuth and the Hungarians, 1848-1849* (New York: Columbia University Press, 1979).

Page 43 Istvan Deak, *The Lawful Revolution: Louis Kossuth and the Hungarians, 1848-1849* (New York: Columbia University Press, 1979).

Page 44 Istvan Deak, *The Lawful Revolution: Louis Kossuth and the Hungarians, 1848-1849* (New York: Columbia University Press, 1979).

Page 47 Dittmar Collection, The Library of the Daughters of the Republic of Texas at the Alamo, San Antonio.

Page 66 Diplomatic Branch, National Archives, Washington, D.C.

Page 67 Péter Bogáti, Budapest, Hungary.

Page 80 Péter Bogáti, Budapest, Hungary.

Page 100 Clara Kalish Madarász, *The Madarasz Book* (Columbus, Ohio, 1911).

Page 101 Clara Kalish Madarász, *The Madarasz Book* (Columbus, Ohio, 1911).

Page 104 *San Antonio City Directory, 1887-88.*

Page 109 Claude Aniol Collection, The Library of the Daughters of the Republic of Texas at the Alamo.

Page 110 San Antonio Museum Association, San Antonio.

Page 112 Institute of Texan Cultures.

Page 119 Amanda Ochse, San Antonio.

Page 125 All three from Milton Varga, San Antonio.

Page 126 The Library of the Daughters of the Republic of Texas at the Alamo, San Antonio—(inset) Ernest Carvajal, San Antonio.

Page 127 *San Antonio City Directory, 1877-78—San Antonio City Directory, 1879-80.*

Page 128 Milton Varga, San Antonio—Mary Ellen Perry, Brownwood.

Page 129 Both from Milton Varga, San Antonio.

Page 133 Ruth Benke, Hondo.

Page 136 Archives of Performing Arts, University of Southern California, Los Angeles.

Page 137 *Art Work in Galveston* (Chicago: W.H. Parish Publishing Co., 1894).

Page 138 *Art Work in Galveston* (Chicago: W.H. Parish Publishing Co., 1894).

Page 139 Archives of Performing Arts, University of Southern California, Los Angeles.

Page 140 Stephen F. Austin State University Library, Nacogdoches.

Page 142 Archives of Performing Arts, University of Southern California, Los Angeles.

Page 145 All three from Archives of Performing Arts, University of Southern California, Los Angeles.

Page 147 Both from Mrs. A.W. Harris, Austin.

Page 149   All three from Mrs. A.W. Harris, Austin.
Page 152   *Men of Texas* (Chicago: A.N. Marquis & Co., 1903).
Page 153   Both from Gary Kent Bartay, Mesquite.
Page 159   Christ Episcopal Church, Tyler.
Page 160   Both from Christ Episcopal Church, Tyler.
Page 165   John Wildenthal, Houston, and Mrs. J. Preston Reeder,
             Rancho Palos Verdes, California.
Page 171   Institute of Texan Cultures.
Page 173   Mrs. John Hrnciar, Shamrock.
Page 175   Mrs. John Hrnciar, Shamrock.
Page 177   Mrs. John Hrnciar, Shamrock.
Page 178   Sallie B. Harris, Wheeler.
Page 181   All three from Mr. and Mrs. Louis Nagy, Boerne.
Page 183   Mr. and Mrs. Louis Nagy, Boerne—Mary Saint-Onge,
             Southfield, Michigan..
Page 184   Both from Mr. and Mrs. Louis Nagy, Boerne.
Page 185   Both from Mr. and Mrs. Louis Nagy, Boerne.
Page 189   B.B. Paddock, *A 20th Century History and Biographical
             Record of North and West Texas* (Chicago and New York:
             Lewis Publishing Co., 1906).
Page 192   The Library of the Daughters of the Republic of Texas at
             the Alamo, San Antonio.
Page 195   Doyle Goebel, Amarillo; Bernice Casey, Waco—
             Bernice Casey, Waco.
Page 201   Mr. and Mrs. Robert L. Tomasini, San Antonio.
Page 205   Eugene Lipstate, Lafayette, Louisiana.
Page 209   Stephanie Schneider, Dallas.
Page 211   Carolyn Holmes Moses with Myrtle E. Lowe, *Hungary Sends
             a Dallas-Builder: The Story of Martin Weiss* (Dallas, 1948).
Page 213   Both from Leon Schmidt, Austin.
Page 215   Jack Roth, San Antonio.
Page 216   Lester Klein, San Antonio.
Page 218   Kansas State Historical Society, Topeka, Kansas.
Page 221   Both from Archives of Performing Arts, University of
             Southern California.
Page 228   Ed Stern, San Antonio.
Page 232   Abbot Anselm Nagy, Irving; Cistercian Preparatory School,
             Irving—Cistercian Abbey, Irving.
Page 233   Both from Cistercian Preparatory School, Irving.
Page 237   Rose H. Safran, San Antonio.
Page 239   Rose H. Safran, San Antonio.
Page 242   The *San Antonio Light* Collection, Institute of
             Texan Cultures.
Page 245   The *San Antonio Light* Collection, Institute of
             Texan Cultures.
Page 246   Agnes Rozsa, San Antonio.

INDEX